FOR THE GOOD OF THE GAME

The Inside Story of the Surprising and Dramatic
Transformation of Major League Baseball

BUD SELIG

with PHIL ROGERS

WILLIAM MORROW
An Imprint of HarperCollins*Publishers*

MLB trademarks and copyrights are used with permission of Major League Baseball.

for the good of the game. Copyright © 2019 by Allan H. Selig. All rights reserved. Printed in the United States of America. No part of this book may be used or reproduced in any manner whatsoever without written permission except in the case of brief quotations embodied in critical articles and reviews. For information, address HarperCollins Publishers, 195 Broadway, New York, NY 10007.

HarperCollins books may be purchased for educational, business, or sales promotional use. For information, please email the Special Markets Department at SPsales@harpercollins.com.

A hardcover edition of this book was published in 2019 by William Morrow, an imprint of HarperCollins Publishers.

first william morrow paperback edition published 2020.

Designed by Bonni Leon-Berman

Library of Congress Cataloging-in-Publication Data has been applied for.

ISBN 978-0-06-290596-3

20 21 22 23 24 LSC 10 9 8 7 6 5 4 3 2 1

FOR THE
GOOD
OF THE
GAME

To my mother and father, and
everyone who made this journey possible

FOREWORD

HISTORY AND BASEBALL—two of my earliest and enduring passions—are the building blocks of this heartfelt memoir by Bud Selig. I first met Baseball Commissioner Bud Selig twenty years ago when I was in Milwaukee to deliver a lecture on one of Bud's heroes, Franklin Roosevelt. Every time we have seen each other since, there has been a happy contest between my desire to talk baseball and his to talk history. So how delighted I am to write the foreword for this memoir that serves both as a work of history and a riveting account of baseball during a fraught and transformative time.

Bud's love of baseball was ignited (as in my case) by a parent's devotion to the game. He was only three when his mother, Marie, an immigrant from Ukraine, began taking him to the park where the minor league Milwaukee Brewers played. Then, during weekends and summer breaks, she arranged magical field trips to Comiskey Park, Yankee Stadium, Ebbets Field, and the Polo Grounds. An intuitive storyteller with a keen memory for the telling detail, Bud recalls a game at Yankee Stadium on his fifteenth birthday. To his glee, a big cake was rolled onto the field before the game began. Bud thought that his omnipotent mother had somehow managed to arrange the celebration just for him. In actuality, the cake marked manager Casey Stengel's birthday.

After Bud graduated from the University of Wisconsin and joined his father's car dealership, baseball became not merely an avocation, but the "essence" of his life. When the Milwaukee Braves stunned the city and state by announcing a move to

Atlanta, Selig and a small group of business and civic leaders fought to give Milwaukee "a second chance at baseball." It took five years to put the money together and gain acceptance from Major League Baseball, but the group was finally able to purchase the bankrupt Seattle Pilots and bring the team to Milwaukee. In honor of the minor league team that had been Bud's first love, they were rechristened the Milwaukee Brewers.

The story of the realization of a new park for the Brewers—Miller Park named for the Miller Brewing Company—is one of intense political drama. After months of struggle with the governor and the legislature, the financing plan was passed by the State Assembly but lacked the votes to survive in the State Senate. The package called for a sales tax in the four-county area that included Milwaukee. After George Petak, the senator from neighboring Racine County announced his support for the legislation, his fellow legislators insisted on adding his county to the four that would be taxed. On behalf of his own county, Petak initially felt compelled to vote no. In the middle of the night, however, he reversed his vote and the bill passed 16-15. Petak knew he would face "a political firestorm," but believed a thriving baseball team would benefit all Wisconsin and didn't believe there was any other way to keep the team in the state. That firestorm was not long in coming. Residents in Racine County forced a recall vote and Petak was voted out of office. To this day, George Petak remains a hero to Bud Selig and to all fans of the Milwaukee Brewers.

Watching the Brewers from the owner's seat, Selig acknowledges, was both exhilarating and agonizing. Like so many rabid fans, Bud is superstitious. When the game was tight in the late innings, he followed a seven-minute rule. He would leave his seat and pace the hallway, hiding behind a girder. There, he could figure out what was happening by the cheers or groans. For some reason he found it less painful to hear what was happening than to actually watch the action. Unless, of course, the cheers rose in volume and then he could race back to his seat!

When Bud Selig was selected by his fellow owners as acting commissioner and then baseball commissioner, a post he would hold for twenty-two years, the game he loved was in drastic jeopardy. He recognized, he writes, that a sport resistant to change had to change, "if it was going to survive, much less thrive." The gap between the big- and small-market clubs was widening at an alarming rate. The same few teams made it to the playoffs year after year, dampening the hopes and attendance of fans in dozens of other cities. In these same troubled years an unprecedented, literally unbelievable number of home runs were being hit. Something more than new workout equipment, smaller ballparks, or dilution of pitching talent because of an expanded number of teams was at play here.

This memoir takes us through each of these significant struggles with vivid detail that enlivens the main characters involved—including the "emotional, combustible" Yankee owner, George Steinbrenner; the L.A. Dodgers' Walter O'Malley, forever a despised figure in Brooklyn, and in Selig's opinion, a leader more concerned with himself and the fortunes of his own team than the good of the game; the union's "bleeping" Marvin Miller, who, Selig believes (despite the immense power he wielded in his fights with the owners), belongs in the Hall of Fame; and Henry Aaron, a giant on and off the field, and Selig's close friend for sixty years.

Indeed, the first chapter recounts the agony Bud experienced when Barry Bonds, a suspected steroids user, was closing in on

Hank Aaron's career home run title of 755 homers. As commissioner, he felt obligated to hopscotch around the country to witness the moment when Bonds hit the homer that would make history—albeit a contaminated milestone.

The watershed process of dealing with steroids in baseball was long and torturous. For years, the players union adamantly refused to allow drug testing, even as the integrity of a game built upon records and statistics was put into question. After much foot-dragging, a series of events finally led to slow progress. A dramatic home run race between Mark McGwire and Sammy Sosa captured the attention of the nation but stoked fresh questions about the sudden increase in their prodigious number of home runs. A few years afterward, players and owners agreed to an anonymous drug testing program and when the tests were conducted, between 5 and 7 percent of the players tested positive. Not long after, four people associated with the game were charged in a 42-count federal indictment of running a steroid-distribution ring that provided performance-enhancing drugs to dozens of athletes. Contentious congressional hearings on steroid use commenced.

Selig persuaded former Senate majority leader George Mitchell to conduct an investigation. Two years in the making, the Mitchell Report gained access to steroid suppliers and accused nearly a hundred players of using steroids. Polls showed that, despite the union's refusal, 79 percent of the players wanted to be tested. Finally, a testing program with harsh punishments for transgressions was put in place. Though it came too late to preserve the record of the great Henry Aaron, baseball's testing program soon became the strongest in any major American sport.

Progress in creating competitive balance was hamstrung from the start by the union's flat refusal to consider a salary cap similar to that in the NFL or the NHL. (This was the issue surrounding the longest strike in baseball history and the cancellation of the 1994 World Series.) Attendance and enthusiasm for the game dropped dramatically. Selig knew that major change had to take place. When he first introduced the idea that big-market teams share some of their greater revenue with small-market teams, however, emotions flared so high that it seemed nothing would get done. But over time, under Selig's patient, yet unrelenting, and ultimately transformative leadership, the owners agreed to both revenue sharing and a luxury tax, bringing an unmatched level of parity to the game.

For the opportunity for a greater number of teams to reach the playoffs, however, additional changes were necessary. Selig proposed that the traditional two divisions be restructured into three and that a wild card (and eventually two wild cards) be added. The proposition met with strong criticism from the media, but Selig brought all the owners around—well, almost all. The final vote was twenty-nine in favor, one opposed. The "no" vote was cast by Texas Rangers owner George W. Bush, a traditionalist who did not want to tamper with the structure of the game. While criticism from purists remains, the wild card has proved wildly popular. With the help of playoff expansion, revenue sharing, and the luxury tax, Selig proudly notes, all thirty teams played postseason baseball during his tenure, and twenty different teams reached the World Series!

The commissioner's battle over instant replay provides yet another instance of the difficult birth of innovation. Traditionalists (at first including Bud himself) worried about losing the human element of the game, the dramatic confrontations between umpires and managers that roused the crowd. But as technology advanced, Selig increasingly came to believe it was wrong to put all the responsibility for close calls on the umpires who would inevitably miss a number of calls. He understood the anguish umpires felt when they blew a call. He cites umpire Don Denkinger's mistaken call at first base during the 1985 World Series that led to a rally by Kansas City and death threats from St. Louis Cardinals fans. A missed call by second base umpire Jim Joyce cost Tiger pitcher Armando Galarraga a perfect game, leaving a shadow on Joyce's career. Selig was finally convinced that the new technology could play a positive role. After a committee studied the situation, an instant replay system was put in place, one that has now expanded to include calls on the bases as well as catches in the outfield.

That something good can come from a fiasco is illustrated by the infamous 2002 All-Star Game that had to be halted after the eleventh inning. Although the game was tied at 7–7, both teams had run out of pitchers. For a number of years, Selig observes, the All-Star Game had lost its allure. Players no longer considered selection to the All-Star team the surpassing honor it had once been. Some players even chose not to participate, preferring to enjoy the break; others would play an inning or two, take a quick shower and then depart the clubhouse before the game ended. How different this atmosphere, Bud notes, from the 1950 All-Star Game he had attended at Comiskey Park where Ted Williams broke his arm early in the game but insisted on playing until the top of the ninth! The eleventh inning stoppage of the 2002 game created an ugly scene. A chorus of catcalls began as fans threw beer bottles onto the field. This embarrassing moment led to MLB's declaration that henceforth, the winner of the All-Star Game would have home-field advantage in the World Series, hopefully restoring a greater import to the game.

Bud's love for baseball and his gift for storytelling shines through every page of this tender and lively memoir which comes full circle when he is elected to the Hall of Fame. His description of the tension he endured while waiting for the call is pure Bud Selig—unpretentious, emotional, authentic. He had been told that the panel in charge of electing executives to the Hall of Fame had included his name on the ballot. The final decision would be made on December 4, 2016 in Washington, D.C., by a sixteen-person panel of Hall of Fame players, executives, writers, and broadcasters. If Bud were elected, the chairman would call at 4:15. Surrounded by his family in Milwaukee, Bud waited. The phone did not ring at 4:15. What seemed an eternity was in all likelihood two minutes later. Bud heard the longed-for words: "You've been elected to the Hall of Fame on the first ballot. Congratulations!" He experienced true joy, he relates, surpassed only by the ceremony at Cooperstown, where he signed his name on the wall behind which his plaque would hang, thereby joining the pantheon he had revered all his life.

—Doris Kearns Goodwin

1

This wasn't the Bataan Death March. Nobody was going to die or be forced into hard labor.

But the summer of 2007 was unpleasant for me, and when I look back, that's putting it mildly. It was one of the few times in my life I wasn't excited about going to ballparks, and if you know me that's all you need to know.

As Barry Bonds closed in on the all-time home run record, I flew around the country and spent my nights in places like the Four Seasons and the Westin St. Francis. I was never far from my next Diet Coke. As far as personal hardship goes, about all there was to worry about was a wait to get on a treadmill in the fitness room before getting a bite and heading out to the ballpark.

There was no way I was going to complain to anyone. Not a scintilla of a chance. But everyone who knew me knew I was unhappy.

They could see it on my face, in my lack of enthusiasm. I was surrounded by people I enjoyed, but even amid good company I felt alone with my thoughts. I was tired, and I'll admit it, I was haunted by regret. My mind raced as I searched for ways I could have avoided these long days and nights.

Bonds was on the verge of breaking Henry Aaron's record for career home runs, and I was doing what a commissioner of a sports league is supposed to do. I was hopscotching around the country to be in attendance when the self-absorbed slugger hit the record homer.

Like Shoeless Joe Jackson and Pete Rose, Barry had brought scandal to the game I'd fallen in love with as a boy and now led as baseball's ninth commissioner. I wasn't going to sing his praises, as I'd done for Mark McGwire and Sammy Sosa when they smashed Roger Maris's single-season homer record in 1998, but I didn't want to be conspicuous by my absence, either.

So in a stretch of sixteen days I watched Bonds and the San Francisco Giants play nine times. It was not one of the highlights of my life.

The Bonds Watch started for me at Miller Park in Milwaukee, where at least I could watch from my own suite and sleep in my own bed. The next stops were San Francisco, Los Angeles, and San Diego, where I was just waiting for Barry to put me out of my misery. He could have done it quicker, but one of the beauties of baseball is you can't orchestrate it.

In the end, the game rewards perseverance; it does not serve up a whole lot of convenience to anyone who makes it their life's work.

After watching Barry go homerless in a series against the Braves at AT&T Park in San Francisco, I traveled cross-country to induct Cal Ripken Jr. and Tony Gwynn into the Hall of Fame. Then I flew home from Cooperstown for a quick rest before moving on to L.A. and Dodger Stadium.

I had hit the road when Barry was two homers shy of Henry, not wanting to take anything for granted. I could have spared myself many nights on the road, because he homered only once in a stretch of thirty-seven at-bats, getting to 754.

Bonds was stuck there—in a slump, actually—and I had business back home, so I flew to Milwaukee for a quick pit stop after leaving Dodger Stadium. That meant another cross-country flight, this time to San Diego to watch the Giants play the Padres at Petco Park.

Along the way, I had a lot of time to think about the differences between Barry Bonds, who simply wasn't likable, and Henry Aaron, who had been such a giant on the field and now was the same way off the field, carrying himself with as much poise as humility. I have called myself a friend of Henry's since 1958 and burst with pride every time I speak about him.

Henry was one of the greatest hitters to ever play the game. He was still a Brave when he broke Babe Ruth's record, but I brought him back to Milwaukee to finish his career as the Brewers' designated hitter. It took Aaron twenty-three seasons to get to 755 home runs, never hitting more than forty-seven in a season.

But it wasn't my friendship with Henry that troubled me as I waited for Bonds to hit the 755th and 756th home runs of his career. It was the way Barry had piled up homers in the second half of his career, at a rate that seemed impossible to Henry and players from baseball's other generations.

We had been caught off guard when McGwire and Sosa passed Maris, but this was almost a decade later. Of course, by then we knew what was going on. This was an age when sluggers found extra power through chemistry, and, of course, Barry was one of the leading men in baseball's steroids narrative.

There is plenty of blame to spread around in this sad chapter, and I'll accept my share of the responsibility. We didn't get the genie back in the bottle in time to protect Aaron's legacy.

Henry knows we tried, but I'll always wish we had been successful in implementing testing for performance-enhancing drugs sooner than we eventually were, as part of labor negotiations in 2002.

If you weren't lucky enough to see Henry Aaron hit when he was in his prime, you missed one of the real delights of my life. You just never saw line drives like the ones Henry hit.

One day I was at a game and Sam "Toothpick" Jones was pitching for the Cubs. I later found out Henry didn't like Toothpick. I was attending the University of Wisconsin at the time. Herb Kohl, my childhood friend and roommate at Wisconsin, and I went to County Stadium to see the Braves play the Cubs. We had seats behind home plate, and I'll never forget what Henry did that day. He hit a line drive past Toothpick's head. I'm thinking it's a single to center, but it just kept rising, not dying, and wound up in Perini's Woods, beyond the center-field fence. Improbably, he'd hit it so hard that the ball, which had looked like it was low enough to take off the pitcher's head, just kept going and going and going. I couldn't believe my eyes. But that was Henry.

Years later, after I got involved in baseball, I asked Warren Spahn about Henry. He was never shy with opinions or anything else, which I think is part of what made him a great pitcher. I asked Spahn how he'd compare Aaron and Willie Mays.

They're both really great players, he said. You start with that. It's like DiMaggio and Williams, Cobb and Hornsby. I guess when you get to that class there are different levels of greatness.

"Bud, there's only two things Willie can do that Hank can't," Spahn said to me.

"What's that?"

"Make a basket catch and run out from under his cap."

Think about that. Henry wasn't as celebrated as Mays in his prime, but he played the game with the same kind of excellence. I'm not saying this to take anything away from Willie Mays—or the great Willie Mays, as they called him. He was a wonderful player. But Henry is right at that level and didn't get the credit when he played.

I'm not sure why. Maybe it was because Hank played in Milwaukee and Atlanta, not New York and San Francisco. I always felt that during that time people didn't fully appreciate Henry's greatness.

When he broke Babe Ruth's record, that was a help. But you look back at his lifetime stats, they're stunning. The consistency was stunning. He outdid Willie Mays in that regard. No question.

Bowie Kuhn, the commissioner, wasn't at the game in Atlanta when Henry broke Ruth's record. I wouldn't have missed that for the world if I had been in charge at the time. There's not a chance I would have been anywhere else.

So even though I didn't like Barry Bonds, I was going from city to city, all over the country, to watch him chase his version of history. I did it because it was my job.

The steroid issue really bothered me. It was a blemish on everything we did in that era, and nobody hated the taint more than me.

Everybody said I was slow to react to steroids, that Major League Baseball was slow to react. Some people actually thought we deliberately turned a blind eye to sell tickets or boost attendance. Still, nobody could make a coherent argument that baseball benefited from steroids. They clearly weren't in the best interest of the game, in any shape, form, or manner. It took us forever to get an agreement with the players union to test for steroids, and an unethical group of players took advantage of the union's protection.

Now here we were, at a new frontier, with Barry Bonds breaking the most famous record in American sports. I longed for the innocence and wonder we all felt when Henry broke the Babe's record.

I first got to know Henry when I sold him a Ford at my family's dealership in Milwaukee. I was a wide-eyed kid then, eaten up by baseball but without any idea I would ever be more than one of the most passionate fans you've ever seen. Henry says I was a certain kind of fan in those days. I was one of those fans that a player knew he was going to have to get to know whether he wanted to or not. He's probably right about that. I was persistent in everything I did and it brought me many rewards in my lifetime, none I treasure more than my friendship with Henry.

He is as fine a man as I've ever known, and, as one of baseball's first African American players, he has endured hatred few of us have known. He once shared with me a box of letters that was full of death threats sent to him as he was getting closer and closer to Ruth's record.

The letters were horrible, as was the treatment that Henry received early in his career. But his belief in himself, his faith, and his country was unshakable.

Henry hit the last twenty-two of his 755 homers playing for the Milwaukee Brewers, when I was the owner. Braves owner Bill Bartholomay and I worked out a trade that allowed us to bring him back from Atlanta to the city where his major league career had begun, and his leadership, his presence, helped Robin Yount develop into a player who could thrive in tough circumstances, as he did in leading us to the 1982 World Series.

I wasn't there when Henry broke Babe's record, but I listened closely to Vin Scully's famed comments. I've listened to them over and over through the years. They give you chills.

"What a marvelous day for baseball. What a marvelous moment for Atlanta and the state of Georgia. What a marvelous moment for the country and the world. A black man is getting a standing ovation in the Deep South for breaking a record of an all-time baseball idol. And it is a great moment for all of us, and particularly for Henry Aaron."

Scully, one of baseball's greatest voices, got it exactly right.

It was a great day for the South, a great day for baseball. It was everything you'd ever want, and it made you proud. Proud you were seeing history made by a man who had conducted himself so beautifully. But what I was experiencing on the Bonds Watch was not making me proud.

Look, Barry was a great player. Let me make that very clear. A great player. He was a Hall of Famer long before he got associated with steroids. But like so many other players, some of them great players, he had made some really bad decisions—decisions that would shape their legacies while complicating mine.

While I felt responsibility to be on hand for Bonds's moment, I'll admit I had a fantasy that I'd be spared when I went to Cooperstown to see Ripken and Gwynn be inducted into the Hall of Fame. Nobody would have blamed me for being there rather than on the road with Barry. But I received no reprieve, so I trudged on to Dodger Stadium and then Petco, the Padres' beautiful home that had opened only three years earlier.

I watched the first game of the Giants-Padres series with John Moores, who owned the Padres. He was a good host, but I'm not sure I was good company.

I trudged up to a box high atop the stadium the next night. I didn't mind being by myself.

I thought I'd experienced every emotion possible at a ballpark. I'd been nervous a lot and angry more often than I'd like to admit. I'd chain-smoked and I'd felt the level of peacefulness that my friends talk about after long hikes at a national park. I'd been exhilarated and had moments of pure joy. But this took me to a place I'd never been before, and I'll admit it.

I was thinking about that and a million other things as I watched Bonds drive a pitch from the Padres' Clay Hensley into the seats in left field in San Diego, setting off a celebration as he tied Henry's record.

I didn't go to the clubhouse to congratulate him afterward. I just couldn't bring myself to look him in the eyes and act happy about what he'd done. I don't exactly have a poker face.

When Barry hit No. 756 at AT&T Park three days later, pulling a fastball from the Nationals' Mike Bacsik over the fence in right-center, I was in New York at a baseball meeting, watching the game on TV. I had planned to fly back to San Francisco the next day, but finally Barry did something I liked. He saved me one trip. It was the least he could do.

After the record-breaking home run, the video board at AT&T Park played a tribute to Bonds from Henry Aaron. He hadn't been sure he wanted to do anything to commemorate the moment, but I persuaded him to record his congratulations, no matter the circumstance. I told Henry I felt it was the right thing to do, and Henry always did the right thing.

This awkward spectacle was the final exclamation point in an era of unprecedented power hitting throughout baseball. I'd seen it all, studied it, and would continue to study it for years.

I know some people will forever link me with Barry Bonds. Some will say baseball's failure to limit the impact of steroids quicker is my failure. They may even call me the steroid commissioner.

That's okay, I guess.

It's not fair, I don't like it, but I've come to understand it.

Did I understand the dimension of the problem from the beginning? No. But did other longtime, well-respected executives, like John Schuerholz and Andy MacPhail? No, they didn't, and they say that.

Steroids became a bigger issue than any of us imagined when we were watching Mark McGwire and Sammy Sosa in the summer of 1998. But through my work with owners—eventually with cooperation from the players union, which was kicking and screaming all the way—we ended up with baseball having the toughest steroid policy in sports.

I couldn't be prouder as I look back. The same is true for the economic overhaul of the sport during my tenure.

On the business side, I inherited a fucking nightmare, if you'll pardon both my language and my honesty. But give us some credit. We identified and corrected our problems, learning how to get all parties to work together for the common good.

Baseball boomed. It had generated $1.2 billion in revenue in 1992 and grew into a nine-billion-dollar-a-year business by the time I stepped away in January 2015, after thirteen consecutive years of growth.

We set attendance records every year from 2004 through '07, after we negotiated a labor agreement without a work stoppage, one that included the first protocols to test for steroids and other performance-enhancing drugs. Teams opened twenty ballparks in my years in charge, and that's no small thing. We gave hope and faith to fans of small- and medium-market teams, at a time when such teams were dying under baseball's hopelessly outdated model. If we hadn't overhauled our revenue-sharing system and made the labor deals we did with the union, there are a lot of teams that would have been out of business. A lot of teams. Ten or twelve teams, maybe. That's how desperate it was. David Glass reminded me of that when his Kansas City Royals won the World Series and back-to-back pennants.

I shudder to think where baseball would be if we hadn't found a way to work together to make these deals. We literally might have been out of business. I'll say that.

Our success, our ability to finally solve our problems, didn't have anything to do with steroids. Instead, it had everything to do with changing a business model that had been largely untouched for half a century.

I know all about change. My life has been full of it.

2

Baseball was the language spoken in the house I grew up in, on Fifty-second Street in Milwaukee. I was the second son of immigrants, but we were a first-generation family of baseball fanatics, in particular my mother and me.

With the closest teams in Chicago, we found our rooting interests at the top of the standings. My brother Jerry, who was about four years older than me, was a Cardinals fan. I was a Yankees fan, and how could you not be? With the exception of a stretch in the middle of World War II, they were a real dynasty. They won the American League pennant twenty-two times in twenty-nine seasons from 1936 through '64, and had the greatest collection of players you can imagine. I was seven years old when Joe DiMaggio had his fifty-six-game hitting streak, and to me he seemed like a god.

I couldn't imagine what it would be like to have a hometown team of my own. That would truly be the American dream realized, not that I wanted for much as a boy.

I did have a running joke with my father. It's one I'd break out in October or November, when I was out shoveling the driveway for the first of what seemed like a thousand times every winter.

Why'd you come to Milwaukee? You couldn't have gone to San Diego or Phoenix?

My father, Ben Selig, was born in Romania in 1899. His father, Abraham, was born there in 1865, and no doubt endured harsh winters and the brutal persecution of Jewish families. My grandfather sought a better life in America, and like so many immigrants he set sail for America and arrived through Ellis Island around 1909, when my father was just a boy.

From there, they moved on to Milwaukee. I never really understood why they chose Milwaukee. Maybe the climate reminded them of Romania. Maybe they had friends from the old country who told them there were jobs in Milwaukee.

My mother, Marie Huber, was also an immigrant. She was Russian, born in Odessa, in Ukraine. Her father, Joseph, was born in 1873 and died young, leaving her to be raised by her mother, Gertrude. She would be the only grandparent I knew. Mom and her siblings left their home on the Black Sea and headed to New York at about the same time as my dad and similarly kept moving west until they settled in Milwaukee.

Why'd they come? I can't tell you for sure. This was a time when coming to America was what you did if you wanted to work hard and build a better life for your family; it was a country filled with immigrants. They arrived with little except the clothes on their backs and their dreams. And it turns out they weren't wrong when they set out on their journeys.

Milwaukee isn't just my hometown; it's the only place I've ever lived, unless you count four years in Madison, at the University of Wisconsin, or a stint in the army, when I was stationed at Fort Leonard Wood in Pulaski County, Missouri, deep in the Ozark Mountains. In 1934, when I was born, Milwaukee was a city of about 580,000, not much smaller than it is today. That may not sound like much, but Chicago's the only bigger city in the Midwest. All that time, though, Milwaukee was the center of my universe. I am so lucky to have started my life here and even luckier to still be here.

I was given the name Allan Huber Selig by my parents, but I've been Bud since I came home from the hospital. My mother gets credit for that. When she introduced my older brother to me she said, "Look, Jerry, you have a little buddy." I've been Buddy, or Bud, ever since.

Jerry and I were raised in a nice, Jewish, middle-class neighborhood on the West Side of Milwaukee. We lived in a trim, three-bedroom home with a stone exterior. My father graduated from North Side High and then went to work selling ads for the *Milwaukee Journal*. My mother learned English quickly upon her arrival in America and soaked up information and culture. She didn't believe in limits and showed that by graduating from Milwaukee State Teachers College, which is now the University of Wisconsin–Milwaukee (one of her classmates there was Golda Meir, who would wind up as the prime minister of Israel). Anything but typical for women of that era, my mother was tough and determined, not gentle and accepting. But she was as nurturing as she was demanding. She was extraordinary, really. She became an English teacher, and you wouldn't be wrong if you said she was strict, both in the classroom and at home. Jerry and I were expected to make A's in school, always. But my mother was kind and loving in everything she did. She was an avid reader, a champion of education, and a fan of the opera and the symphony. She was a traveler and—this would prove very significant to me—an outstanding, devoted, committed fan of baseball.

My dad was a great salesman. He was very present, and people really liked him. One of those people was Ray Knippel, who was one of the first big car dealers in Wisconsin. The dealership was Mertz-Knippel, in West Allis, and Dad had that account for the *Journal*. They must have advertised a lot, because Dad became really close to Ray Knippel, who offered him a job as a sales executive for the dealership. He went to work there in 1921, and the following year Knippel asked my dad to become his partner. Otto Mertz, who had been the more garrulous of the two partners in the dealership, had drowned. Knippel was not really a salesman—he was more of an inside guy. He needed somebody on the outside, dealing with people, and that was where my dad could make a difference.

My dad and Ray built the business into the biggest Ford dealership in Wisconsin, eventually outgrowing their location on West Greenfield Avenue. They expanded into a bigger location on West National Avenue in 1946. When they did that they changed the name from Mertz-Knippel to Knippel-Selig, and Dad bought out Knippel when he was ready to retire. Then it became Selig Ford. My dad was also a pioneer in the leasing business. He may have been the second or third person in America in the lease business. By 1960, it was big. We would have ten thousand, twelve thousand cars under contract.

My parents were great with all kinds of people. It didn't matter where you came from or what you looked like. People were always people and were to be treated respectfully. I lived in a household where I never heard a word of prejudice ever, about blacks, Hispanics, Asians. Nothing. Our neighborhoods and schools were effectively segregated—white only—and I'm sorry to say I never really thought about it. That's just the way it was then.

Milwaukee was home to a minor league team, the Brewers. I was only three years old when my mother started taking me to see them play. They had been a staple of life in our city since before my parents arrived, and in my childhood played in the American Association, only one step away from the big leagues. Their affiliations changed over the years, but for a long time they were tied to the Cubs.

That was great for me because I listened to a lot of baseball on the radio, especially the two Chicago teams. The Brewers played at Borchert Field, named after the team's colorful owner in the 1920s, Otto Borchert. It was quite a stadium, notable for not having any seats where a fan could see both foul poles. That sounds like an impossibility, I know, but it was true.

I would go to a lot of games with my mom, who rooted for the Brewers as hard—and loudly—as anyone there. When I got older, I could take the bus and go on my own. Kids would pick their favorite players. Mine was switch-hitting outfielder Hershel Martin. Don't ask me why Hersh Martin, but he was my guy, for sure. I took particular delight when he played for the Yankees in 1944 and '45, when DiMaggio was on military duty in California and Hawaii.

The Brewers had a run of great managers while I was watching them. First was former White Sox catcher Ray Schalk, who would later be elected to the Hall of Fame by the Veterans Committee. Then there was "Jolly" Charlie Grimm, who had managed the Cubs in the World Series three times, and Nick "Tomato Face" Collup, a legendary minor league slugger. Even Casey Stengel came through for a season managing the Brewers before his twelve seasons with the Yankees. It was minor league baseball, sure, but it was great entertainment.

We had a lot of fun playing in our neighborhood, too. I was fortunate in that I always had someone to play catch or a game of pepper with. Herb Kohl lived on Fifty-first Boulevard, about a half block away from me, and we went back and forth between our houses all the time. We were in the same grade in school and shared lots of the same friends.

Herb would go on to grow his family's supermarkets and retail chain, dive into a successful career as an investor, become a U.S.

senator, and purchase the NBA's Milwaukee Bucks. But we didn't talk about our ambitions when we got together. We talked about baseball and we played baseball.

We'd play games behind the school, in the park, wherever. We'd play with any kids who showed up, and if there weren't a lot of kids that was okay, too. Herb and I or some of our other friends—Shelly Gash, Buzzie Grossman—would play strikeout. I don't know if it was played everywhere, but it was played in the Midwest. Kirby Puckett told me about playing it in the Robert Taylor Homes housing project where he was raised in Chicago.

We would use chalk to draw a strike zone on the wall at school, and one of us would pitch and the other would hit. It was simple as could be, but that's always been part of the beauty of baseball. One kid can play; two kids can play. These variations on baseball were great ways to pass the hours. They let us imitate our heroes. I walked the streets of Milwaukee knowing I was going to replace DiMaggio, Mickey Mantle be damned. In truth, I wasn't the greatest player, but I could run a little bit and I was certainly competitive. As Lew Wolff, one of my college fraternity brothers, remembers it, I'd be the thirteenth person chosen for a nine-man team.

Milwaukee had this sandlot league, the Stars of Yesterday League, that was sort of like Little League or Pony League. I played on the Cuckoo Christensens, named after a former Cincinnati Reds outfielder who late in his career hit over .300 for four years in a row for the Brewers. I played center field but couldn't exactly hit like Cuckoo, especially not when pitchers started making the ball bend. I was about fourteen the first time I saw a curveball, and that's when my delusional dreams died. Luckily, by then, I was thoroughly hooked on the game.

One of the experiences that impacted me the most came at Wrigley Field in 1947, before my thirteenth birthday.

Jackie Robinson had broken baseball's color barrier on Opening Day that year, when the Boston Braves played the Dodgers at Ebbets Field in Brooklyn. The Dodgers were coming to Chicago in May. My parents said I could go as long as I brought a friend, so they put my friend Herbie and me on a train the morning of May 27. An older cousin, Sidney Rolfe, met us at Union Station. He had little interest in sports, but like so many people in my family he humored me, for whatever reason. And that day we watched history being made on the North Side of Chicago.

Even as a boy I knew the impact that could have on American society, how it was going to bring our divided world closer together. Jackie's debut drew a huge crowd to that great ballpark with its ivy walls and iconic center-field scoreboard. We were lucky to get tickets in the upper deck, as the paid crowd was 46,572, a record, with an estimated twenty thousand congregated outside, near the intersection of Clark and Addison.

I can just about recite the Dodgers' starting lineup that day from memory. Eddie Stanky led off, followed by Jackie, Pete Reiser, Carl Furillo, Dixie Walker—who was known as the People's Choice and wasn't exactly a supporter of Jackie's, as we learned later—then Cookie Lavagetto, Bruce Edwards, Pee Wee Reese, and the pitcher, Joe Hatten. We cheered just as loudly as anyone up there when No. 42 came to bat in the first inning, facing Johnny Schmitz, a left-hander who had played his high school ball in Wisconsin. He would lead the National League in losses that year, including one to the Dodgers that day.

Jackie took a called third strike the first time up. The Cub fans below us cheered, but there were nothing but groans in the upper deck. It wasn't a great day for Jackie. He lined one hard to center field but ended the day 0 for 4, without ever getting a chance to show the speed that helped this son of Georgia sharecroppers earn letters in four sports at UCLA. But he was on the field alongside his white peers, no longer assigned to the Negro Leagues, and that was what mattered.

I didn't want the game to end, but it did, and afterward Sidney returned Herb and me to Union Station, to catch the North Shore train home. None of us would ever forget what we experienced that day. On the ride home, I felt so many emotions—not only was I a little wiser from my time in the upper deck, but I could see plain as day that even though Jackie had gone hitless, he was a great player whose presence was going to change baseball.

Baseball wasn't everything I did growing up, of course. I'm not completely one-dimensional, although I'd have to plead guilty to being obsessed from an early age. I followed the Packers, too. Everyone in Milwaukee did, I think. They went to the NFL championship game four times in my first ten years under their great coach, Curly Lambeau.

In fact, my father and I were listening to Chicago radio—a game between the Bears and the Chicago Cardinals at Comiskey Park—when Pearl Harbor was attacked. The Packers were off that week, waiting to find out if they would go to the championship game or have to play a one-game playoff with George Halas's Bears, who had given them their one loss during the season, and several of the players were in Chicago watching. It was a Bears game, sure, but it was being followed almost like a Packers game here. That's when news of the Japanese bombing of Pearl Harbor was announced. It was shocking, but life in Milwaukee went on almost like normal.

I went to school on Monday, as usual. And on the following Sunday Sid Luckman led the Bears to a 33–14 win over the

Packers in maybe the most famous game in their great rivalry. Not a great time for America, and an especially bad one for those of us in Milwaukee. It was hard to study, to focus, but the teachers at Sherman School kept us in line. I never was a problem for any of them. All the teachers knew my mother, so she'd be unhappy if I did anything wrong.

School was always an important part of my life, but I cared a whole lot more about my teams, the Yankees and the Packers in those years, than I did my future. My dad took me to a lot of baseball games in Chicago. Sometimes he'd drop me at Wrigley Field or Comiskey Park in the morning and then join me for the end of the game, after he'd had his meetings with automobile dealer Zollie Frank or someone else. Once we went to a Sunday doubleheader at Comiskey Park to see the White Sox play the Yankees. In the eighth inning of the first game, Joe DiMaggio was up with the bases loaded. The feeling was electric—this was what you came all this way to see. I looked over at my dad and he was reading *Time* magazine. The second game he was snoozing a little bit. But he was a great sport.

When my mother and I went to games together, she certainly wasn't reading *Time* magazine—she was watching the ballgame. In fact, I'll always thank my mother for one of the greatest trips any mother could ever give her son.

The 1949 baseball season was such a glorious time in American history that David Halberstam would remember it with his bestseller *Summer of '49*. In a bit of serendipity, that was the time when the fabulous Marie Huber Selig took me on a six-week trip to the East. We experienced everything New York City had to offer and added an equally memorable side trip to Boston. I turned fifteen that summer, and I have always considered that trip the most magical gift I've ever been given. We saw the New York Giants play at the Polo Grounds, the Dodgers play at Ebbets Field, and the awe-inspiring Yankees play at Yankee Stadium, which was so majestic it took my breath away. I could barely believe I was there in the House That Ruth Built, where Lou Gehrig gave his famous speech.

I hadn't been that lucky in Boston. When we were there, my mother wanted to go to places like the Athenaeum and the art museums. She wanted to go to the North End and stroll through the famous graveyards. I had eyes only for Fenway Park, of course.

I was beside myself on June 28. The Yankees were in Boston and DiMaggio was coming back after being sidelined all season with an Achilles injury. The stars were lined up just right with me in town.

But when my mother and I stepped up to the ticket window, the guy there slammed it down.

"Sold out!" he bellowed in his best Boston accent.

"You can't do that!" my mother told him. "I just brought my boy here from Milwaukee."

"Sold out!" he repeated.

That was that. This guy could not care less. We never got in and ended up walking around outside Fenway that afternoon. It was a delicious torture. Close enough to feel the excitement, practically to hear the crack of the bat, but no idea what Ted Williams and Joe D. were doing inside. Luckily for me, that first trip to Fenway wouldn't be my last; it remains one of my favorite places to watch a game. (Thirty years later, in 1979, when I owned the Milwaukee Brewers, my mom joined me in Boston for a big series against the Red Sox. Our traveling secretary, Tommy Ferguson, escorted my mother down to the club seats, next to the visiting dugout. When she saw me she said, "Well, this is a little different than in 1949.")

In New York, we stayed at the Hotel St. Moritz, at 50 Central Park South, on the east side of Sixth Avenue. On July 30, my fifteenth birthday, we had seats in the upper deck at Yankee Stadium, where a White Sox team built around Luke Appling was playing the Yankees. This should have been no contest, but the great thing about a baseball game is you never know what you're going to see. The White Sox won 9–2 that day, over a Yankee team that featured DiMaggio, Yogi Berra, and Phil Rizzuto. The Yankees' leadoff hitter, of course, was Snuffy Stirnweiss. Trust me.

But my biggest memory of that day was about my own self-involved naïveté. I looked down on the field before the game and they were rolling a huge birthday cake out. I turned to my mother and said, "You're embarrassing me!" I really did think the world revolved around me. She just laughed, and pretty soon I realized the cake was for Casey Stengel, who was in his first season as the Yankees' manager.

I got to know my way around New York well enough that my mother would sometimes let me ride the subway to the game by myself. To see these cathedrals in person—Yankee Stadium, Ebbets Field, and the Polo Grounds—was magnificent. In those days, you mainly listened to games on the radio. There was a little television here and there—but nothing in color. And here were these grand ballparks, so vivid in their bright colors and wonderful smells.

It was heaven going to all these places I'd read about and seen pictures of but mostly only imagined. It was as overwhelming to see the ballparks as it was to see the ballplayers. And there I was, seeing the great DiMaggio, my favorite player, in gleaming white pinstripes. Little did I know that soon, I'd be able to see games in color a lot closer to home—not just on TV, but in person.

3

On March 13, 1953, Lou Perini shocked baseball—and me, in a good way—by announcing that he was moving the Boston Braves to Milwaukee, pending approval of the National League. It was a monumental change—both for our city and, ultimately, for me as well.

At the time, I was a freshman at the University of Wisconsin in Madison. Eighty miles is about all it is between Milwaukee and Madison. You can drive it in an hour and fifteen minutes now on Interstate 94, but we didn't complain in the fifties when it took us a little longer, navigating state highways and back roads.

It hadn't been preordained that I would attend the University of Wisconsin, but it was always where I saw myself continuing my education. My mother had wanted me to go to Michigan, where her niece was going. But there was never a doubt in my mind that I wanted to go to Madison, and in the end it was my call. It was the best decision I ever made.

Leaving Washington High behind and moving on to Madison was a huge development for me, especially in terms of making new friends and learning how to live on my own. I wasn't yet a complete person. Not even close. It's that way for most kids, I guess, and it sure was for me. I'd been shy in high school, very shy. Once I went away to school, a lot of that just seemed to leave me. I wasn't always aggressively outgoing, as I gradually became after I left home. There was a big difference in me between high school and college. I'm not sure why.

I loved Madison from the start. I thought it was the best college town in the country when I was there, and it still seems the same now. Two of my grandchildren earned degrees there, and I returned to teach a history course, Baseball & American Society since WWII. I even have my own office in the Department of History. Madison is one of those vibrant American cities that are home to both a large state school—UW has grown to an enrollment of almost forty thousand, including graduate school—and also the state capital. It's anything but a sleepy town, as generations of graduates will tell you. The population is a little over 250,000, and it grows when the Badgers play a game at Camp Randall Stadium.

I never missed a Badger football game, and I also went to a lot of basketball games. Boxing, too. You have to be of a certain age to know this, but intercollegiate boxing was once huge. It was big at Wisconsin and a lot of schools. You couldn't get a seat in the field house when we had a boxing match. It was the death of a Wisconsin student, Charlie Mohr, from injuries suffered in the 1960 NCAA championships, held in our field house, that made school officials rethink the viability of the sport. But I think of it almost as much as football and basketball when I think about my years in college.

When I wasn't watching sports, I dove into my studies in American history, especially the New Deal, and had my eye on eventually returning for graduate school and then maybe even joining the Wisconsin faculty. I was fascinated with Franklin D. Roosevelt's presidency, both its substance and its politics. FDR and his influential first lady, Eleanor, were giants to me. I think I've read every book there is on FDR. He was the first president to use technology—the radio, actually—and it was brilliant. His fireside chats were huge in our household. He was a man of action when America needed decisive leadership, and he wasn't afraid to tell you what he was thinking. It was a model for so many of us.

I was flourishing in Madison when I got the incredible news that the Boston Braves were relocating to Milwaukee. This was stunning. No major league baseball team had moved to a different city in fifty years. Bill Veeck was making noise about moving the St. Louis Browns to Baltimore but had been denied approval from the American League. Yet here was Perini, setting his sights on my hometown, and on March 13 he received approval from the NL.

A team built around Warren Spahn and kid third baseman Eddie Mathews—already getting MVP votes and barely older than me—would be making its home in Milwaukee, with the opener set for April 14, only a month away. I was beyond thrilled. Just like that, I became a Braves fan overnight. And even better, I could still be a Yankee fan, too, because if they played the Braves it would only be in the World Series.

The World Series! In Milwaukee. Talk about a dream.

There were two reasons this was happening. One was that the popularity of Ted Williams had swung Boston toward the Red Sox and away from the Braves. The other still makes me proud to live in Milwaukee.

Coming out of World War II, a group called the Greater Milwaukee Committee was established to consider the city's future. It included Edmund Fitzgerald, who was head of Northwestern Mutual and father of Ed Fitzgerald, who would later be my partner with the Brewers—and, no, it's no coincidence that his name was the same as the one in the famous Lake Superior shipwreck; the ship made famous by Gordon Lightfoot was named after him as a tribute to his family's history of ship captains—and Irwin

Maier, head of the Journal Company. They proposed and the city and county built an art museum, an arena, and a stadium.

Think about this on the stadium: no team had moved since 1902, no expansion had ever taken place, and they had the courage to build County Stadium, with thirty-six thousand seats. That's vision. That's courage. Somehow they knew that baseball would grow and change to meet them where they were—and then, suddenly, it did. It was a level of foresight that made a big impression on me.

As it turned out, County Stadium was what prompted Perini to move the Braves to Milwaukee. He wouldn't have done it if the stadium wasn't being completed in 1952, when he brought the Braves here to play their Triple-A affiliate, our Brewers. The Braves and Brewers played an exhibition game at Borchert Field on August 18. The minor leaguers beat the big leaguers in that game, but what mattered the most was the impression that was left with Perini.

He was losing money in Boston and felt he could change that by coming to Milwaukee.

In an Associated Press story in September, he telegraphed his intentions.

"There is a new stadium in Milwaukee that is unequalled in baseball," Perini said. "It is so located that it is in the center of north-south and east-west traffic arteries and there will be facilities for parking 10,000 cars. And where can you match that?"

While Williams enjoyed godlike standing in Boston, the Braves had fallen on hard times after winning a National League pennant in 1948. They had drawn almost 1.5 million fans in '48, leading the NL in attendance, but stumbled along in the ensuing years, becoming less and less popular with fans. They couldn't even draw three hundred thousand fans in '52, when they were 64–89.

Perini was said to be losing five hundred thousand dollars per year in those days. That's a lot of money in 1950s dollars.

"I don't intend to (stay) here when people don't want to see the Braves," Perini told the *Boston Globe* after the last game in '52.

Perini was Boston through and through, from a prominent family. Few Bostonians took his threats to move seriously. But Fred Miller, head of Miller Brewing, and others in Milwaukee were quietly working to point him to County Stadium. It turned out Perini was listening.

My friend Herbie and I were home from college that spring when the news that the Braves were moving hit the airwaves. He and I drove to Story Parkway, the parkway above County Stadium. We just looked at the ballpark, thinking that major league baseball would be played there, and it was like a dream come true. I can still remember standing there looking at County Stadium with all that red brick and envisioning baseball's future there.

School kept me away from Opening Day, but Herb and I did shoot into town on April 8, when the team was welcomed to Milwaukee after traveling from Florida via train. They played the Red Sox in two exhibition games but before then were celebrated with a parade that ran from the train station to the ballpark.

I was thrilled that Milwaukee had a team. Even better, they turned it around that season, thanks to Mathews, Spahn, Lew Burdette, and others. I went to a lot of games that summer when I got home, but even in Madison I didn't miss a game on radio. Earl Gillespie and Blaine Walsh were the announcers.

I could walk from the library to the Pi Lambda Phi house and listen to the game the whole way, without even having a radio of my own. It was on in every dorm and every car. Braves baseball was an obsession.

The Braves won ninety-two games that first season in Milwaukee, finishing second to the Brooklyn Dodgers. They drew more than 1.8 million fans, setting a National League record, and in each of the next four years would draw over two million, including 2.21 million in 1957. It was an unbelievable beginning, one that caused other teams to think differently about baseball's future out west.

I was picked to serve as president of my fraternity my junior year in Madison. I don't know if I wanted to be the Pi Lambda Phi president. It just happened. Some of the older guys who had been running things came to me and said, "You're the next president of the fraternity." They took a vote and that was it. I was the REX. It took a fair amount of time, but I enjoyed it.

Charlie Thomas played on the football team. He was a backup to Alan Ameche, who had led Wisconsin to the Rose Bowl the year before and was on his way to winning the Heisman Trophy as a fullback and a linebacker.

Charlie worked as a waiter at the Pi Lam house to earn a little money. He was African American, and he was a great guy.

I had a routine in those days. I'd go to the library to study after dinner every night. One day he said, "I know you go to the library every night, can I go with you? Would you wait ten minutes, let me clean up?" We walked to the library, studied, and afterward walked to this place, Greasy George's, and had hamburgers. It was appropriately named. It was plenty greasy.

Charlie and I got to be really good friends. I got the idea one day that he should join Pi Lam, breaking the color barrier in our fraternity the way that Jackie Robinson had in baseball. That had happened in 1947, eight years earlier. Integrating a college fraternity didn't seem like such a big deal, at least not to me. It was the right thing to do.

Of course, civil rights events around the country were starting to shape my thinking—it wasn't just Jackie. These were simple times in Madison, for sure, but complicated ones in America. The landmark school desegregation case *Brown v. Board of Education* was handed down on May 17, 1954, and it wouldn't be long before racial issues rightfully would become impossible for anyone to ignore.

Emmett Till, as I would learn later, was a kid from Chicago who loved little more than to play baseball on the South Side's sandlots. His mother, Mamie, used to tell stories about the time she sent him to the store for bread only to find him playing baseball with friends as it got dark.

Emmett had family in Mississippi, near the tiny Delta town of Money, outside of Greenwood, and as a fourteen-year-old traveled there by train in the summer of 1955. He was there to help in the fields and to enjoy himself in the country, where he could fish and relax before returning in the fall.

When Till returned, he was in his coffin. He had been beaten, shot, and horribly disfigured before being thrown into the Tallahatchie River, where his body was discovered. His so-called crime was being friendly with a local white woman while visiting her store. It was a horrible tragedy and quickly became a national story, thanks in part to graphic photographs and persistent reports on radio and television from Chicago, where Mamie directed that Till receive an open-casket funeral.

Lynchings were nothing new, sadly. But this one was different because of the attention it received. A TV news bulletin even interrupted scheduled broadcasts after the body was discovered. Till's heartsick mother seized the opportunity to use her son's death as a call to action for African Americans and whites with a mind for fairness.

In terms of where I was and how my life was going, I was a million miles away from these horrors. But I can remember being shaken by how anyone in our country could treat a person like this. It just horrified me.

The funeral home where Till's body was taken in Chicago was at Forty-first and Cottage Grove, not too far from Thirty-fifth and Shields, where the White Sox played at Comiskey Park. I'd been there a lot, especially for Sunday doubleheaders against the Yankees, and I think that connection really brought home the meaning of the story to me. I looked at it as a different world down south, but this was a kid from Chicago.

I couldn't believe the color of someone's skin could matter this much. That was not how I was raised. So, I sounded out some of my closest friends in Pi Lam and lots of others about Charlie pledging. They told me there would be some opposition from some of our brothers, which really saddened me, but I thought we could pull this off. I was determined not to let that old mind-set take hold. The guys knew Charlie and they liked Charlie. That was the thing I kept coming back to when I considered whether this could work.

One day walking home from Greasy George's I said to Charlie, "You get along so well with all the guys, it's like you're one of the guys." I didn't really think much about how I was white and he was black. I didn't have any bias. I never heard my parents talk about it, nothing. He was a wonderful guy, and I really liked him a lot.

I said to him, "You ought to pledge." He looked at me like I was nuts. I had studied our fraternity bylaws before I talked to them. They were silent on the subject of race and, if anything, the history of our fraternity suggested inclusion, not exclusion.

About two weeks later, Charlie said to me one day, after Greasy George's or on the way there, "Were you serious about that?" I said, "You bet I was." He said, "Well, I'm thinking about it." I said, "I wish you would."

He was one of the guys. He said to me a day or two later, "Well, if you want to take it on and do it, I'm willing." I said, "Charlie, it's my pleasure."

We had a big fraternity meeting to discuss Charlie and the other pledges. Of course, that's not all there is to the story. It was the night a few of our guys got in trouble, and I had to go dig 'em out of jail. That was my lot in life.

Five or six of them dressed up as Hollywood producers, and convinced an eighteen- or nineteen-year-old young lady to pose for photos, saying they could get her a job in Hollywood. Except it turns out she was engaged to a Madison policeman. Here I am in the midst of this very dramatic meeting and I look up and there are two policemen at the door. I thought, well, we're making too much noise and the girls next door complained. It turns out I had to take our house fellow, the faculty adviser, a man named Art Hillman, who was in law school, with me to get these jerks out of jail.

By this point we'd already had one vote and Charlie hadn't gotten in. I wasn't willing to quit on Charlie, so I told the guys, don't go anywhere. I'm going to the jail, but I'll be right back.

We went to the jail and there were our nitwits. They had hats on that said phot ogr apher, and stuff like that. You couldn't write a script like this. Well, Art helped me and we got the guys. Then I got back to the house.

I said, I know it's late, but we're not leaving here, no matter how long it takes, until we get this vote. After many tries, the last vote we took passed. Charlie was in.

I remember calling Charlie to tell him. He was a wonderful guy. He went on to become superintendent of schools in Evanston, Illinois, had a wonderful career. He was as fine a human being as I ever met. He had the misfortune to be behind Ameche, probably the greatest football player Wisconsin ever had, probably the best football player I ever saw. But Charlie was a great friend to have, and we were friends for a lifetime.

A few days later, I got a call from Fifty-second Street in Milwaukee. It came into the fraternity house, where we all took our calls. Usually it was my mother calling, but this time it was my father.

"Buddy, I've had some calls from parents, and they're unhappy."

"Yeah, what's that about?"

He said he was just calling to tell me that these parents didn't like Charlie Thomas in the fraternity. He said it was my decision, he wasn't saying there was anything wrong with it, and that my mother didn't even want him to call, but he thought I needed to know what was going on. He said it was the right thing to do, that he was proud of me, but that some of the parents didn't think it was time yet for a mixed fraternity.

"Well, Dad," I said. "I'm going to graduate next year. This is our time. I'll be gone. I understand some people are unhappy, but it's too bad. It's done. It's over."

And I'm so glad I did exactly what I did. It was the right thing to do, without a hint of a doubt, and it was a great lesson for me in how to get the votes necessary to make change even when there's resistance.

And as it turned out, it wouldn't be the last time I'd need this skill.

4

"Just fo r a year."

I can still hear my father's words, asking me to come work for him at the auto dealership. I was hesistant, since I had other plans. Of course, if I'd known that selling cars would be a crucial step to me becoming involved in Major League Baseball, I would have jumped at the chance.

At the time my father said these words to me, I'd just gotten out of the army, which had been a story in itself. I'd enlisted after graduating from Wisconsin and headed off to Fort Leonard Wood, in Missouri, near the Ozark Mountains, for basic training. The Korean War had ended three years earlier, but Israel had just invaded Egypt in a tug-of-war over the Suez Canal, so if you were a man of draft age you had to consider the possibility that the armed forces could be in your future.

Fort Leonard Wood is about three hours southwest of St. Louis, and you wouldn't call it a tourist attraction. I reported there for basic training, under Sergeant Nelson Morris. I liked him, liked the guys—a lot of them were from Milwaukee—and saw the whole thing as a necessary adventure, doing my part. I tried hard at everything but didn't always bring a lot of skill to the tasks I was assigned. This was clear on the shooting range, as rifles were new to me. "Do me a favor," Sergeant Morris said one day. "Put the gun down. You're shooting at everyone else's targets!"

After about six weeks at the base I wasn't feeling well. I was weak. I was skinny. I'd lost a lot of weight that summer. One

Friday night we were cleaning up for inspection the next morning and it was clear something was wrong with me. Sergeant Morris sent me to bed. I think I ate two hamburgers that night, with raw onions, and had two big Cokes. That's not too smart when your stomach's a mess, and my stomach was a mess.

Luckily for me, my commanding officer, Major Beliveau, was a doctor, and he recognized that there was something significantly wrong with me. It turned out I had a bleeding ulcer, which had apparently started my senior year at Wisconsin. I remember having stomach issues then but never thought it was serious. Major Beliveau ordered blood transfusions for me. He told me afterward that I might have died if it had gone untreated one more day.

I became close to Major Beliveau. He had me work as his administrative assistant after I got released from the hospital. He said I could get a medical release to go home, but I didn't want to be seen as shirking my duty. He taught me a lot about medicine, which I'd think about when I got involved in baseball and was dealing with the health of players.

I enjoyed what I was doing at Fort Leonard Wood, but when my time was up I knew going home to Milwaukee was the right thing to do. I had responsibilities there.

For one thing, while I was in basic training, my longtime girlfriend, Donna Chaimson, came to visit me and we impulsively got married. Her sister Marsha had married my brother Jerry and we'd been dating in Milwaukee and during my time in Madison, so we'd been together for a while by that point. It was what we wanted to do, even if it didn't thrill everybody back home. My mother strongly felt I was too young to get married, but I was ready. I never really asked myself if I was too young to make such a commitment, even if that was the summer I turned twenty-two. In those days that was what you did. You went to school, got a degree, and got married. I never thought anything about it. I just did it.

For another thing, my original plan had been to return to Wisconsin for graduate school, but now my father was presenting me with a different idea, asking me to join him in the auto business. It wasn't what I had in mind, but his words "just for one year" made sense. In those days when your father asked you to do something, you did it.

So just like that I was a newlywed working in a new job, doing anything and everything my dad needed at the family business. He was a hard worker—six days a week, five nights a week. So that's what I did, too. I never really sold cars, but I did everything else. I worked hard and rooted for the Braves just as hard.

They had finished behind the Brooklyn Dodgers all four years they had been in Milwaukee, finishing second in the National League three times and third once. They had won ninety-two games in 1956, only one less than the Dodgers.

Not surprisingly, my mom was as big a fan as I was. One time during my senior year at Wisconsin I was speaking to a big luncheon at school. There were a lot of kids there and many of their parents. In the middle of my talk, there was a commotion in the back. There was my mother holding a radio to her ear and she shouted, "Buddy, [Joe] Adcock just hit a homer to beat the Dodgers!" That's the kind of fan she was.

The '57 season was the first time I was able to be in Milwaukee for a full season. I couldn't have picked a better year. They were loaded. Hank Aaron, only twenty-three but already in his fourth season, had an MVP year, leading the league with forty-four homers and 132 RBIs while hitting .322. It was truly a privilege to have a chance to watch Henry hit.

The Braves' infield had Frank Torre at first, Red Schoendienst at second, Johnny Logan at short, and Eddie Mathews at third. Warren Spahn told me years later that they never would have done what they did without Schoendienst, who was acquired in a trade at the deadline (it was June 15 then).

Hurricane Hazle became part of the story late that summer.

Bob Hazle, a left-handed-hitting outfielder promoted from Triple-A Wichita, picked up the nickname Hurricane when he went on a two-week tear in August, hitting .473 with five homers and nineteen RBIs in fourteen games. The Braves were already in first place but being threatened by the Cardinals. Hurricane Hazle served noticed against\them in a three-game sweep in St. Louis, pushing the Milwaukee lead to five games, and the state of Wisconsin was thrown into a raging case of pennant fever.

I was at County Stadium as much as I could be and always had the game on the radio when the team was on the road. I was taking an accounting class, at my father's urging, but the last place I wanted to be that fall was a classroom.

There was a class scheduled the night of September 23, when the Braves had a chance to clinch the pennant against the Cardinals. I'd almost never skipped a class in my life. Maybe never. But I did that night, after first starting to drive to the school. I pulled the car off the freeway and headed to County Stadium, which was beyond capacity. I think I parked nine miles away and the only ticket I could get was an obstructed-view seat behind a big metal post. It was cold that night, but I loved every minute.

It was a 2–2 game through nine. The Braves had a chance to win in the tenth, loading the bases, but Billy Muffett got Torre to hit into a double play. I about died. But it only made the eventual ending even sweeter in my memory.

In the eleventh inning, Aaron hit a laser to center field, the deepest part of the park. Wally Moon chased it, but the ball cleared the fence. Milwaukee had clinched the pennant. We were going to the World Series.

This was big. Enormous. Gigantic.

The image of the great Aaron, deliriously happy, being hoisted onto the shoulders of his teammates was burned into my memory and hasn't faded. That photo was carried on the front page of the *New York Times* the next day, opposite a picture of the National Guard being ordered into Little Rock because Arkansas governor Orval Faubus was defying courts by not letting nine courageous African American children enroll at Little Rock Central High School.

Those two contrasting photos, one showing unity in Wisconsin and the other showing division in Arkansas, made the same kind of impression on me that the Emmett Till murder had. I'll never forget looking at that front page and seeing the sociological significance. My father would teach repeatedly, "Nothing is good or bad except by comparison." The comparison between the ideals being shown by Aaron's place in baseball and the ugly politics of race in America couldn't have been any clearer.

I was as joyful in the first weeks of October as I'd ever been. My first child, Sari, a beautiful daughter, was born on September 30, the day the Braves were heading to New York for the World Series.

My emotions were thoroughly tested by both events, I'll admit. I put in a full week at work, too, although the day games didn't help. I was hardly alone in being preoccupied by baseball, however, as Milwaukee essentially shut down when the World Series games were televised on NBC, with Mel Allen and Al Helfer providing commentary.

Here's an amazing fact about the support the Braves received in 1957: they not only outdrew the Yankees; they outdrew the

Yankees and New York Giants combined. That sounds crazy, doesn't it? Milwaukee is a great baseball town, which was why Aaron and many of his teammates settled here to raise their families rather than returning to their old hometowns in warmer parts of the country.

In fact, Milwaukee was such a great baseball town in '57 that fans booked all the hotel rooms downtown for the World Series. Casey Stengel was furious when his Yankees wound up staying in Browns Lake, a tiny community thirty miles southwest of town, which prompted Stengel to call our city "Bushville," as in bush league.

Stengel wasn't happy at the end of the World Series, either. Lew Burdette beat Whitey Ford 1–0 in game 5 and came back on two days' rest to shut out Mickey Mantle and the Yankees again in game 7. The Braves had given us a championship in their fifth year in town.

While our family wouldn't always sell Fords, it turned out to be fortunate for me that we represented Ford when I got into the business. In the summer of '58, I was sent to Ford School in Detroit for six weeks, and there I met Carlos Nelson, a Ford dealer from Puerto Rico. He was a baseball junkie like me and filled my ears with stories from winter ball in San Juan. We stayed at the same hotel and became very good friends. He told me at some point that he'd like to come to Milwaukee and see our dealership on his way home. That way, I could show him my hometown and we could go see the Braves, who were on their way to winning a second pennant and facing a rematch with Mantle and the Yankees in the World Series.

It turned out that Carlos had met a couple of the Braves players during winter ball: Don McMahon, a relief pitcher and a great family man, and Frank Torre, the first baseman who was then one of Milwaukee's leading bachelors. The four of us went out together when Carlos was in town and became friends. Suddenly I didn't just have a major league team in my town, I knew some of their players.

Joe Torre, who was eight years younger than Frank, came from Brooklyn to watch his older brother play that summer. He was having such a good time in Milwaukee that he convinced Frank to let him stay when the Braves left for a road trip, and Frank asked me if he could stay with me, Donna, and little Sari. I said sure, and it turned out that Joe was a lot less trouble than Frank would have been. It was the start of a remarkable friendship between me and Joe.

The 1958 World Series also went seven games, like '57, but this time my old favorite team, the Yankees, prevailed. The Braves jumped to a three-games-to-one lead, but Spahn and Burdette ran out of gas pitching on short rest. They started eleven of the fourteen games in those two Series, which sounds crazy, but it almost got us two parades.

There was almost no competitive balance in those years. The Yankees won the pennant fourteen times in sixteen seasons beginning in 1949, and nine times won the World Series. The New York Giants and Brooklyn Dodgers had combined to win the National League pennant seven times in eight years before the Braves broke through.

Between the Yankees, Giants, and Dodgers, New York teams won twenty-one pennants in a sixteen-year period that's remembered as the golden age of baseball. Maybe it's remembered that way because so many of the most influential writers and broadcasters were based in New York, not in cities with lesser teams.

Going head-to-head with the Yankees did a lot for Milwaukee's self-image. This was a downtime for the Packers, between the reigns of Curly Lambeau and Vince Lombardi, and baseball was king in my city. I wasn't doing badly for myself, either, in part because I was beginning to do a lot of business with Braves players.

There was a Dodge dealer in town, Wally Rank, who had been getting the Braves' business from their first year in Milwaukee. He had loaned a car to Del Crandall and then lots of other players, but I figured two could play that game.

Don McMahon and Frank Torre opened a lot of doors. I got to know Henry Aaron and a lot of other players and front office people, and I was happy to help players with cars. It wasn't even a lease. I just gave them a car to use when they were in Milwaukee. Joe Torre was such a good young catcher that the Braves signed him in 1959 and he was in the big leagues in '60. He had a Ford convertible, and he liked it so much, he bought it. Henry bought a car from me but says that his buying it from me was so good for my business that I still owe him money. I don't know about that, but I do know I loved doing business with the Braves. And I loved Henry.

He had grown up in Mobile, Alabama, and was thirteen when Branch Rickey signed Jackie Robinson. We were about the same age. I was a product of American immigration; he was a product of American integration. We were both becoming proof that all things can be possible, dreams can come true.

When I got to know Henry, I had no idea he would eventually break Babe Ruth's home run record. But I knew he could really hit (so did anyone else lucky enough to see him up close). I knew he was as wise as he was intelligent. I knew his smile could light up a room.

Henry and I started going to Packers games together after the 1958 season. You didn't have to go up to Green Bay to see them because they played a couple of games a year at County Stadium. Henry and I developed a pattern that worked for both of us. We'd get together the morning of a game, go to a place called Ace Foods on West Wisconsin Avenue for an early lunch, and then head over to the game.

Thanks to the Braves clubhouse guys, we had passes that got us access to the field. One day we were standing right behind the Packers' bench during a game against the Rams. There was a lot of fighting going on and the game was going against the Packers. We looked up during the second quarter and here came the young Lombardi, laying into his players as they came off the field. "What the hell is going on around here?" he yelled. He really let them have it. He got so worked up, he broke a clipboard. That was enough for Henry and me to see. We didn't want him to see us staring at him with our wide eyes. He might've made us his next target. So we hustled away from the bench, down to a quieter spot.

Henry would root for his friend Jim Brown whenever Cleveland came to town. I had become friends with Willie Davis, a Green Bay defensive end from Grambling State in Louisiana. He was as big as a meat freezer, but he could really run. Great player. Henry and I would trade barbs the whole game about Willie and Jim Brown whenever the Packers were playing Cleveland.

When the Packers started winning under Lombardi in the early sixties, with superstar players like Bart Starr, Paul Hornung, and Jim Taylor, the Braves very quietly slid into the status of a middle-tier team. The turning point was losing general manager John Quinn to the Phillies after the '59 season, though Perini did well to recruit one of baseball's best young executives, John McHale, to replace Quinn.

It's hard to pin down what the Braves were missing after the back-to-back pennants in '57 and '58. Aaron and Mathews remained as dangerous as any combination of hitters in baseball. Crandall was solid behind the plate and guys like Bill Bruton and Joe Adcock were very reliable. Time took a toll on Spahn and Burdette, more than anything else, and the front office couldn't add any more All-Star arms to complement them.

So the Braves went from first place into the middle of the pack as the NFL became a glamorous league under Pete Rozelle, who was only thirty-three when he stepped in as commissioner, after the death of Bert Bell. The Braves' attendance went into free fall—from just under two million in '58 to 1.75 million in '59, 1.5 million in '60, 1.1 million in '61, and all the way down to about 767,000 in '62. The team wasn't doing anything to market itself and alienated a lot of fans by not doing more to protest a city ordinance that prohibited fans from bringing their own beer into the park.

It seems like common sense now not to allow fans to bring their own beer into the ballpark, but it was a big deal in Milwaukee in 1961, when the ordinance went into effect. The original Washington Senators had also moved to Minneapolis for the '61 season, which probably cost the Braves some fans who had been traveling from the western parts of Wisconsin to attend games.

Perini had never been a hands-on owner, remaining in Boston to run his construction business when the team moved to Milwaukee, but he did react after attendance dropped almost 25 percent in 1961. He cut his payroll by selling Frank Thomas and Johnny Antonelli to the expansion Mets, introduced a corny slogan—"Something new in '62"—and raised ticket prices. He also allowed a limited number of games to be televised, the Braves becoming the last major league team to put its product on television.

When attendance fell again that season, Perini bailed out. He sold the team to a group of Chicago investors led by thirty-four-year-old insurance executive Bill Bartholomay for $5.5 million. There were rumors that Bartholomay's group bought the team with the idea of moving it to Atlanta, where a municipal stadium was in the works to open in 1964 or '65. The change of ownership certainly had done nothing to regain the trust of fans who felt they were being taken for granted.

Under both Perini and Bartholomay, the Braves were better on the field than in the community. If you ascribe to the (hopefully) extinct theory that you merely need to open your doors and win, you'll lose. An owner can never take the fans for granted. An owner must never forget that the fortunes and popularity of a club are fragile. An owner must never forget that people ought to feel appreciated. The Braves made all of these mistakes, and when the wins dwindled, the effects became visible, and eventually insurmountable.

5

Unlike a lot of owners of professional sports teams, I never set out to own a team. At least at the start, all I wanted was to do my part to show the Braves that Milwaukee wanted them to stay right where they were. I had already put my money where my mouth was, but the problem was that I didn't have a lot of money. I had to borrow to buy two thousand shares of stock at ten dollars a share when Bill Bartholomay, the Braves' owner, made a limited offering to the public, attempting to broaden the team's hold on Milwaukee. It was one way that Bartholomay tried to offset the perception that he had just bought the team to move it. No one in Milwaukee was more invested than me in keeping the team here. I didn't know it at the time, but afterward I found out I was the largest shareholder of public stock. It wasn't true ownership, but it was the first time I had a financial stake in a team.

Unfortunately, it didn't help matters much.

On an idyllic September day in 1964, I went to lunch at the Milwaukee Athletic Club with Bill Anderson, who managed County Stadium. We were talking about what locals had talked about every day since 1953, the Braves, but now this wasn't just about Spahn's brilliance in attacking hitters' weaknesses or how Johnny Logan turned the double play. It was about whether we could do anything to stop the team we loved from moving to Atlanta.

A lot of people didn't want to believe the Braves would leave, but this was a time of great movement in baseball, after the Dodgers and Giants had left New York to go west, and the climate here was bad. It wasn't just Atlanta, either. There were also whispers that Phoenix and Toronto were trying to get our team. Bartholomay had pursued the White Sox before buying the Braves. But he saw Milwaukee's limitations, not the spirit that I knew was here.

"We were so happy to finally buy the club," Bartholomay said. "It was like when you chase the girl, and she finally says yes. You're just so happy. Now, once we had the club, you stop and look around and see that the American League had just moved the Washington Senators to Minnesota. So we have the Twins in the west, a lake to the east, a border to the north and two clubs in Chicago to the south. Any way you sliced it, it was a small and finite market."

People talk about quality of life, and I'm a big believer that baseball adds to that for a city. But for me baseball hasn't ever been about quality of life; it's been the essence of my life. All around America, major league teams were popping up in new places. The Dodgers and Giants moved to Los Angeles and San Francisco, respectively. Texas got its first team with the expansion Colt .45s in Houston. The American League awarded an expansion team to Southern California—the Angels—to keep up with the Dodgers. Even Washington, D.C., got an expansion version of the Senators after Calvin Griffith turned the original Senators into the Twins.

I wanted to make a difference but couldn't do it on my own. The key, I knew, was to get some of Milwaukee's business leaders involved. And that day at the Athletic Club I had the good fortune to have lunch at the same time as Bob Uihlein.

He was the president of Schlitz Brewing Company, one of the biggest businesses in the city, and his family controlled the two biggest banks in the state, M&I and First Wisconsin. He was a Harvard grad who had picked up a law degree at the University of Wisconsin, and was known around town as a legendary polo player. I certainly knew who he was, even if he didn't know me.

I had been talking to Anderson about how Milwaukee needed to get a group together to save the Braves and Uihlein was someone who could actually help. Anderson knew Uihlein and approached him. He told him that I was the fellow who was trying to keep baseball in Milwaukee and asked if he had time to meet with me.

"It's quarter to one," Uihlein said. "How's one thirty?"

Anderson came back to our table and asked me what I was doing after lunch. I told him I was going back to work, but he shook his head. "No, you're not," he said. "You're going to see Mr. Uihlein at the brewery."

In forty-five minutes? I'm having the most important meeting in my life and I've got forty-five minutes to prepare for it?

That's crazy, even for me. But I was thrilled that I was getting time with Uihlein, so now it was a matter of making the most of it.

My mind was going a mile a second as I drove my Ford sedan toward Schlitz's headquarters, in a huge building in the heart of the city that I'd passed a thousand times but never been in. I had to make the most of this chance. I had to convince him that there's something special, something sacred even, about the relationship of a city and its baseball team.

Once his secretary showed me in, I was struck by how Uihlein carried himself. He was this big, tall man but he made me feel comfortable immediately.

He knew what I wanted to talk about but at the start didn't share my concern.

"Our people don't think the Braves are leaving," he said.

"Mr. Uihlein," I said, "they're leaving."

I poured my heart out to him, passing along what I'd picked up from being around Bartholomay, Anderson, and even the team's players, including Aaron and Mathews. They knew the situation was dire, and that's what I worked to get across to Uihlein.

After about an hour, he was sold.

Uihlein said he would help if I could put together a group that would buy the team to keep it in Milwaukee. He walked around his desk, stuck out his big hand, and said, "Well, partner, we're in."

When I walked out of the Schlitz headquarters, I was stunned, almost speechless. I was also happier than I'd been in a long time. Maybe this could work. Our Braves were leaving, which was heartbreaking, but something else was happening and I was right in the middle of it. Here I was, on the verge of devoting my life to baseball, and it felt like what I was supposed to be doing.

In that first meeting, Uihlein had told me we needed a lawyer and a banker in our group. He had recommendations—a lawyer named Richard Cutler and a banker named George Kasten. I went to see both of them that afternoon and they enthusiastically jumped aboard.

Kasten was a gentle man and a people person who had been educated at Williams College. He was chairman of First Wisconsin, and he loved Milwaukee the way I did. He was waiting for me on the street after Uihlein called to tell him I was coming over to meet him. It was the first time a bank chairman was happy to see me.

I remember being really proud of myself when that day ended. When I told my dad that I had met with Bob Uihlein and George Kasten, he couldn't believe it.

With Uihlein's support and our new line of credit, I decided to go for it. Bob and I wrote a letter to Bartholomay, offering him seven million dollars for the team.

In our eyes, that could have been a classic win-win situation. The Braves' new owners would earn a tidy profit for their short time in baseball and we'd have local ownership of the team, determined to ride through the tough times that the franchise was facing. But we were naïve to think they'd sell us the team when there were so many other cities talking to Bartholomay about relocation.

We got a one-line response to our proposal, and it was a polite rejection. "Thank you for your interest in the Milwaukee Braves," it read, but that was only the start for us.

We recruited another of Milwaukee's civic leaders, Ed Fitzgerald. He was the head of Cutler-Hammer, an electrical manufacturing giant. His father was Edmund Fitzgerald, who had been active on the civic commission that got County Stadium built. Ed would become an invaluable friend and partner. A coalition was forming, and it would become a tight group.

Ed's sister, Liz, was married to our lawyer, Dick Cutler. He had graduated from both Yale and Yale Law and was a managing partner at one of Milwaukee's most prominent law firms, Quarles & Brady.

We also reached out to Ben Barkin, a brilliant advertising and public relations man. He was like Uihlein. He knew everybody in town and from the start he grasped both our vision and the urgency of our actions.

We decided to give our organization a name. Ben came up with "Teams Inc.," which was an acronym for "To Encourage All Milwaukee Sports." This had become a second full-time job for me, and I was already following my father's example by working long days and nights.

I might have been working alongside him, but my father didn't really understand what I was doing. Because my mother loved baseball the same way I did, she got it, but she was worried about me. Donna and I had two daughters now, as Wendy was chasing Sari around the house. She was born March 18, 1960, and was a ball of fire from the start. She would become my baseball girl. Eventually my mother made me start taking Wednesday night off, so I could have one family night in the middle of the week.

I had gone to New York myself in October, a month after Uihlein and I got the ball rolling. I sent myself to the World Series—Cardinals–Yankees—to represent our group.

While I was there I managed to visit Commissioner Ford Frick in his office. I cold-called him, of course, and he must have felt our conversation would be harmless.

I was nervous riding up the elevator, scared. Here I was, just a kid, and he was the commissioner of baseball. I was surprised he was seeing me, to be honest, but I told him how much I loved baseball and how worried I was about the Braves leaving Milwaukee. He was actually very nice to me. Really nice. He thanked me for coming in. I wasn't there long, but I left feeling good. He said he understood why I was unhappy and wished me well. That was something, even if it didn't mean anything.

And believe me, it didn't. Bartholomay was steaming ahead with his plans to move the Braves, and his board of directors voted 12–6 to move to Atlanta. The *New York Times* had written in July that this was their plan, and it was happening.

Atlanta Stadium was being completed, and the Braves planned to play there in 1965. We worked behind the scenes as Milwaukee County and the state of Wisconsin tried to stop the team from moving.

Suing a major league team—and, in effect, the National League—was a bold thing to do, especially for a city that wanted to get another team if we lost the Braves. We worried that we were going to alienate people and that the suit could boomerang back on us, making what was happening even worse. But the only other option was to watch our team leave, and that wasn't an option we could get behind.

We used our local law firm, Foley & Lardner, and brought in a Washington law firm because we had decided to attack it as an antitrust case. This sounds a little crazy now, but I really thought we had a good case, that what the Braves were doing wasn't just wrong but illegal. I wouldn't say I got cocky, but I definitely thought they might crack because they didn't want to get sued. I thought we could win if it did go to court, and we almost did.

In the end, we did win an injunction that delayed the Braves from moving by one season. The case had been heard by Elmer W. Roller, who ruled in our favor. I enjoyed the ruling immensely.

I got to know Bowie Kuhn, an outside counsel who was representing the National League. He would go on to become baseball's fifth commissioner, replacing Spike Eckert in 1969, and served sixteen seasons. We got along well even though we were on different sides of this case.

Bowie always called Judge Roller a "hometown judge." I would encounter plenty of those myself in later years, but for now I was fully on board with Judge Roller's wisdom. The NL appealed the ruling and won a split decision, by a 4–3 vote, in the Wisconsin Supreme Court. The judges on that panel were actually very sympathetic to the Brewers, but they just didn't think state antitrust laws were applicable in this situation.

By then it was clear the Braves were going to play at County Stadium for one more season and that would be it. They would be in Atlanta in 1966 and forever more, no matter how much it hurt me and the Milwaukee community.

That was the weirdest year ever. It's safe to say that a franchise with one foot out the door isn't going to get much support. The Braves muddled through an 86–76 season under manager Bobby Bragan, getting the usual excellence from Aaron, Mathews, and the Torre I had babysat when he was Frank's little brother. They were fifth in the standings and last in attendance, drawing 555,584 dispirited fans.

The Braves front office was gearing up the operations in Atlanta and barely paid attention to what was going on in Milwaukee. There was so much bitterness here that the team's staffers didn't even want to stick around to run the club.

One of the strangest sidelights is they offered our group—Teams Inc.—a chance to essentially run the operation during that final year in Milwaukee. They paid us a nickel per ticket sold—a whopping $27,779.20 for a full season of involvement. We weren't doing it for the money, of course. It was great experience that would benefit us if we could ever land another team.

For some reason I believed we would, but there wasn't an abundance of positive thinking in the community. Even my father echoed the skepticism.

"Buddy, it's Milwaukee," he told me. "People say we can't support a major league team. You're wasting your time."

6

Bringing baseball back to Milwaukee became my life. As the one fully committed staffer for Teams Inc., I changed our name to Milwaukee Brewers Baseball Club. I'll admit that move didn't get banner headlines in the *Milwaukee Journal*. We were a company without a baseball team, major or minor league. But for me it was a method of making something happen, of moving the chains, which, as a lifelong Packers fan, I've always understood.

I chose *Brewers* as the name because it was the name of the minor league team my mom and I watched so often when I was a boy, the team that played at Borchert Field. I figured it would make people smile when they remembered life before the Braves, who, in complete hindsight, exploited our city and robbed any future efforts of the goodwill of baseball fans.

I understood what fans were feeling because I was one of them. But I had my foot in the door and became something of a squatter at County Stadium. I used County Stadium as the mailing address for the Milwaukee Brewers Baseball Club, which kept me from mixing my baseball business with my work for my father or life at home with Donna and the kids. The Braves' comptroller had abandoned his office, moving his work to Atlanta, and I moved in. It would be my home away from home until 1998, when I was named baseball's ninth commissioner.

If the MBBC was going to be viable, we had to raise money to secure a team whenever one became available, either through relocation of an existing franchise or expansion. Bob Uihlein,

Dick Cutler, and others involved in the effort drew up a list of prospects in the Milwaukee business community we could tap for the money that would help Milwaukee get a second chance at major league baseball. I drove from place to place visiting these Wisconsin business leaders in person to sell them on the significance of Milwaukee having a team in the majors. One by one I landed the pitches, gaining serious financial commitments from individuals and companies until we had an impressive group with deep financial roots to get baseball to take us seriously.

But even with this group, it was hard trying to envision baseball's future in the city, just as it was heading out the door. Sandy Koufax pitched against the Braves in their last home game here in the fall of '65. We have a photo of Aaron and Mathews walking from the dugout to the clubhouse for the last time. It was so sad.

Once the Braves were gone and County Stadium was eerily quiet, I knew we had to do something to keep Milwaukee in the conversation around major league baseball. Because the city's lawsuit against the team was still ongoing after the '65 season ended, it gave me the tiniest bit of standing to attend baseball's off-season meetings. I went, but I can report that I was treated like I had leprosy. Most of the old-line owners looked at me with contempt, and even the nice guys seemed to feel sorry for those of us from Milwaukee, and that wasn't what we wanted from them. We wanted to be taken seriously.

We'd work the lobby and I'd introduce myself to everybody who came by. I hit it off with the Baltimore delegation better than any of the others. At the winter meetings in 1965, we traveled to Miami to make a presentation about Milwaukee's situation and desire to get baseball back at County Stadium, where we had set attendance records.

I don't know what showing up for meetings like that turned

out to mean, other than that we showed that we weren't going away. I would continue to deliver that message over the phone, talking to anyone who would listen, but I can understand how my dad thought I was wasting my time. We weren't getting anywhere.

I was in my car the night the Braves had their opener in 1966. They were playing the Pirates, and I had a good signal from KDKA radio in Pittsburgh, listening to legendary announcer Bob Prince. He said, "Welcome to Atlanta, Georgia. We're a long way from Milwaukee, Wisconsin," just pushing the dagger in deeper.

Meanwhile, Packer fever had swept Wisconsin. Vince Lombardi had built a football machine in Green Bay, and it seemed to be all anybody talked about in Milwaukee. Fans here were mad at baseball and in love with Pete Rozelle's NFL, especially the Packers. I knew I had to do something to get baseball back into the minds of my neighbors as well as Spike Eckert and the owners who controlled the major leagues. My idea was to stage an exhibition game and draw a bigger crowd to County Stadium than teams like the Braves were getting at their games.

It probably wouldn't have been too tough to get teams to play here in March, on their way to their home stadiums from spring training. But you are delusional if you count on good weather in Milwaukee in March, and I wasn't delusional. I knew I needed to get a game during the summer, and that would be tougher.

After studying schedules, I saw that the White Sox and Twins shared an off day on Monday, July 24. I circled that on my desk blotter calendar and headed off to Florida during spring training. I billed it as a way to take ten-year-old Sari and seven-year-old Wendy to the beach, but of course that was really subterfuge for the trip's true mission.

I knew that Rudie Schaffer, a Wisconsin native who had

worked for the Triple-A Brewers, was one of the White Sox' marketing guys. Rudie told me the only way he could consider a game was if the White Sox were guaranteed money. "What if it was a hundred thousand dollars?" I asked him, pulling a figure off the top of my head.

Schaffer arranged a meeting with Arthur Allyn, the owner of the White Sox, and he was interested if I could get another team. This started a nice relationship with Art.

Calvin Griffith from the Twins, on the other hand, wasn't interested. He told me he felt badly about what had happened in Milwaukee but that his team didn't do exhibition games in midseason. Then I told him I could pay him a hundred thousand dollars. I thought he was going to kiss me.

My partners were surprised I'd given the teams a two-hundred-thousand-dollar commitment, but it would turn out to be a wise investment. We put tickets on sale about six weeks before the game, hiring three former Braves employees to staff the windows and handle the tickets. I got myself on radio and television as much as I could, but a week before the game we had sold only about ten thousand tickets. I was stopping off at the box office twice a day, morning and night, and one of the women I'd hired told me we were starting to do a little better. On the Thursday before the game we'd hit twenty-five thousand, and there were lines at the stadium to buy tickets. I was thrilled.

The lines continued over the weekend, with the staff busier than hell. By the end of the afternoon on Saturday we had an unexpected problem. We didn't have any good seats left. My supervisor asked how long we were going to stay open. I could hear my father in my ear, quoting Harry Gordon Selfridge's line about the customer always being right.

"Until every customer is taken care of," I said.

I wound up calling the commissioner's office for permission to add standing-room-only spots in a roped-off area around the warning track. I was told it was okay with the league if the teams approved it, and after I gave them an extra five thousand dollars they were enthusiastic supporters of the idea.

We sold 6,250 standing-room tickets for the outfield, and wound up drawing 51,144 fans on a beautiful night. It was serendipitous how everything worked out. There are turning points in everyone's life, everyone's career, and this was one of mine.

If I'd overestimated the support we could receive, if the anger toward major league baseball kept fans away, it could have been devastatingly bad for me. I could have had one of the shortest careers ever in baseball—over before it really started—but in the end that one night would be a real launching pad.

We had done it. I had done it. And the timing, it turned out, was key.

The summer of 1967 was painful across America because there were ugly race riots in many cities. Milwaukee wasn't spared. Protests broke out over police brutality and housing discrimination less than a week after crowds packed County Stadium. A fight between teenagers turned into a riot on July 30 and grew so bad that the city instituted a round-the-clock curfew for July 31.

I watched in horror, ashamed at the conditions that angered African Americans and disappointed with the behavior on both sides of the riot. But timing always plays a role in success, and it did for me, as we had made our statement about Milwaukee baseball a week before the front page was dominated by events of much more consequence.

We had momentum and it was time to ride it.

The White Sox had a very good pitching staff in '67—the rotation had Gary Peters, Joel Horlen, and a young Tommy John, and the bullpen included knuckleballer Wilbur Wood and my old friend Don McMahon—but there were no stars in the lineup. Chicago fans were starting to fall in love with Leo Durocher's Cubs, at the expense of the Sox. They hadn't drawn a million fans since '65 and attendance seemed likely to continue to decline, so Art Allyn was ripe for my pitch.

I persuaded him to have the White Sox play nine home games in Milwaukee, one against each AL opponent. I was excited to be able to pull this off and sought to promote the games on the County Stadium scoreboard when the Packers played games there against the Falcons, Vikings, and Browns.

One day at County Stadium, eating lunch with Ockie Krueger, whom Lombardi had put in charge of the Milwaukee operation, I asked if it would be possible to advertise our White Sox games on the board. I wanted to put the phone number for tickets up there—933-8650, weird but I still remember it—and asked Ockie what he thought. He said you got to talk to the coach.

I inquired about Lombardi's schedule for the game that weekend. "He'll be here Friday, ten o'clock," Ockie said. "But if I was you I'd be here at nine thirty. Vince works on army time." I was there at nine. My phone rang about nine twenty. Ockie said, "Coach is here and he'll see you."

Well, Coach Lombardi couldn't have been nicer. We talked about baseball, all the games he saw at the Polo Grounds. He was really a good baseball fan. He congratulated me for getting the White Sox. I told him what I needed and he said to Ockie Krueger, "What do we have?" "Not much," Ockie told him.

"Bud, we'll help you any way we can," Lombardi said. "We'll put it up on the board."

I'll never forget that game.

It was Rams versus Packers to advance to the NFL championship game. The sports editor of the *Milwaukee Journal* was a guy named Ollie Kuechle, and I don't know why but he hated baseball, hated the Braves, hated everything, really. He was nasty. He saw our ads on the scoreboard and he went nuts. "What's all that Brewer crap on the scoreboard?" He got in this fight with other Packers people in the press box. "Baseball! Who cares about that game? Nobody cares about it."

Robert Cannon, a Milwaukee judge who was serving as a legal adviser to the Players Association and had close ties to the Packers, came and got me, told me about the ugly scene in the press box about our ads. Now it was after the game and the Packers won big. I was still at the stadium well after the game, in the little hospitality area we had, and up came Vince. I told him congratulations and walked away. Later I got up my courage and went over to apologize about the stupidity in the press box. He knew everything about it before I told him. He thought it was funny.

"Young man, there's only one person who runs the Green Bay Packers, and it's me," he said. "I don't care about Ollie Kuechle. I don't care about anybody else. I wish you well. I have one condition. I love Mantle. Will you invite me when Mantle comes with the Yankees?"

You bet I would.

The Packers were a true dynasty in that era, rolling toward another championship. I was in a better mood that winter than I had been a year before, and was excited as any fan when Lombardi's team landed a rematch with the Cowboys in the championship game. They had beaten Don Meredith, Bob Hayes, and Chuck Howley at the Cotton Bowl by 34–27 the year before, and the rematch was scheduled at Lambeau Field on New Year's Eve. We'd gotten good tickets, near the forty-yard line or so. It was an unbelievable day.

We had driven up the night before and checked into a hotel. I got up in the morning and it was sunny, a beautiful day. One of my friends said it was really cold out. I said, "Oh, it looks like a gorgeous day." After all, it had been nice the day before. At least I'd thought it was nice the day before. The high was twenty-one, but we had some sun and it wasn't too windy. Not bad by our standards.

On the drive to the game, we had the radio on and a report came in that it was already sixteen below zero at Lambeau Field, with the wind chill more than fifty below. That gets your attention, even when you've spent your whole life in Milwaukee.

What an experience that day was. It was a helluva game. We were there all the way to the end, when Jerry Kramer threw that block that allowed Bart Starr to get into the end zone. I know everybody from Dallas thinks that was a game they should have won, but the 21–17 victory was a classic Packer win. It was such a battle of wills, from the start until Kramer's historic block.

Once the celebration ended at the stadium, I got back to our Green Bay hotel, turned the water on as hot as I could get it, and climbed into the bath. I didn't feel anything. I was worried about frostbite after the game, but at the time I was so cold I didn't know what I was thinking. I wasn't dressed warm enough, but neither was anyone else. You couldn't dress warm enough, but we never once considered going someplace warmer. That would have been deserting the team, and I'm not a deserter, not a quitter.

We drew well when the White Sox played in Milwaukee—23,510 for the first game against the Angels but more and more as the summer arrived, including two games above forty thousand. County Stadium was rocking. But I was distracted all summer

because there were whispers about a likelihood of expansion under embattled commissioner Spike Eckert, who was in trouble
because the NFL's popularity was soaring and baseball was beginning to be viewed as staid, with scoring and attendance down.

Charlie Finley had moved the A's from Kansas City to Oakland, which had brought on the wrath of powerful Missouri senator Stuart Symington. His threats to call hearings on baseball's
antitrust exemption led to expansion in the American League,
which seemingly happened overnight. Art Allyn told me it was
coming when I saw him in Milwaukee for a White Sox game, and
shortly thereafter came word that Kansas City and Seattle were
getting teams. I was disappointed but I wasn't shocked.

The upside to two new teams in the AL was that the NL might
follow suit and add teams. That became my latest obsession. I
started working National League owners as hard I could, remind-
ing them we'd had over fifty thousand at a game here the previous
summer and telling them how well the White Sox games were
being supported.

I hit the road to meet with owners when they would take
meetings, bringing with me any prominent resident of Milwaukee who happened to have a relationship with that owner. I was
pulling out all the stops because there was no time to waste. The
NL moved almost as fast as the AL, calling a meeting for May
27 at the Executive House hotel in Chicago, on Wacker, near
the river.

I went there hopeful of bringing home a team. Cubs owner
Phil Wrigley and the Cardinals' Gussie Busch were in our camp,
expected to campaign for us with their fellow owners once the
boardroom doors closed.

The meeting dragged on and on, and the longer it went, the
more hopeful I got. Finally, the owners left the room and Walter

O'Malley came into a side room to make an announcement. "The winners are," he began.

His lips were forming the letter "M," and to me this was happening in slow motion. It was a surreal moment I've never forgotten. I was thinking, My God, we've got it. But when time started to move again he was saying "Montreal." Then "San Diego." My heart dropped.

This was crushing. I was devastated that we got so close but couldn't get across the finish line. I really thought we were getting a team that day in Chicago. I was really optimistic.

Later I was told that it was the Atlanta Braves who blocked us. We needed all ten teams to support us by the rules at that time and had nine votes. Everyone in the room voted for us except my old friend Bill Bartholomay.

It's funny, but I've never told anyone that until now. Some people—Pete Rose, for instance—don't believe it, but I don't hold grudges. I learned from my father that in business you turn the page, move on to what's next. You keep looking forward, not backward.

I didn't hate the Braves. I really didn't. In fact, as early as 1972 we brought the Braves back here for an exhibition game with the Brewers. Henry Aaron was in the middle of that. Bill Bartholomay and I developed a really good relationship through the years. He's become one of my very best friends.

Let's face it. Milwaukee isn't a large market. It's like Baltimore or St. Louis. It's a baseball town, but it's not a big market. There's no question that hurt us trying to get another team. Milwaukee had this great run with the Braves, but our attendance had dropped off. The Braves had a lot of complaints and people in baseball bought 'em. As hard as we tried, it did not seem like we were making progress. We had a lot of ups and downs, but mostly downs.

The White Sox played at County Stadium the night after that vote, so I couldn't pout long. We wound up averaging almost thirty thousand per game for the nine relocated White Sox games—pretty impressive considering that their games at Comiskey Park averaged only about nine thousand. Art Allyn didn't have to think hard to renew our deal for 1969, this time with eleven games moving from the South Side to Milwaukee.

Eckert was quietly convinced it was his time to "retire." Bowie Kuhn, my friend from our days in litigation, was picked to replace him.

The Seattle Pilots paid us a visit in 1969, along with their manager, Joe Schultz. His marvelously profane vocabulary would be immortalized by Jim Bouton in *Ball Four*. I didn't give the Pilots much of a thought when they were passing through, but I could see what an uphill fight it was for those expansion teams to compete.

Still, I watched the expansion teams with envy. Anything's possible when you have a team, even if it's a bad team. The Sox games in Milwaukee weren't quite as popular in '69 as they had been the summer before, but still drew about three times as many fans per game as they averaged at Comiskey Park.

When I approached Art Allyn about renewing the deal for the 1970 season, he shocked me.

"I may sell the White Sox," he told me. "Are you interested?"

Of course I was interested. I hadn't seen this opportunity coming, but I was ready with my group of partners. We began a process that would lead to months of negotiations. We offered $10.8 million for the team, but he wanted a little more. He eventually accepted our offer of $11.5 million on Labor Day. We shook on the deal, and it seemed like all that was left was to decide whether to keep the name *White Sox* or change it to *Brewers*.

But the deal fell apart quicker than it came together. Art called me and said his brother John wouldn't let him sell the team. John was buying out Art's share and keeping the team in Chicago. I think Art was embarrassed. I know I was gutted. But only for a brief instant.

You won't believe this, but it's true.

At the very moment Art Allyn was giving me the bad news, I was reading the *Milwaukee Sentinel*. There was a story in it saying that the Pilots were having serious financial troubles. One of their owners, Dewey Soriano, was quoted saying that they weren't willing to keep losing money on the team, which was playing in a horrible ballpark.

I figured why not give Soriano a call.

He was happy to hear from me, let me tell you. He wanted to know when I could come out to Seattle to meet him. I asked him if he was really serious about selling the team, because I couldn't stand the thought of having the rug pulled out from under my partners again. Dewey put his brother Max on the phone and he assured me that they would love to find a buyer and get out of the baseball business.

After a trip to Seattle and some back-and-forth with the Sorianos, we struck a deal to buy the Pilots for $10.8 million, which had been our original offer for the White Sox. It would have been the largest price ever paid for a team. It was just before game 1 of the World Series and we were in Baltimore for the game. I saw the commissioner, Bowie Kuhn, before game 2 and brought him up to date on our deal. He wasn't happy, telling me he wanted to keep a team in Seattle.

I don't know if I was bluffing or not, but I told him that if we didn't get this team we were out. I couldn't keep putting my partners through the drama, and it was taking a toll on me and my family.

"If you guys don't want us, then you don't want us," I told him.

"Oh, no, no, no," he said. It wasn't us, but that baseball didn't want to get dragged into court again after spending two years involved in litigation with Milwaukee. I had a hard time arguing with him.

Kuhn immediately began an effort to find an ownership group that would keep the team in Seattle. It was the right thing for him to do, and I would have done it if I had been the commissioner. But it was painful waking up every day wondering what was going on in Seattle.

The process was still going on when the Pilots went to spring training for their second season. There was a report that the American League had advanced the franchise $650,000 so it could stay in business. Things clearly weren't going well. As I'd later learn, the Pilots were going into bankruptcy. Our $10.8 million would pay off their debts and give them a clean break. One snowy day in March, I got a call from AL president Joe Cronin asking me if we were ready.

"Believe me, we're ready to go," I said. "We have a ballpark. We have the money. We're ready." I didn't know what to think when I got off the phone. I thought this was a good sign, but we knew we couldn't count on anything, especially something as crazy as getting a team in the middle of spring training.

The month of March dragged by with no resolution. Finally, on the night of March 31, about ten thirty, I got a call from Lloyd Larson, sports editor of the *Milwaukee Sentinel*.

"Ya got it!" he said, then hung up to get his newspaper out.

My lawyer, Bud Zarwell, called two minutes later saying he had good news. I told him that Lloyd had already called, and we both had a laugh.

The bankruptcy judge, Sidney C. Volinn, had awarded us the team. I asked if anything could go wrong from here and he told me we were in the clear. Our group really did own the Brewers. I was thirty-five years old and owned a piece of a baseball team that I was going to run. Opening Day was a week away.

7

Don't ask t o o many questions about the Brewers' first season in Milwaukee. It was a blur when I lived it and much of it is still a blur. But I remember being happy. Very, very happy. I barely even noticed that we lost ninety-seven games. This was the only time in my life I was a good loser.

I didn't have any extra time or energy to agonize over the outcome of games. I was finding out how fast they come at you when they're your games.

When Judge Volinn awarded us the team, the equipment truck had already left Arizona. It was parked in Salt Lake City awaiting word whether to take Interstate 15 north toward Seattle or veer east on Interstate 80, through Wyoming, Nebraska, and Iowa toward Milwaukee. The Pilots' traveling secretary, Tommy Ferguson, had worked for the Braves. He was about the only person with the franchise I knew.

We were the Brewers from the start, not the Pilots, but we had no uniforms, so we'd have to modify the ones on the equipment truck that were designed for the Pilots. The Pilots' colors were blue and gold, and those became the Brewers' colors. We wore the uniforms that they had planned to wear in Seattle. We changed the logos on the caps, switching out the letter *S* for an *M*. Real creative, huh?

I was getting so many phone calls, I needed a switchboard operator. I hired a woman named Betty Grant to help with the phones, and she would stay with us for forty years. That's the kind of franchise I wanted to run—a solid business that was built around its people. I wanted familiar faces, not constant turnover.

One thing I'll never forget about that time is that Coach Lombardi took time to send me a telegram congratulating me on getting a team. That keepsake is still on display in my office. It's a wonder it didn't go in the trash can, because those were crazy, crazy days.

We didn't just have to sell tickets for a season that was starting in a week; we had to print tickets. But when the day arrived—in the blink of an eye, after a wait that until a week earlier had seemed endless—somehow we accommodated a crowd of 36,107 on Opening Day. Andy Messersmith and the Angels would beat us 12–0. But I was the one lighting up a victory Tiparillo.

I was leaving the park that night and a fan said something I've never forgotten. "Well, you wanted baseball in the worst way, and that's what you've got," he said. I laughed like I hadn't even looked at the scoreboard. The city was happy to have a team to call its own but slow to trust us. I didn't blame them, either, because I longed for the days of Hank Aaron, Eddie Mathews, Warren Spahn, and Red Schoendienst as much as anyone. We knew we faced a challenge creating a tradition of our own that would make fans proud.

One tradition did start that year, although maybe not in the way you'd think. Bernie Brewer was created accidentally when we took up one of our fans, Milt Mason, on his crazy idea to remain atop the County Stadium scoreboard until we drew a crowd of forty thousand fans. I still don't know why Milt did it, but he was retired and loved the team. He went up on the scoreboard in late June, with some of our people figuring out how to get a camper up there for him to sleep in, and he stayed until Bat Day against the Indians, on August 16. We drew 44,387, and after the crowd size was announced Milt slid down a rope. The fans loved it.

Three years later our marketing guys—probably Dick Hackett, who had left the White Sox to join us that first season—got the idea to honor Milt by creating a mascot who would wear lederhosen and descend down a slide into an oversized beer mug. I never did go down that slide myself, but I know a lot of our players did over the years.

About a week after I got the team, Bowie Kuhn called. I think he was relieved we'd finally gotten a team, because he'd seen what we were doing from the start, when he was an attorney for the National League. Once we got the team he was great with me. He was calling this time to tell me about an upcoming owners meeting in New York.

I was the new guy, there to listen and not to speak, but I'll never forget what I heard and saw at the first owners meeting I attended. Marvin Miller, who had been a leading negotiator for the United Steelworkers, had been hired to lead the players union in 1966. He was having an immediate impact in baseball. I'd heard about it from the Orioles' Jerry Hoffberger and my other friends in ownership, but now I was about to see it for myself.

Curt Flood had been traded from the Cardinals to the Phillies the previous October. He responded by sending a letter to Bowie saying he planned to play baseball in 1970 but not necessarily for the Phillies. He was challenging the reserve clause, which essentially tied a player to his club on a perpetual basis, and there is no question he was right to do that. Baseball should have modified the reserve clause years earlier, maybe decades earlier. But these guys were behind the times. Because Flood hadn't gone to spring training, I was expecting us to talk about him at the New York meeting. But it barely even came up—instead many owners were focused on the union. We were in negotiations on a collective bargaining agreement, and funding pensions for players was the issue that was the focus for my fellow owners.

It was as nasty a meeting as I've ever been in. Messy, really messy. Bowie seated me right between Gussie Busch and Phil Wrigley at that meeting, and Gussie was mad. He kept pounding his cane so much he actually broke it.

"Not another goddamn cent," Gussie said. "Do you understand that, Bowie? Not one more goddamn cent."

Bowie got red in the face, but he was no match for Gussie Busch and those other old-school owners, who seemed to think Kenesaw Mountain Landis was still the commissioner. They couldn't get used to the fact that players were now represented by a union and had a say in the business. That wasn't the way it used to be. These owners were determined to stay in the Stone Age. They just wanted the game to stay exactly as it had always been.

It was an education, and the first of many encounters I'd have with people who wanted to keep this game exactly as it was— regardless of the impact that would have on the players, on the fans, or even ultimately on the game of baseball itself.

The scene was one that I'd encounter over and over again, and one that came to take more meaning after one of my first such meetings as an owner. While on our way to LaGuardia Airport, I learned a lesson I would never forget from John Fetzer, the owner of the Tigers, who would become my most important mentor.

During the meeting, Mr. Fetzer had voted in favor of a proposal I had thought he would oppose. It seemed to me it worked against the Tigers. But when I asked about it, in the cab to LaGuardia, he had a quick answer.

"This is good for baseball," he said. "If I always do what's in the best interest of baseball, it will be in the best interest of the

Detroit baseball club. Remember that. If you do what's in the best interest of baseball, it will be in the best interest of the Milwaukee baseball club."

Though I had much to learn about ownership, one thing I knew from the start was that scouting and player development are the keys to a successful operation, especially in a market like Milwaukee, where you can't really shop for free agents like the Yankees and Red Sox.

One of my more questionable moves on that front was when I hired Bob Uecker to be a scout for us in the early days. When I was attending Washington High, Bob was across town at Milwaukee Tech. He was signed by the Braves while I was in Madison and he spent six years climbing through the farm system. We met in '62, when Bob was the backup catcher behind Del Crandall. It didn't take long for us to become good friends—he has an infectious personality and is the funniest person I've ever known. We stayed in touch.

After a journeyman career as a backup catcher, he came back to Milwaukee with a .200 batting average after six years in the National League, finally running out of teams that needed a wise-cracking backup catcher. I hired him as a scout and our general manager, Frank Lane, sent him up to the Northern League, with teams in places like Fargo, Duluth, and Winnipeg. Not exactly the big time, but a good organization needs eyes everywhere.

One day Frank comes steaming up the stairs into my office with a bunch of paper in his hands. "What the hell is wrong with your guy, Uecker?" he says. "He just sent in his first scouting reports and there's mashed potatoes and gravy all over them!"

Turned out scouting wasn't Bob's calling. Broadcasting was.

We put him on the air in '71 and he's been doing play-by-play for the Brewers ever since. His knowledge of the game shows up every inning he's on the air.

It was probably for the best that we got Bob off the road and into the booth, because given the size of our market, we needed scouts who could find talent. From the start, I was looking to emulate the Orioles and the Royals more than any other teams. Baltimore and Kansas City were similar markets, and from the top down were really well-run organizations. The early years were tough for us because the team we bought was woefully short on talent. There were some nice people who came from Seattle, but we were way behind the teams we were competing against.

The Royals were in the same type situation but had a head start on us. Those guys were so smart—Joe Burke, John Schuerholz, Whitey Herzog—that it was no surprise they started winning their division every year from '76 on. They had struck gold with George Brett in one of their first few drafts. We were hoping to do the same.

I only stuck with Frank Lane as GM for two seasons before promoting a scout named Jim Wilson to the position. Wilson had brought a young man named Jim Baumer with him from Houston when we hired him, and I made Baumer the scouting director. This was the team that was tasked with helping us draft our way into the competition.

The draft that changed things for us was '73. We had the third pick, behind the Rangers and the Phillies. Wilson and Baumer both spent the spring flying all over the country to see high school and college players, mostly high school, because college baseball wasn't very good in those years.

As the draft approached, there were split opinions in the front office on our first pick. Baumer wanted us to take this kid from

Woodland Hills, California, Robin Yount. But Wilson, who was Baumer's boss and the guy who'd brought him to us in the first place, was pushing for Rich Shubert, a big left-handed pitcher from New York. The two of them got into this huge fight—fierce, loud, and filled with expletives. It was really, really heated. Baumer wouldn't back down, even though his boss was telling him he was making the wrong choice. Eventually Wilson told him he could make the pick he wanted, but he was still angry. I don't think they ever really spoke again, and Wilson resigned after they'd worked one more draft together.

Thank goodness Baumer won that battle. Yount and Paul Molitor, a University of Minnesota shortstop we took with the third pick of the '77 draft, would change the history of our franchise.

Robin's older brother, Larry, had pitched at Arizona State and been drafted by the Astros in 1968. He'd helped Robin grow up early, and the seventeen-year-old we got was already a man. Robin played only sixty-four games in the low minors in that '73 season and was such a good shortstop and so mature that Wilson and Del Crandall made him our Opening Day shortstop in '74, when he was eighteen.

No one was more surprised than Robin. He thought he was about to be cut when Crandall summoned him during a bus ride late in spring training. Instead, Crandall told him, "You're our shortstop," and he was for the next eleven years (and then our center fielder for nine more years).

It sounds a little crazy to put an eighteen-year-old in the big leagues, but some players are just different than the rest, and Robin was certainly one of those. He would collect 3,142 hits and two MVP Awards on his way to Cooperstown. When you've got a player like that on your roster, you've got something big, especially when he's also the toughest, most reliable guy on the team.

It took a long time for us to get the team going in the right direction, too long, maybe, but baseball is hard. It always has been, always will be. I hated every loss back then, believe me. Just ask Robin.

Robin told me that I used to make him nervous, especially after he moved from shortstop to center field. He said he'd look in to home plate at County Stadium and see me pacing on the catwalk in front of my box. That's how he knew it was a tight game. I'd be walking back and forth, like a madman.

But there was one time nobody could find me. That was when we had a lead in the ninth inning and needed three more outs to close it out. I've got to give Lee MacPhail and Chub Feeney credit. They taught me what I call the Seven-Minute Rule.

When a game is on the line in the last inning, you don't watch it for seven minutes. If you're at home or in the car, you turn it off for seven minutes. Then you turn it back on, and if it's still being played you know you're in big trouble. I believed in that. Much easier on the nervous system. At County Stadium I'd walk behind my box and look the other way, not at the field. I'd basically hide behind a girder. You could tell by the crowd what was happening, but it was easier hearing the cheers or the groans than watching what was happening.

During those early seasons, let's just say I spent my share of time behind my box listening to the bad news rather than watching it.

One thing I understood early on was if you're going to own a team, you'd better have somebody there every day, preferably yourself. This is not a toy. It needs somebody watching it every day. That wasn't the case for most owners when I got into baseball.

They just didn't pay much attention to the business side, at least not until the end of the season when they found out they'd lost a bunch of money. Then they paid attention, fired people, but it was too late.

I'm good with numbers, even though I hate math. I was a history major, with no accounting background, but I am good at knowing how to run a business. I've always made sure there is more money coming in than going out. Well, except the first few years of the Brewers.

Initially I had put only about three hundred thousand dollars of my own money into our ownership group, so mostly I was managing money for other people. We were struggling financially in '71 and '72. At times we had bills coming in faster than we could pay them. There were some cash calls where I put in more money and all of the partners put in more money. I really hated those meetings. Anybody would. I was always more sensitive about other people's money than I was my own.

But I understood what a good player was worth, and if you wanted to have a winning team you needed good players. Once my phone rang and my father said, "Your mother just told me you signed your first baseman and you paid him a hundred thousand dollars."

"Well, Ma's right," I told him.

"I thought I raised a smart kid," he said. "You're going to pay a player a hundred thousand dollars a year? What are you, crazy?"

He was serious, and he hung up. That was the end of that conversation.

But eventually the team got better and we began to understand how to run a baseball franchise as a business. There weren't a lot of great examples to follow at that time. In fact, I didn't know of any.

One day in the '75 season, probably in July, I was on the phone with John Fetzer. I told him I was really happy because I had just hit my break-even mark in attendance, so everything the rest of the year was profit. He was astonished that I knew that. He wanted me to talk to Jim Campbell, general manager of the Tigers. Campbell and I were good friends. Campbell didn't want to hear about it but said the boss had told him to talk to me. I explained how I made my budget. It wasn't rocket science.

I projected our attendance on a game-by-game basis—I did it on all these scratch pads, and kept them on my desk so I could adjust them all the time—and I knew pretty well what our fixed costs were, in addition to our little bit of guaranteed revenue from radio and TV. The variable was player salaries, the payroll. I added that on to fixed costs and made sure the total was below what I projected we'd make in revenue from the crowds. I had a set figure for average ticket price and averages for concessions and parking.

This seems basic, I know, but nobody was doing it in baseball. That's how I came to be known as Budget Bud. That nickname got thrown around in the newspapers a lot in the 1990s, when the game was in crisis and I was in charge. It would get used by writers as a pejorative, as if I were the little penny-pincher from Milwaukee, but believe me, within ownership it was first used as a compliment.

Jim Campbell must have mentioned my budgeting to Edward Bennett Williams, the brilliant Washington lawyer who had purchased the Orioles from Jerry Hoffberger. I got a call from Ed, asking what I was doing. He wanted me to come see him, so I did. We had lunch at Duke Zeibert's and I met Art Buchwald, the humorist who wrote for the *Washington Post*.

We eventually formed a small group of owners and I tried to teach them what I was doing while also learning from them.

Word got around and we eventually grew to a group of sixteen to eighteen.

We talked about the best ways to run a team and how it had become essential for owners to be involved. I knew that if we were going to grow as a sport—survive, even—we had to start doing a better job on the business side. The NFL seemed to understand that from the start, but let's be honest here. It's a lot easier to conduct business when you have sixteen games a season, all carried by national television, than it is playing 162 games with local television. And in the end, it's not good enough to do just a decent job, because fans hold baseball to a higher standard than other sports. They just do.

I understood back in the seventies that it's hard work, not just fun, to be a successful owner of a team. That was the mind-set I was trying to help my fellow owners develop.

While I focused on the bottom line, I wasn't like George Steinbrenner or Charlie Finley. I hired baseball executives to run the team and then stayed out of their way. Usually I did, anyway. But there were exceptions.

After the Henry Aaron deal, there was only one other but it would prove to be a big deal. I personally conducted the trade talks that got us Cecil Cooper, and he would be an important piece as a left-handed hitter alongside Yount and Molitor.

We were at the winter meetings in 1976, in Los Angeles. Dick O'Connell was running the Red Sox for Tom Yawkey, whom he always called "the old man." Dick was one of those guys who moved fast.

Jim Baumer was our general manager, but O'Connell came to see me. He said Yawkey wanted him to make a deal to get back George "Boomer" Scott, whom we had acquired from the Red Sox in a trade after the '71 season. Scott was really productive, leading the league in homers and RBIs in '75, but had dropped off in '76.

He was a very good player, but we were anxious to bring in new blood. He was getting older. So I was all ears. I walked over to our scouting director, Dee Fondy, who was nearby, and told him we could trade Scott to the Red Sox and asked who we wanted back.

"We want Cecil Cooper," Fondy said. "He hasn't hit his stride yet but I have no doubt he will."

We also wanted them to take Bernie Carbo, who wasn't happy in Milwaukee and couldn't stay healthy. So I went to tell O'Connell we'd do Scott and Carbo for Cooper, and he said done! Just like that. The whole thing took five, six minutes.

Scott had good years back in Boston, but Cooper turned out to be one of the best hitters in baseball for eleven seasons. He hit .300 with us and delivered fifteen or twenty homers every year—when you needed them, not when they padded his stats. He was a high-character guy, too, and became a good friend.

After the Aaron deal, that was the only time I ever made a trade, so I can honestly say I never made a bad one.

We had losing records our first eight seasons, but I could tell things were close to turning in '77. Robin was starting to be a threat at the plate, as well as the best athlete on the field, and we believed Molitor was going to be able to help us in short order. I knew I needed to change management again, however, so I thanked Baumer and Alex Grammas, the manager, for their service and turned the page.

We made the firings on a Saturday, and they came to be known locally as "the Saturday night massacre." I never liked that part of the job—nobody does—but the timing called for decisive action.

I knew who I wanted to hire, but he wasn't available. Harry Dalton, who had run the Orioles' farm system and then essentially been their general manager as director of player personnel, was at the time the GM of the Angels.

I wasn't sure who was my second choice behind Dalton. But one day I picked up the newspaper and read that the Angels had hired Buzzie Bavasi away from the Padres to run their operation.

As soon as I could get to a phone, I called Gene Autry and asked if I could interview Harry for the job here. He was wonderful. All he wanted was ten minutes to call Harry and let him know I'd be calling. It was a long ten minutes, let me tell you. But when I called I told him right away I wanted to hire him, and he was anxious to make a move.

I knew this was going to be great for us. I had known Harry for a long time and I really had faith in his ability. I knew we had the beginning of a very good young team, but there was just something missing in the front office. And frankly, he was the guy I wanted, the only guy I wanted. I was excited. By the way, he didn't disappoint me, either.

It was Harry's call on the manager. I was at the University Club in January, at a luncheon, and Harry said to me, "I got George Bamberger coming in. I think he's our guy, but I want you to meet him."

Bamberger had spent the last decade as the pitching coach for all those great teams in Baltimore, working for Earl Weaver. I had huge respect for him as a baseball man, not just a pitching coach. So I went up to meet Harry and George. I met George and I liked the idea a lot.

George was blunt. I said, "George, delighted to meet you, glad you're here, and hope you're going to come with us."

He said, "Why would I come here? You guys are a bunch of losers."

"Well, I don't think we will be," I said.

That was it. He got hired that afternoon. We were starting to put something together, and I could feel it.

That year, I was excited going to Sun City for spring training, and it turned out to be one of the best camps we've ever run, thanks to the talent we'd assembled and a manager who cussed like nobody's business.

One day I walked into the manager's office and Bambi was there. I was just getting to know him. He said, "Hi, boss."

"Hi, George. How are you?"

"Well, I told you about that fucker."

He couldn't complete a sentence without calling somebody a fucker, so I was just listening to him, enjoying his way with the English language. He kept going.

"I'll tell you what I'm calling the fucker."

I didn't know who the hell he was talking about. No idea.

"The guy is the Ignitor. He'll ignite us. That fucker will ignite us."

Now I got it. He was talking about Molitor, who was in his first spring training. I was surprised how excited Bambi was, so I asked him what he was going to do with him.

"What am I going to do with him?" Bambi replied. "He's going to lead off. He's going to ignite this fucking club."

No manager was ever more correct about any statement he made. For the next fifteen years, on his way to the Hall of Fame, Paul Molitor did exactly that.

He was such a special player that even Ted Williams noticed.

I spent some time with Ted late in his life, really getting to know him when Major League Baseball celebrated its All-Century

Team at the 1999 All-Star Game at Fenway Park. There were a lot of events and we had a great time talking baseball.

From then on he'd just call me out of the blue. My phone would ring and Ted's son would be on it, telling me his dad wanted to talk to me. Then Ted would come on the line. We had great conversations.

"You have the worst fucking job in America," he said one day. "How do you put up with all those assholes?"

He was talking about the owners. We got through that and then he said, "Your guy has the most beautiful stroke." I thought he was talking about Yount, but he was talking about Molitor. He said, "He's got the best stroke in this game since me."

Wow. That's saying something when Ted Williams compares you to him. I immediately called Paul to tell him what Ted had said. He didn't believe it. But that's the kind of hitter Molitor was, and when you had him and Yount in the same lineup you really had something.

8

Marvin Miller.

Or Marvin.

Sometimes just Miller.

Put those names together any way you want and they were sure to make the hair on the arms of baseball owners stand up in the 1960s and '70s. After all, because he was the first head of the players union, Miller's name was generally said with an adjective in front of it, and that adjective was not *brilliant* or *dashing*. It was *bleeping*.

That bleeping Marvin Miller. Or Marvin bleeping Miller.

Needless to say, he wasn't real popular when I got into baseball. But it's easy to see now, looking back, that few men have had such a profound impact on the business of baseball. His role shaping the game, pushing it forward to become a more player-conscious enterprise, fundamentally changed the way owners and fans viewed the players on the field—for better and worse. Marvin Miller should be in the Hall of Fame—no question about it—and I can't explain why he isn't. I do know this: it's not because there is some conspiracy among baseball's blue bloods to keep him out—that's just not true. Regardless, he deserves to be honored for what he did to help players. But his prolonged all-out war against steroid testing caused him to lose support, even among some of the great players.

When Marvin was put in charge of the players union, he'd left the most powerful union in the United States—the United

Steelworkers—to essentially create one from scratch. It's been written that it had only a fifty-four-hundred-dollar bank account and one old filing cabinet when he arrived. He grew it into the most powerful union in sports—probably in America, to be honest—in a period of about fifteen years. That's having an impact.

Robin Roberts, Jim Bunning, Bob Friend, and Harvey Kuenn were among the players who realized early that it was time for them to organize. They'd been represented as a group in the past, but the only issue that was ever really discussed was a pension plan, which Happy Chandler, the second commissioner, had agreed to fund through money generated from World Series radio and TV money. That was essentially found money when it arrived, but the growth of broadcast revenues would continue through the decades, becoming a battleground for first owners and players and later among owners themselves, with the dividing lines being the size of their markets. In fairness, the players probably realized the role that TV money could play quicker than most of the owners.

Miller was the players' choice to lead them, and he was brilliant. He had graduated from high school at fifteen and earned a New York University economics degree at nineteen. Marvin dove into the challenge of representing the players the same way that I jumped into baseball—with both a passion and people skills. He did a wonderful job both leading and educating players.

Marvin empowered players. They had been raised in a culture that often didn't make them feel valuable. But Miller banged away at them when he visited camps in spring training or held meetings of player reps, selling them on their value and power. He encouraged them to come by the Players Association offices—he didn't like to call his group a union, even though that's what it was—when they were playing games at Yankee Stadium or Shea

Stadium. He wanted them to understand exactly what they were a part of, to show the players that they mattered.

Miller's initial focus was negotiating a new pension agreement—this was playing out while I was working behind the scenes to try to bring baseball back to Milwaukee. But it's safe to say owners weren't throwing open their doors to Marvin. They were so stuck in the past, the distant past. Most of them could not imagine change, let alone embrace it.

The owners at the time were relentless in their belief that they should control all of the power in the sport. These were barons of industry who enjoyed having things their way. I'll never forget a meeting that we had in St. Louis with Gussie Busch when a casual mention of changing the reserve clause in player contracts to give the players more freedom led to Gussie slamming his hands on the table and screaming. That reaction was symbolic of the sentiment of that era among the owners. Gussie was honestly expressing what he felt about the division of power between the people who owned baseball teams and the men who played for baseball teams. It was the way most owners felt in the 1960s. They didn't see anything wrong with controlling a player's rights throughout his career, with the only guideline being the minimum salary.

Phil Wrigley, whose family had owned the Cubs since 1921, spoke for many owners of that era with his description of the enterprise. "Baseball is too much of a business to be a sport and too much of a sport to be a business," he once famously said.

That's the way it was when I came into ownership.

Walter O'Malley, who had owned the Dodgers since 1951, did a lot of talking at every meeting. He had inherited Dodgertown, the state-of-the-art spring training facility built by Branch Rickey, and then oversaw the building of Dodger Stadium in Chavez Ravine, which was a palace when it opened in

1962. They hated O'Malley in Brooklyn but not in National League meetings. He was powerful.

Calvin Griffith, who had moved the Senators to Minnesota when Washington fans stopped supporting him the way he believed they should, was pretty much the stereotype of the baseball owner. His family had been in baseball since 1919 and he mostly thought like his father, Clark, who had signed checks for Walter Johnson. I loved Calvin personally, but he was the prototype of the old-time owner. He was a great baseball man, really wonderful in so many ways, but stuck in the past.

Phil Wrigley was really a nice man. He loved the game. He was quiet, very quiet, and he really was an advocate of the fans. He started the "friendly confines" feeling at Wrigley Field. He was never out at the park with his chest stuck out, instead generally staying in his office in the Wrigley Building when the team was playing. But I did hear that sometimes he'd go to games and sit at the back of the grandstand, just wanting to be left alone.

He had a really good relationship with Ernie Banks and some of his other players, but he wasn't pushing for a change in how baseball treated its players. The system was the system. That's the way it was with just about every owner.

One guy who saw things differently was Charles Finley, who had bought the Kansas City A's in 1960 and moved them to Oakland in '68. He was creative, resourceful, and really destructive to baseball. He was all over the place on issues and, like too many owners, too concerned about himself and his team. He had a lot of crackpot ideas. He really hated Bowie Kuhn and didn't think twice about taking on the game or his fellow owners.

There were some remarkably good men in the group of owners, of course. I loved George Steinbrenner when he bought the Yankees from CBS in 1973. We had a great relationship from the very start.

I helped introduce him to the owners the way that Jerry Hoff-berger, John Fetzer, and Dan Galbreath had helped me.

Oh, Charles Bronfman, too. The Expos owner was great. He encouraged me a lot early on. He was born wealthy because of his father's empire, which was built around Seagram spirits, but spends his time and his money in wise, caring ways. He's dedicated to so many social causes, one of the finest human beings I've ever known.

We became great friends when we both were young owners in the game. We were very close. The thing I always admired about Charles—a lot of people say it but they don't mean it—is that he believed, as did Mr. Fetzer, that the best interests of the game always transcended his own. That's very unusual.

We had a lot of fun together. We'd talk on the phone every Sunday morning.

Carl Pohlad, who owned the Twins, was another invaluable asset as a friend. I got to know him well after he bought out the Griffiths. We had an 11:30 in the morning call on Saturdays for many, many years, through a lot of our tough times.

Carl was influential in ways a lot of people never really knew. He informally assembled a group of small- and medium-revenue teams seeking change, which we came to call the Pohlad Com-mittee. He had a wonderful way about him. He's another guy who never got the credit for not only being influential in baseball but also really serving the game.

Carl was the kind of owner who if you were commissioner, trying to get things done, you wanted around. He was aggres-sive; he was also a great partner. You want people who under-stand what you're trying to do and are willing to take pains to get it done. Dick Jacobs, who owned the Indians, was exactly like that. When he was selling the Indians, he told me, "You know,

Commissioner, a lot of blood is going to be spilled, and it's going to be yours, but you're doing the right thing."

You want to be a great owner? Yeah, you have to run a successful franchise, but you also have to understand, as painful as it might be, that the game is bigger than you are, and that's how you ought to make your decisions. Hard to do. Really hard to do.

Marvin Miller was the enemy to a lot of these guys. They were not interested in listening to the discussion with an open mind. As we went through the 1970s, we made a lot of mistakes, as did the union. I don't know how else to say it. Lack of enlightenment was one of the reasons we made mistakes. Marvin ran into a lot of opposition, a lot of anger. Unfortunately, a lot of that was the fault of our people. That hurt us, and it hurt us for decades to come.

In the Brewers' first season, the major league minimum salary was $12,000 and the average $31,543. Ten years later, with Marvin doing well for his players, the minimum had grown to $32,500, and the average to $185,651.

The tide had turned the players' way, thanks to fundamental changes in the economic system that Miller brought in while proving himself to the players, who began to trust the union implicitly. While owners were divided, players were united behind Marvin to an unbelievable degree.

I was there for all of baseball's disputes with Marvin's union, but in the 1970s I was just another face in the hotel conference room. Marvin called the first player strike in the spring of '72, over a demand for inflation increases in the pension system. The amount of money we were fighting over is laughable—not just because of inflation, it was laughable back then, too—but owners didn't like to be told what to do. The start of the season was delayed about two weeks before owners cracked and settled.

We called a lockout the following spring, with John Gaherin representing the owners. Ted Simmons had declined to sign his contract, saying he'd play without one and let an arbitrator decide afterward what he'd been worth, and owners decided the situation needed to be clarified before camps opened. We had already accepted Marvin's push for an independent arbitrator to decide certain issues that had previously fallen to the commissioner, and during the lockout that delayed spring training in '73 we negotiated the basics of the salary arbitration that still exists.

Arbitration was something of an outlier in the disputes of those days because most of the owners supported the idea just as much as players did. It was presented as a better alternative than free agency—so a way to enforce the old system—and had the support of most owners. Offering it got the players to sign off on a three-year collective bargaining agreement without losing any games to the '73 lockout. We didn't address the elephant in the room—free agency.

We should have understood our economic system was from a different time and no longer worked. It was an anachronism, and we should have found a way to work with players to replace it. We weren't smart enough, unfortunately, and all we did was make the union stronger.

Instead we had to learn the hard way—by losing in arbitration and in court on several separate grievances filed by the union throughout the 1970s. Things were changing, but few of the owners could see just how far we would be planted on the wrong side of history.

We couldn't make progress even when we really tried to work with the Players Association. When the issue of free-agent compensation became contentious in 1980, we came out of an all-night session at the Doral Hotel in New York agreeing to form a one-year joint study committee, which seemed helpful at the time.

It was a four-person arrangement, including two members from management and two players. I was pleased because it was a heavily Milwaukee group, with Harry Dalton and Sal Bando working alongside Frank Cashen and Bob Boone. They met eight times but couldn't bridge the gap, as the dynamics between Miller and our negotiator, Ray Grebey, were unproductive.

"The four of us felt we had a good early rapport," Dalton recalled in the book *Lords of the Realm,* by John Helyar. "But every time we seemed to be making progress, either Grebey or Miller would confuse the issue."

These talks extended into the 1981 season. Players went on strike on June 12 and we didn't get an agreement until July 31, making it by far the longest work stoppage in sports history.

The fifty-day strike wiped out 712 games and cost the owners an estimated seventy-two million dollars in losses (although forty-four million was offset by strike insurance) and cost the players twenty-eight million dollars in lost salaries. But this was arguably Marvin Miller's finest hour, as players rallied together with spirit through the long negotiations—sometimes as many as twenty-five or thirty players would show up to support the union at bargaining sessions—and rarely questioned the union's leadership.

For our side, we had a new labor leader in Grebey, but he proved ineffective, in large part because owners were divided on the significance of compensation for departing free agents but also because he lacked the authority that Miller had on the other side of the table. We would crack just before our strike insurance was scheduled to run out. That was probably predictable, in hindsight, and we didn't really achieve anything for all the pain that we suffered that summer. Marvin would claim that he'd brought about complete surrender, and he wasn't wrong. As strong as the Players Association had been going into this round of bargaining, it was even stronger coming out of it.

The strength of the players flew in the face of what was happening in America at the time. The power of most unions was being diminished with Ronald Reagan in the White House, and the NBA was quietly working toward a peaceful negotiation with its union on a new collective bargaining agreement during our dispute. The next NBA deal would include a limit on each team's payroll. That salary cap—along with the arrival of Michael Jordan—would help the NBA have tremendous success, but Miller would always be appalled by the willingness of unions in basketball and football to make concessions to their owners and commissioners.

For my part, I couldn't help but recognize the horrible PR position that owners were in during these public fights with our players. We couldn't win. You don't want the fans to get mad at your players. You don't want them thinking, I love Bud Selig, but I hate Robin Yount. What does that do for you? It only hurts you.

I knew there was no way we were ever going to win with the public. We couldn't expect any sympathy when we wound up in the headlines. Bowie Kuhn had given me a lesson about that in 1971, when I was just getting into baseball.

Bowie had invited me to lunch on one of my trips to New York. We went to a place he picked—Rose's on West Fifty-second Street, an Italian spot that had been a baseball hangout since the days of John McGraw—and after we'd been seated for a few minutes in walked Pete Rozelle, by himself. He came over and sat down at our table, joining us for lunch. I knew I was going to have a good time, and I did.

For one reason or another, the New York press was killing Bowie that day, which wasn't really unusual. Bowie was always getting killed by columnists and reporters, while Rozelle was constantly patted on the back. He owned New York. He owned pro sports, and I personally was a Rozelle fan. I loved the guy.

Again, I don't remember what the issues of the day were, but it struck me that Rozelle was getting a pass while Bowie got crucified. It didn't seem fair to me. Bowie liked his Scotch, and he'd knocked back a couple at lunch. He and I just sat talking for a while after Rozelle left.

I said to Bowie, "It's not fair, you're getting killed on this and Rozelle can't do anything wrong."

He looked at me across the table and told me something I've never forgotten.

He told me I was right, but also that it didn't really matter.

"Remember, Buddy, we're always held to a higher standard," Kuhn said. "Baseball always somehow gets held to a higher standard. It's a compliment, except when you're commissioner. Then it makes life tougher."

Bowie was 100 percent right, and I've never forgotten it. I certainly experienced it when I was commissioner, and I kept it in mind when we got back on the field after the 1981 strike. I couldn't imagine baseball would ever go through anything worse than a fifty-day strike. But as it turned out, the fights were only getting started, both with the union and among owners, and publicly we would always be held to a high standard.

9

The owners might have been stuck in their ways, but in 1981 the Brewers were moving forward in all the right ways. I'm not sure when I knew the Brewers had officially become contenders, but it was probably around the time George Steinbrenner made a reservation for me at the New York restaurant and institution '21.'

George was emotional, demanding, controlling, and as combustible as a Molotov cocktail. He was also, believe it or not, a gentleman. I'll never forget that even as our teams were in the heat of battle he took a few minutes to make this reservation for me at '21,' which is Sue Selig's favorite restaurant in New York.

I had known Sue in high school. We had a lot of the same friends. She was a baseball fan from the time she was a kid, going to games at Borchert Field with her dad. Sue went away to college, first to Colorado and then the University of Minnesota. She eventually moved back to Milwaukee and was going through a divorce about the same time as me.

We played tennis together. She was a very good tennis player and I was very competitive. She still kids me that I deliberately smashed a ball off her once when we were playing doubles.

About the time I was making my last trade—the Cecil Cooper deal—I was kicking the door on some free agents represented by the agent Jerry Kapstein. I traveled to Providence, Rhode Island, where Kapstein's office was, and took Sue along.

We were considering Gene Tenace and Joe Rudi, who had been

important players for championship teams in Oakland but were never taken care of by Charlie Finley. I wanted Kapstein to know they'd be more than just players to me if they came to Milwaukee, but instead Tenace signed with the Padres and Rudi became an Angel.

It was still a great venture, because of Sue. She got along great with Jerry and his brother Dan, which made the trip a success. Sue is very outgoing, extremely social, very aggressive.

We did sign another Oakland player that year, Sal Bando. And Sue was great in making Sal and his wife, Sandy, feel comfortable in Milwaukee. Sal would like it so much that he would have a long run as the Brewers' general manager in the 1990s.

Everybody loves Sue. I remember the first baseball meeting she attended. People who I didn't know were outgoing were raving about her. The whole Griffith family loved her. Calvin came over and said, "This young lady you married, I really like her."

Mr. Fetzer liked her. She fit in beautifully, which isn't always the case.

Sue liked to travel, and she had known me most of my life. She certainly knew what she was getting into. She still says I make her nervous at baseball games, but I've always known that I could be myself around her. That's such a blessing with anybody, especially your wife.

The first years that Sue and I were together were great ones for me and the franchise. We had put together strong teams that would be competitive year in and year out, and now suddenly we were right there with the biggest teams in the game. This was what I'd been working so hard to experience, and in 1981 we were in the thick of the postseason.

The Brewers were 31–25 when players went on strike, third in the AL East behind the Yankees and Orioles. We remained consistent after returning to play—a credit to Yount, Molitor, Ted Simmons, and our pitchers, the best of whom were Pete Vuckovich and Mike Caldwell, with Rollie Fingers always there to protect leads—and a 31–22 record after the strike was good enough to grab the first playoff spot in franchise history.

During the 1981 playoffs, I had one of those moments I will never forget, as long as I live. It was a little thing, but when you own a team, and when you're competing against a powerhouse like Steinbrenner's Yankees in those years, you never forget the moment. It was that sweet, like something you would script.

When George made us a reservation at '21,' I'm sure he thought I'd be there drowning my sorrows after the Yankees had eliminated us. But we were tougher to put away than George thought we'd be. The Yankees had won the first two games of this best-of-five series in Milwaukee, which killed me, but then we went to Yankee Stadium and won games 3 and 4, forcing the series to the deciding game.

I stayed around for a long time after game 4, just enjoying myself, and as I prepared to leave, I took the elevator down to the basement of the old Yankee Stadium. It could be like a tomb down there, like the catacombs. But when the elevator door opened, George was right there.

It was just me and George. He said, "Well, Buddy, I guess this is the way it's supposed to be. We'll play for a spot in the championship series tomorrow." His demeanor had changed since the first two games in Milwaukee, that's for sure.

I heard later that he had been in the clubhouse after game 4 and had a battle with his catcher, Rick Cerone. George went in and said he was embarrassed. He was fuming that the Yankees couldn't beat the Brewers. I could tell he was still mad when I saw him, but he tried his hardest to be gracious.

That moment—just making the owner of the New York Yankees sweat a little—meant so much to me, with where I came from and all it had taken to get here.

To have beaten the Yankees would have been such a thrill for me. We were close to doing that in game 5, after Sue and I had so thoroughly enjoyed our dinner at '21' the night before.

We took a 2–0 lead on Ron Guidry but couldn't hold it. We would lose 7–3 but were down only 5–3 in the eighth inning and nearly gave Fingers a lead to protect.

Two men on, two outs, eighth inning, Don Money up against Goose Gossage. He had just walked Sal Bando and Roy Howell and looked nervous as hell on the mound. I could relate. I'd been pacing back and forth in the back of the press box because I can't sit still.

Money hit one to left and everyone in the press box thought it was gone, including me. Dave Winfield leaped at the wall and caught it. I won't say it was a phenomenal catch, but it was a good one. Everyone thought the ball was in the seats from the time Money hit the ball. We would have had a 6–5 lead to turn over to Fingers, but instead the Yankees scored two in the eighth, essentially putting us away.

It was a terrific series and a disappointing end, but it wasn't long before we were really looking forward to '82.

We started the season with high hopes. Buck Rodgers was our manager, in his second season. We staggered out of the gate, much to the surprise of me and our GM, Harry Dalton. We had felt so good in spring training, but April was a different story. It was right around Memorial Day when Harry called me at home. He said, "Boss, I think we've got to make a change." I was really surprised. This wasn't Harry's style, and it wasn't my style, but the AL East was loaded and we were getting in a hole.

I wasn't against changing the manager. Sometimes that can make a difference. Harry told me he thought we had the guy here to replace Buck. He thought Harvey Kuenn was the guy. Everyone here called him Archie. He had been a starting forward on the basketball team in addition to his role as shortstop at the University of Wisconsin. He was Milwaukee through and through, and had been the Brewers' hitting coach for years.

Players liked Arch, and it was a really smart move, the right stroke at the right time. We were in Seattle when we made the change, having gone 7–14 in this stretch. Right after the change, that's when Harvey's Wallbangers, as the team came to be known, took over. Man, did they go on a tear. We played Oakland the first weekend and Roy Eisenhardt, president of the A's, called me that Sunday and said, "Stop it, please." We had killed them Friday and Saturday, and we killed them again on Sunday.

We were in first place in July and led most of the year. Wonderful team. Wonderful hitting team. Robin had a phenomenal year. Molitor was a great player. The guy who was underrated, people outside of Milwaukee never understood how good he was, was Cecil Cooper. Boy, could he hit. He never got the credit he deserved. I think he's a borderline Hall of Famer. You look at the ten, eleven years he was in Milwaukee. I know it's not enough, but man, he was great. He was huge here. Big favorite here.

Late August we needed a pitcher, and we got Doc Medich from Eddie Chiles and the Rangers. But Doc was no longer Doc Medich, if you know what I mean. He was at the end of his career. Great guy, but not much help.

Harry came to me. He'd been talking to my friend Al Rosen, who was general manager of the Astros, and said, we can get Don

Sutton. He said our guys think he can help us. We would have to give up Kevin Bass, a good young outfielder, and some other future pieces to get him. Neither one of us liked the price we were going to pay, but when you have a chance to win, you have to do it. For us, this was like the deal the Cubs made in 2016 when they picked up Aroldis Chapman. There are times you just have to make a deal. Theo Epstein said it well with Chapman—if not now, then when? That was the question for us as it was getting late in '82.

So we made the deal, and the next thing we were playing a doubleheader with Cleveland in early September. Fingers had gotten hurt in the first game. Little did I know that would be the last time he would pitch that season. He had won the Cy Young and the MVP in '81. Rollie was a great pitcher and huge for us. Not having him would be a big blow. But that day I wasn't that worried because I didn't know that he had torn a muscle in his forearm. I was walking up the ramp at County Stadium for the second game, and I heard this big ovation. I couldn't figure out what was going on. It was Sutton walking in from the bullpen. That's how happy fans were to have him on the Brewers.

Sutton said for years that that would happen only in Milwaukee. He loved playing here. He was tremendous about it. He told me that every player should get a chance to play in Milwaukee.

We entered September four and a half games ahead of Boston and five up on Baltimore. Things got tight, of course, because it's never easy, right? I was really worried because we played the last thirteen games of the season against the Red Sox and the Orioles, with the last seven in Boston and Baltimore. It was a wonder that my bleeding ulcer didn't return.

We've got Earl Weaver's mighty Orioles in Milwaukee for our last home series. Before the Friday night game, I'm in my office, the phone rings, and it's Harry. He says, "You better get down here, your kid is acting up."

The kid is Yount. That's what we all call him. I go down, Dr. Paul Jacobs is there, Harvey Kuenn, Harry. The door is closed. I'm thinking, What's the problem? Dr. Jacobs, who was a very close friend of mine and is to this day, says Yount's got a bad shoulder and a bad knee. They're both puffed up. I have to take him to Mount Sinai to get cortisone shots in those two joints. Maybe he can play next Monday or Tuesday.

I'm stunned. "Doc, wait a minute . . ."

He reminds me that I've always said the health of my players comes first. I say, "Yeah, but Doc . . ."

I know that Dr. Jacobs is right, of course. Yount's gonna have to do what the doctor tells him to do, and I have to support the doctor. There's not a moment of question about any of this. It's what has to happen, even if Rob Picciolo plays shortstop in the biggest games of the year, not Robin Yount.

Archie is sitting behind us. He looks like he's ready to check out. He's beyond distraught. I go out in the clubhouse and it's very quiet. Robin is sitting down. I say, "I'll see you when you get back from the hospital," and pat him on the back. He says, "Wait. Wait. Wait a minute. What do you mean? There's nothing wrong with my knee and my shoulder. Boss . . ."

I say the doctor told me he told you. He says again, "There's nothing wrong with my shoulder and my knee." Other players are sitting there, staring.

"Rob, we're not going to have any debate."

"What are you talking about?"

"You're going to the hospital. He'll bring you back and I'll see you when you get back. You'll come up and sit with me."

"No. No way."

So now I'm going out the clubhouse door, people are coming into the ballpark. It's six o'clock. He's in uniform and now he's walking after me, in the middle of all these people, vendors, fans. We're going back and forth.

"You can't do this to me," he says. "This is not right. We got to win."

What an attitude. Now we're halfway up the ramp and we're still arguing. We're discussing things emotionally. Finally, he says to me one of the best lines.

"What do you mean, I can't play? I'm a ballplayer. That's what I'm here for."

I look at him and I can see it would just crush him to go to the hospital. He's won the argument. I finally say, go ahead and play, I'll take the responsibility. I get up to my office and call the manager's office. Arch answers the phone. I say, you've got him in the lineup.

He's like, "Oh, man." You can hear the relief. And Robin never misses a pitch all the way through the rest of the season, the play-offs, and the World Series.

If you ever want to doubt what an athlete can do in these situations, think about Robin Yount.

That night we beat the Orioles 15–6. Robin homered in the first inning off Mike Flanagan and in the sixth off reliever Don Stanhouse. He drove in six runs. The sellout crowd started chanting "MVP!" Robin was hurting. He wouldn't admit it. He would never admit it. My only fights with Yount in twenty years were about his health. I so admired his toughness.

We go to Boston to start the last week of the season. We win the first night in shocking fashion. Our backup catcher, Ned Yost (who would manage the Brewers before winning a World Series as the Royals' manager), hits a homer in the ninth to win the game.

We win the next night, lose Thursday, and go into Baltimore three games up with four games to go—starting with a makeup doubleheader. We were swept, and now the lead is one. I'm dying.

We play a game on Saturday afternoon, Tony Kubek and Joe Garagiola announce the game, and we get killed. We go back to the Cross Keys Hotel in Baltimore, where the team stays. We've got the kids with us, but they're smart. They all go out on Saturday night while I just sit around and stew.

The tension, you could cut it with a knife. I'm up all night and Sue's up all night. I watch *The Dirty Dozen* twice. I'm nervous. I'm thinking, all these years, what if we blow this? The club may never recover.

About eight thirty in the morning, I've finally fallen asleep, and there's banging on the door. I say to Sue, "Why did you order breakfast? We have a 3:05 game."

"I didn't order breakfast," she says.

This is not a good thing. I go to the door and it's Howard Cosell. He's come down to do the game. He walks in and he says, "I knew Sutton in Vero Beach, 1966," and goes into this long tirade.

"You're going to win today because this guy won't let you down," he said. "Look out the window. I just saw him."

Sure enough, in this little park across from the Cross Keys, there's Sutton and Simmons, sitting at a picnic table going over hitters. We order breakfast, Howard leaves. I don't know why, but I feel better. I wanted to feel better. (I only found out later that he'd told the opposite version of the same story to Edward Bennett Williams, the owner of the Orioles. When Williams and I called Cosell on it, his reply was: "Well, I made you both feel better, didn't I?" As much as it pained me to admit it, he did.)

It was a huge crowd at Memorial Stadium, a very emotional

day, and the only fans the Brewers were going to have were the few people sitting by the dugout. It was terrifying. The place was a madhouse when I walked in. The Orioles were pitching Jim Palmer and we were going with Don Sutton. Two Hall of Famers. And the team that won would capture the AL East after a great race. This is the kind of stuff that I loved when I was a kid, the kind of game that people remember the rest of their lives.

Before the game, I asked Harvey and Harry, do you mind if I talk to the players? I had never done this before in my years with the Brewers. I told them I wouldn't take much time and Harry liked the idea. Harvey was thrilled.

I said, "I love you guys, I wish you well today, just do the best you can." That was it.

Yount hit a home run in the first inning and another one in the third inning. Palmer is still mad about those homers. He tells me they were just two fly balls. I tell him they were fly balls, all right, but they were 410-foot fly balls.

Cecil Cooper hit a homer off Palmer in the sixth, giving us a 4–1 lead. Sutton was pitching great, and all of a sudden it was the eighth inning, we were up 5–2, but they got a couple men on. We didn't have Fingers, so Harvey stuck with Sutton. Joe Nolan came up as a pinch hitter and hit a long fly ball into the left-field corner. Ben Oglivie made a great catch. I mean, a great catch. I wanted to kiss him.

That was the end of the Orioles. We blew it up with five runs in the ninth, including a three-run homer by Simba, Ted Simmons. It was 10–2. Somebody counted the number of Tiparillos I smoked. There were thirty under my seat. I had 'em going all the time. I lit one, lit another. You talk about nervous.

There are great pictures of Coop and me in the clubhouse. We were drinking champagne. No wonder it became my favorite drink. It was such a great moment.

I'll never forget the fans when we got back to Milwaukee. We went by under the bridge on Wisconsin Avenue and you saw all these people. I said, "I wonder what happened?" never dreaming they were all out there because we won.

We played Gene Mauch's Angels in the AL Championship Series. They were very good—the lineup had Hall of Famers in Reggie Jackson and Rod Carew and a cast of tough veterans that included Don Baylor, Bobby Grich, Brian Downing, Bob Boone, and Doug DeCinces—but so were we. Our lineup was just tremendous.

Oglivie had a big year. Simmons. Cooper. Molitor. Yount. Gorman Thomas. Even Charlie Moore was a very good player. We were tough. One thing about that team, they could hit. We lost the first two games in Anaheim, putting us in the same situation we had been in a year before, down 2–0 in a playoff series. But this time we were going home to County Stadium, and it's like my security blanket.

Sutton pitches great on a Friday, and we win. Saturday we have a big debate. It's raining. Lee MacPhail, the American League president, is there. Bowie's there. Bowie thinks we should call the game. It's raining on and off. Lee says, no, we can't call it off. Bowie's not happy with Lee. I'm grumbling a little bit, but I always grumble. We play the game and we win. Mark Brouhard, who's in left field because the Angels started lefty Tommy John, gets three big hits and we win. Now we're down to another Sunday game to decide the series.

We still don't have Fingers, of course. I keep thinking about Yogi Berra's comment that if you don't have relief pitching, you don't got nothing. We have Pete Ladd. He's out of our farm system, a big guy, and he's been okay. But Rollie was great.

That fifth game is one of the best games I've seen. I don't think I've ever seen a crowd more into a game. You can't hear yourself think.

In the seventh inning, we're down 3–2. But after Robin walks to load the bases, Coop lines a hit to left-center, scoring Moore and Jim Gantner, and the place is up for grabs. Bedlam. I can still see Coop waving the ball to get down, get on the grass, as he's running to first base. Then Gantner slides in behind Moore. They're going crazy.

By the ninth inning, I'm hanging on for dear life. There's two outs, Brian Downing is on second, Ladd is pitching, and it's 4–3. The place is wild. You can't hear. I'm smoking. I've got one lit here, I've got one in the ashtray, I've got another here. I burned myself. I'm just lighting up. I don't know what I'm doing, and I admit that.

The only thing I can think of after all these years: Why does it have to be the great Rod Carew coming up to hit? Why can't it be some stiff who can't hit?

Carew hits the ball hard but right to Yount, who comes up throwing to Coop. The game is over. What a finish. I go downstairs and they dump everything on me. Vukie and Ted Simmons are waiting for me. I'll always remember this. Now I get home, happy, it's about ten o'clock at night, the game was over at seven. I'm still sitting in my den, with my little radio.

This voice says, "It's the seventy-ninth World Series, between the St. Louis Cardinals and the Milwaukee Brewers." I'm not ashamed to tell you I cried. Oh, my goodness, the Brewers are in the World Series. It was a great feeling.

St. Louis is a great baseball town, but so is Milwaukee. You have two really great baseball cities. We head to St. Louis first to play the mighty Cardinals and we get off to a big start. We win 10–0. Molitor and Yount have nine hits between them at the top of the order. I think we have a better team than the Cardinals, but I'm biased. A lot of people thought we would have been clearly a better team if we had Fingers.

In later years I would kid Whitey Herzog about it, and he didn't deny it. He had Bruce Sutter and we didn't have our guy.

The next day we lose 5–4. That's where we miss Fingers. Ladd is great. Gives us everything he has. But it would have been great to have had Fingers.

With the World Series tied one apiece, we come back to Milwaukee. Bowie's here. Bob Lurie, the Giants' owner, and his wife. The Bronfmans came. That meant a lot to me.

The Cardinals win game 3 on Friday, but we win on Saturday to get it even again. After the game I take a big group to our regular pizza place, Zaffiro's. It's a good time. We win Sunday, and now we're ahead 3–2. We're going back to St. Louis, and Sutton's ready to pitch.

That's it. We lose game 6, get killed 13–1, so we go to the seventh game. Vukie, as it turns out, is pitching with a torn rotator cuff. We don't know he is, but he is. He's tough, a real competitor. We're ahead until we have one tough inning. After that it's all over. We lose 6–3. I don't need to tell you how crushed I am.

Dick Hackett, our marketing guy, says to me, "I just talked to the Association of Commerce people; they want a parade tomorrow."

"What? Are you crazy? We lost. What are we celebrating?"

This goes back and forth. Robin Yount is in the back of the plane, sobbing, and I'm going all around the plane, back and forth, talking to our players, making sure they're all right. Now here comes Hackett again. He's smart. He talks to Sue. Naturally she says of course, you can't tell 'em no.

Hackett comes over, and I'm saying, "I'll tell 'em no. We lost." But by the time the plane lands in Milwaukee, I agree. I even apologize to Hackett. But I'm thinking, The heartbreak of losing game 7, nobody's going to come, you're going to be sorry you did it.

The next morning we get to the ballpark, and they have little buses taking us downtown. When we get to the park, there are some sheriff's department guys there. I know 'em well because they used to work the ballpark.

"Oh, hi, Bud, sorry, but we're so proud of you."

I say to one of the sheriffs I know very well, "Eddie, this will be quick. I'm sorry you have to work." He says, what are you talking about?

I say, "We lost, why would anybody come out?"

He says, "I don't know, but we've just closed downtown. There must be a million people here. I don't know where they've all come from." The streets are jammed, the buildings are jammed. And, of course, Sue is beaming, just as she should be. It takes us four or five hours to get up Wisconsin Avenue. It's unbelievable.

At the ballpark Robin rode his motorcycle in. There was a huge crowd there. It was such an emotional day. It was everything you could ever expect, and even in losing you could see how much this group and this team meant to the city. Much as I had said during the years after the Braves left, Milwaukee was indeed a baseball town.

10

As electric as the season had been, there were things going on behind the scenes that even I, as involved as I was with the players, had no idea about. Perhaps the biggest one was an issue that demonstrated how quickly the culture around the game was evolving beyond anything we'd seen before, one that all of baseball would end up confronting numerous times in the months and years ahead: cocaine.

For my part, I learned of the trouble from a single phone call. Sometimes it can only take one phone call to lose your equilibrium. I had an acquaintance who worked for the FBI. I think he was a friend of Bob Uecker's. He was looking out for me when he called one day and said I needed to come meet him somewhere we could talk. I knew immediately this was serious, and I went right there to meet him.

He told me Paul Molitor was involved with a big cocaine dealer, Tony Peters. I was surprised and disappointed, but I don't know if I was stunned. Cocaine had become a big problem in America, especially with young people who had the means. Paul was single and popular in Milwaukee, very popular. I knew he liked the nightlife. Paul was one of my favorite players then, and through it all remains a personal favorite.

In terms of his fame, his situation was not unique. Around the country, players were going from being blue-collar heroes to true celebrities, subject to all the adoration and temptations that come with superstar status. The more money the players made, the more apparent this became. With players signing bigger contracts out of free agency, their private lives became flashier. The celebrity culture around the game was changing, and the off-field dangers escalated right along with it. Like so many other young people around America, especially those with money and access to glitzy clubs and the wrong kind of people, cocaine was creeping into baseball. And now, apparently, it was at the doorstep of my team and one of the Brewers' biggest stars.

This was bad, very bad. The FBI guy let me ride with them that night and I was nearby when they moved in on Peters. Paul was there, as the FBI thought he would be. He wasn't arrested and would never have to testify publicly in the case that landed Peters a sentence of twenty-two years.

But can you imagine what a shock it was for him to look up and see me? He and I were very close.

I still shake my head about what might have happened to Paul if I hadn't been there that night. I was a part of a group that bought a team never dreaming everything would change like this, this fast. Seeing how rapidly the culture around the players was evolving, you began to worry. But I would have been downright petrified if I had known what was starting to happen with players.

As I'd learn over the years, this was not Paul's first time getting into trouble. In his 1993 book *The Game Behind the Game,* Paul's agent Ron Simon wrote about the police being called to his house on Christmas Day, 1980.

"They had to break in to see if Paul Molitor was inside, dead or alive," Simon wrote. "Molitor was in my house, sleeping off a wild night of cocaine abuse."

Needless to say, Simon didn't bring up Paul's cocaine problems when we talked about contracts or the future.

When Paul was inducted into the Hall of Fame on a gorgeous

July day in 2004, he stood at the podium, in that beautiful field in Cooperstown, and told the world he "had problems with drugs early in my career."

He once admitted to *USA Today* that he'd had bad judgment in that era. "I tried cocaine but that was it," he told the newspaper. "It was a long time ago and I regret it, but those things come back to haunt you. Part of it was peer pressure. I was single and in Milwaukee and I hung around with some wrong people. I was able to get out before I got into serious trouble."

I was proud of the way that Paul addressed his problems. He was caught up in what you could probably describe as an epidemic in professional sports. Here was a great young player with everything to live for and to achieve in baseball. Thank God he worked around it. I think he would tell you that I helped him, a lot.

We had a problem here, and so did many other teams. The FBI case against Peters disclosed the scope of the problem on those Brewers teams of the early eighties. We had an outfielder here in 1977–80 named Dick Davis. He later played for the Phillies, Pirates, and Blue Jays, then extended his career playing in Japan. Testimony in Peters's case showed that Davis was purchasing cocaine and marijuana from Peters and passing it on to teammates and other players around the league.

But this was hardly a Milwaukee story. As we'd be reminded throughout the 1980s, cocaine use impacted many teams in baseball, as well as other sports. A three-month investigation by the *New York Times* in 1985 showed that players on almost every team had been named in connection with cocaine use. Many of those named were kept out of the public record, but baseball found itself with ugly, horrifying drug trials in Kansas City and Pittsburgh. Vida Blue, Willie Wilson, Willie Aikens, and Jerry Martin were handed prison sentences after admitting to cocaine use in Kansas

City in 1983. As many as twenty-one players, including future Hall of Famer Tim Raines, testified against Phillies clubhouse caterer Curtis Strong in 1985. They'd all been granted immunity for their testimony, which was common in those cases.

Baseball's embarrassment could have been much worse, but the government was going after the dealers, not the ballplayers. I felt our sport was lucky, and so were the players like Paul who realized they needed to clean up their off-the-field habits. Unfortunately, the leniency shown here by law enforcement allowed the league, and perhaps more problematically the players union, to move on from this black eye without implementing the changes necessary to make sure issues with drugs—be they recreational or performance enhancing—didn't arise again.

The owners did seek help from the union in stemming a serious problem, but that was one area where Marvin Miller wasn't any help to anyone. Peter Ueberroth, who had replaced Bowie Kuhn as commissioner, was used to having unilateral powers in his business dealings. He decided he was going to do something about our cocaine problems, instituting mandatory testing of players.

He dropped this bomb on the union shortly before the start of the 1986 season, saying that every player would be subject to testing four times a year.

"Someone somewhere has to say, 'Enough is enough,' to drugs," Ueberroth said. "And I've done that."

There was one problem, however, as I would be reminded repeatedly in future years. Drug testing couldn't be implemented without consent of the Players Association. It was subject to collective bargaining, and Donald Fehr, who had been named executive director of the union after Marvin Miller retired, was quick to point that out.

Marvin handpicked Fehr, his assistant since 1977, as his successor, after Ken Moffett served for less than a year, and even though Marvin was retired he remained highly influential in the union. Marvin had us on the run for most of the previous two decades with his in-your-face style, but in the aftermath of the '81 strike he'd celebrated his biggest victories. Salaries had soared since the fifty-day strike. The average salary had been $185,651 in '81, and by 1984 it was already $329,408. That, to Marvin, was an example of winning a strike, and I don't think owners would have disagreed. Having Fehr inherit the mantle from Marvin ensured that the union would be run for most of the next two decades the way Marvin had run it, with owners and players constantly fighting about one issue after another.

The biggest issue was drug testing.

Even after baseball's obvious problem with illegal drugs, most notably cocaine, the union regarded a drug testing policy as an invasion of privacy, which did nothing to solve the problem that guys were abusing their bodies and putting their health in danger. If teams didn't know who had the problems, if they were kept deliberately in the dark by the players union, then there was no way to help them deal with the possible fallout from addiction. Immediately after Ueberroth announced his plan to test for cocaine, Fehr filed a grievance, and in short order baseball's arbitrator, Tom Roberts, ruled for the union. So that was that.

After that initial ruling, players wouldn't agree to any form of testing for sixteen more years. Whether it was PEDs or so-called recreational drugs, the union's ironclad opposition to testing left us with no consistent, defined way to reel in players with serious problems, like Steve Howe and Darryl Strawberry.

You remember Howe, right?

He'd been Rookie of the Year with the Dodgers in 1980 but couldn't beat his demons. He wound up being suspended seven different times, by three different commissioners, including a lifetime ban from Fay Vincent on his seventh strike.

That came after an off-season arrest in Montana, where he was in the process of buying cocaine. Howe would ultimately plead guilty, and in June 1992, Vincent suspended him for life. But Howe still had the power of the union behind him.

My friend Dick Moss was his agent and argued the union's case. The hearing turned into an ordeal unto itself—Fay angered George Steinbrenner, Gene Michael, and Buck Showalter by overreacting to testimony they'd given that seemed to support Howe, who was then a Yankee—and arbitrator George Nicolau would eventually overturn the suspension.

Howe would play for the Yankees from 1993 through June '96, pitching until he was thirty-eight. He died at age forty-eight when he ran his pickup truck off the road in the California desert in 2006, and an autopsy found methamphetamine in his bloodstream.

No one won in protecting Steve Howe or other players from the cocaine epidemic of the 1980s. Every time the owners tried to get testing, we were turned down flat. The union leaders were dug in, there's no question about that. For some reason they were adamant that drug testing was harmful to the players—even as the league's drug problem exploded in newspaper headlines. It was a horrible health problem, an integrity problem, a problem in so many ways, and they just didn't care.

In so many ways, the cocaine abuse during the 1980s foreshadowed the later issues we'd confront around performance-enhancing drugs. Both the arbitrator's ruling and the union's refusal to budge on the issue laid the groundwork that allowed for the growth of steroid use a decade later.

As dangerous as it was, baseball's problem with drugs was only beginning. This initial stonewalling of drug testing meant there was no accountability for players using drugs of any kind, leaving us no way to combat the burgeoning science behind anabolic steroids, human growth hormone, and other performance-enhancing drugs that would become all too apparent in the years ahead. No one seemed to truly understand the stakes here—whether it was the risks to the league, to the union, or to the players themselves.

11

Change comes hard to any institution as entrenched as baseball. And as the 1980s progressed, it became clear that the league was facing serious issues—both economic and systemic. Something had to give, and it started at the top, with then-commissioner Bowie Kuhn.

While Major League Baseball certainly didn't do itself any favors back then, it was hard not to look at the NFL with quite a bit of envy. Even though the football league wasn't anywhere near the juggernaut that it's become today, it still seemed like it was the model for all professional sports leagues to follow. This was true largely because of the work of one man: Pete Rozelle

Rozelle epitomized what a commissioner should be, what a commissioner can do for his sport. As a baseball fan and then an owner, I was always envious of the magic he was making for the NFL. Pro football was a shaky proposition when he took over as National Football League commissioner, and he turned it into the slickest, most popular operation in sports. He'd merged the leagues and instituted revenue sharing in 1961, which was a remarkable display of foresight. I know the league was poor, but still, the fact that someone had the vision to understand that the teams were going to need revenue sharing is very remarkable.

By comparison, baseball was stuck in neutral and Rozelle took advantage of that. No question about it. He was extraordinary. He knew how to market his sport. He understood television and its relationship to sports. He was way ahead of us. I'll say that very bluntly. When you look back at his career, he was brilliant. His vision was really remarkable.

There was just no will to do things differently in baseball, which was most unfortunate. Perfect example: Here's something nobody knows. It was about this time that Major League Baseball missed a great opportunity.

We had a group that explored our television rights—Kuhn, Eddie Einhorn, and Bill Giles. We called it KEG.

ESPN was struggling financially in its early years. We had discussions about buying it from Getty Oil. Einhorn and Giles were very interested. Eddie actually thought it would be the best thing ever, and he was right, but Bowie didn't want any part of it.

I was on the Executive Council when it came up. Bowie just said, we're not going to buy it, and that was that. The concern at that time and in ensuing years was about what critics called the oversaturation of games on television. The Cubs were on WGN, the Braves on WTBS, so-called superstations that went into every market, and the other teams weren't happy about it.

It's hard to say what would have happened if we had bought ESPN. But I think history says we would have had tremendous success. We would have been able to market our game even better than the NFL marketed its game, and maybe later on we would have sold it for a few billion dollars. But instead of us, ABC bought the network from Getty Oil in 1984.

Missed decisions like these allowed football to take off at our expense. Rozelle was a PR guy. He understood. There was nobody like that in sports before him. He was a true revolutionary.

Baseball owners were generally like Walter O'Malley. They wanted what was good for them and their teams. Football owners were different, at least back when the NFL was growing into the powerhouse it is today. You look at Wellington Mara, Art Rooney,

George Halas, Clint Murchison, lots of others. Rozelle worked with their willingness to think about the league, not just their teams, and that was why they were able to get so much done. Later on, like everything else, it began to pull apart. But the NFL was amazing in the early years.

Bowie was our commissioner for fifteen seasons, and he didn't run the game as much as preside over it in an era when Marvin Miller and the union were making giant strides. Bowie, of course, was in office when free agency and salary arbitration were instituted. He knew the effect those changes had on player salaries. He could see we were headed for difficult times but didn't address the reality. Bowie was involved, but under him we didn't do anything to help our economic outlook.

This didn't exactly endear him to the owners. I always liked Bowie personally—he loved baseball—but he didn't build the relationships he needed to effectively lead the owners. Some owners always saw Bowie as a stuffed shirt, an elitist. He could be distant, and when he tried to make conversation it seemed he talked down to you—unless you got to know him well, as I did. There weren't many owners who were comfortable talking to Bowie, but I was.

Seeing Bowie's strained relationships with some of the owners taught me something that would be very helpful later—that the commissioner can't have his favorites. If he is going to be effective, he has to talk to all the owners all the time. That's what I did. I was on the telephone all day, every day, it seems.

With salaries escalating and the players union only growing in strength, there was a growing internal frustration that we weren't solving our problems. We had all these work stoppages and resulting settlements and none of our problems were being resolved.

Bowie's tenure came to an end at the winter meetings in 1981, when a group of ten owners said they wouldn't vote for him to be reelected as commissioner when his contract was up. I was the one who delivered the news to Bowie. And oh, it was painful. Just like that, he became a lame duck.

The next year was bad. He was in office but he didn't have the power of the office. That's not a great situation for anybody. At an owners' meeting the next November, a group put together a compromise to give him a three-year extension. The final vote was 7–5 in the NL and 11–3 in the AL—both in favor of Kuhn. But reelection required a supermajority, which was ten votes in the sixteen-team AL and nine in the NL. He was left to serve out the rest of his term until the following August.

Of all the comments from the owners after the vote, one stuck with me. Eddie Chiles of the Rangers, an oilman who didn't like to be told what to do by anyone, said he voted against Kuhn because he felt "the commissioner system has outlived its usefulness." He wanted to see the office be restructured.

He wasn't wrong. The commissioner system needed change. A lot of people never understood that, even later, when I became commissioner.

People would say, "If Kenesaw Mountain Landis were still alive," referencing the commissioner who cleaned up baseball following the Chicago Black Sox scandal in 1919. You need a commissioner with a lot of authority. I took a lot of authority. I admit that. I don't know what Eddie had in mind. I don't even know if Eddie knew what he had in mind. But he was right in this regard—this was not the commissionership of 1940, '50, '60, '70, or even '80. It needed change.

I was appointed to lead the search committee for a new commissioner. Eventually, we had three finalists, and we spent a long time getting to know all of them. The finalists were Bart Giamatti, James Baker, and Peter Ueberroth. Giamatti, who was the president of Yale, was pretty easily accessible for us, but the other two were tricky. Baker was then chief of staff for President Reagan and Ueberroth was knee deep in preparations for the upcoming Olympic Games in Los Angeles.

Those were three great candidates. I fell for Giamatti, who loved baseball the same way I did, but it was impossible for owners to ignore the great job Ueberroth was doing with the Olympics. We didn't know it at the time we chose Ueberroth, but those Olympics would return huge profits (as much as 31 percent, according to some reports) while showcasing Los Angeles in a way that we wanted baseball to be seen.

Ubie wasn't a friend of many owners. He led with a sharp tongue and an iron hand. He knew he had been hired because our economics were in bad shape, and that drove everything he did. He got the ball rolling on a lot of good things, including the marketing and merchandising of the game. He brought our business side into the modern world, more than it had ever been.

But he didn't mind calling owners names in our meetings. Even worse, to some of the owners who had been staying away and sending representatives in their place, he required that the owners themselves come to the meetings, which he changed from two a year to four.

I got along great with him, but the meetings were very tough. You may quarrel with his style and how he went about it, but anybody who looked at the numbers, looked at what was going on, knew there was an institutional problem, a very serious one.

But Ubie thought he could dictate the terms. He didn't go about trying to make changes in a way that would make them happen. I could see that. Years later, in the 1990s, it was moments like this that helped me recognize that if there was to be change, the kind of change that I knew we needed, you were going to have to work at it with all the owners. But that wasn't how Ubie operated. He'd get them in a room and say, "Hey, we're going to do this and do that." Then the meeting would be over and he'd be off doing whatever else he did. There was no follow-up with everyone else, no politicking to make sure people actually implemented his decisions.

That said, Ubie did have his areas of focus. Ubie didn't just worry about growing our revenues. He worried about our growing payrolls, specifically what we were spending to sign free agents. He liked confrontation. "Hey, what are you doing?" "You gonna sign this guy?" It was tough.

This became a cause for him, generating a lot of discussion at meetings and eventually the creation of an information bank that kept teams up to speed on what was happening with free agents. An undeniable change was happening in the market for free agents. These developments would be the basis for the union's charges of collusion, and the owners were found guilty by arbitrators Thomas Roberts (1985) and George Nicolau (1986 and '87 free agents).

Eventually these cases were settled with owners agreeing to pay $280 million, divided equally, and a group of players were given new-look chances at free agency. I testified in those hearings and said the Brewers weren't looking to sign free agents. That happened to be the truth. I believe that Nicolau and Roberts both drew inferences not supported by the evidence. But what happened in the market was a manifestation of our serious problems.

There were all these charges about this guy did this, that guy did that. Look, the system was broken. Owners were desperate. Instead of solving the problems at the table, we solved nothing.

I could honestly say, when I went to testify, that I never said to another club—"don't sign my player, I won't sign your player." I never did any of that. As close as I was to all the owners, closer than anybody else, I never had that conversation.

The collusion rulings were frustrating to me. They were a manifestation of the system being broken. Salaries were rising dramatically and people were concerned. There's the phrase "acting in concert," which is prohibited in our Basic Agreement. It is prohibited for both sides. I always thought it was odd that the agents had more information on what everyone was doing than anybody. There was the sense that if our guys had the same information it was collusion. I often used to joke that if we're colluders, we're the worst colluders in the history of mankind. Because look what was happening with salaries.

Clubs are always going to make their own economic decisions. I have never understood why that was so hard to understand. Ubie talked to us all the time about fiscal responsibility. I did the same thing when I was commissioner. I used to say in my many speeches, "I'm not telling you who to sign, what to sign, but I ran a club. You sweat every game out." To do that and lose money, what sense does that make?

Ueberroth had other issues with owners, of course. As Bowie had done in 1976, he killed any leverage owners might have had during a player strike in 1985. He didn't want a prolonged strike to stain his record with the public, so he made sure it ended after two days.

Players had gone on strike August 6. We were represented by Barry Rona and were attempting to get the kind of salary cap mechanism that the NBA had ever so quietly gotten its union to approve years earlier. That was always our goal in negotiations during those years, and it was always a nonstarter for the union.

We weren't sure players could hold together again as they had in 1981 because their salaries had doubled since then. But it didn't matter, because Ubie dived in after one day, telling our guy and Fehr they had till two o'clock to get a deal done or he was going to order players back on the field, without a deal.

Nobody wanted that, so a compromise was pounded out. Ueberroth had killed us.

After a while, everyone knew Ueberroth would be a one-term commissioner, gone when his deal was up. As usual, for whatever reason, I was in the middle of things.

When Peter decided he was done, he called me to meet him at the Regency Hotel in New York and negotiate the terms of his departure. I don't know how I got these jobs, but I got them.

One of the biggest pleasures I've had, and one of the biggest heartbreaks, came from getting to know Bart Giamatti, who would succeed Ueberroth. The time hadn't been right for him to leave Yale when we interviewed him in the earlier commissioner search. He eventually told us he'd given the school a longer commitment and needed to keep it. But when he did leave Yale, he was a great fit for a job we had open—National League president, replacing Chub Feeney.

Bart was a lifelong Red Sox fan, a Ted Williams man through and through. The first time I met him, we debated the merits of Williams versus DiMaggio and wound up in a delightful dissection of the 1949 pennant race between the Yankees and the Red Sox, which was decided when the Yankees beat Boston in the last two games of the season.

Bart loved baseball so much that he wrote an op-ed piece for the *New York Times* during the 1981 strike, essentially demanding that the players get back on the field and start giving us baseball. I loved everything about the man and was so happy when we got him involved in baseball. He was the easiest choice ever as a replacement for Ueberroth.

There was a romance to Bart that you didn't see in most others involved in baseball management. He was a wordsmith and did a lot of writing about baseball, the game's charm and its nature, its integrity. But Bart was smart and he was tough. He had dealt with a lot of tough labor situations at Yale. I think he could have been a great long-term commissioner. I think he would have brought about a lot of the change that wouldn't happen for years.

One of the many qualities that pointed to Bart Giamatti's potential to be a great commissioner was that he wanted to discuss issues, not just dictate change. He understood that being commissioner requires you to persuade people to see your point of view, not order them to do your bidding. He also understood that he represented owners—who, after all, had hired him and could fire him—and not the players. He understood that the union represented the players. He understood that his influence as commissioner would go only so far in labor issues, because, to quote him, "I only have suasion over one side."

He and I had spent endless hours talking. He understood the problems and what the commissioner's role should be in resolving those problems. Now, every commissioner in every sport is knee deep in labor and business, and should be. You can't say "I don't care," because you're the commissioner and it's your job to stay involved.

When we named Bart as commissioner-elect, we had another labor agreement to negotiate. The Basic Agreement expired in 1990. Bart knew he'd have to hit the ground running. He also knew he could use all the help he could get. That's why we created a new position under him—deputy commissioner. He wanted someone with a strong business background and brought us Fay Vincent.

They'd been friends for ten years, drawn to each other's intellect, passion for literature, and love of baseball. Fay was a New Yorker who had been hired as an outsider to run Columbia Pictures. His success there put him in Bart's orbit. He got Bart onto the board at Coca-Cola, which had purchased Columbia, and Bart returned the favor by giving Fay a chance to work in baseball.

We needed strong leadership more than ever, leadership that would focus on the economic issues, which were becoming bigger by the year. They thought they'd love working together, and from the outside it seemed they did. But they couldn't have really enjoyed that period, as it was largely occupied by a much more public drama they'd inherited from Ueberroth: Pete Rose.

Reports of Rose's gambling and dealings with shady people made their way to the commissioner's office when Pete was a player-manager with the Reds. Ueberroth called Rose to New York to confront him in February 1989, about a story dealing with Rose's alleged gambling that was set to run in *Sports Illustrated*. When the *New York Times* got wind of the meeting, Ueberroth told Murray Chass that "there's nothing ominous and there won't be any follow-through."

Ueberroth had his foot out the door and essentially turned it over to Giamatti and Vincent, both of whom believed the issue merited a full investigation. Vincent hired a lawyer he knew well, John Dowd, a former federal prosecutor who had gone after mobsters in the 1970s, to build a case. There was no way to get around the issue. It had to be addressed. But the shame for our sport was that it turned into such an ugly chapter for everyone. It's to Bart's everlasting credit that he took on the weight of holding the Hit King accountable for his actions, but it was one more bad story for baseball. Because of Rose, there was little romance in baseball for Bart during his brief tenure, and that's a shame.

From the very start of MLB versus Rose, the sides had squared off, creating a battle royale that would result in no winners. Dowd was extremely aggressive throughout his investigation. He got to the bottom of the matter, proving beyond a doubt that Rose, as a manager, had bet on baseball. He did it by turning some of Rose's acquaintances against him. But his investigative style blew up on everyone on the MLB side when a Cincinnati judge read a letter that Dowd had drafted seeking leniency for one of the men who provided information on Rose. The wording of the letter made it seem as if baseball had prejudged Rose, rather than merely gathering information on him, and Judge Carl Rubin—a Reds fan who, like almost everyone in Cincinnati, worshipped Rose—took his concerns to Rose's attorney and to the press. Bart had signed the letter, so there was no wiggling out of having a hand in this. Before Bart could call Rose to a meeting, Rose sued him. He wanted the process to be shut down and even for Bart to pay damages.

Vincent and Dowd should not have put the commissioner in this terrible position. I think that greatly impacted the relationship between Giamatti and Vincent. Bart felt that internally we had mishandled the Rose situation. He was unhappy with some of the letters and details of the investigation.

Bart eventually prevailed upon Rose to sign off on a deal that made him permanently ineligible to participate in baseball but allowed him to apply for reinstatement provided he had lived up to his side of the agreement, including a requirement that Rose "reconfigure" his life.

It was August 24 when the deal was announced. Several days

later, Bart headed to his home on Martha's Vineyard to take a little break. He died there on September 1, after suffering a massive heart attack.

I had talked to him the night before. I called about ten o'clock at night and he returned the call after having dinner with Senator Bill Bradley.

"Buddy, you sound so forlorn," Bart said. "Are you okay?"

I told him I was fine. We'd beaten a good Oakland club that day, so I was in a good mood, actually. We talked from about midnight until around one in the morning. We just gossiped. Bart loved to hear what was going on with the owners and other people.

That was the last time we spoke.

The next day, he went shopping for a wedding gift for my daughter Lisa and wrote a beautiful note. Then, in the blink of an eye, he was gone.

Fred Wilpon, the Mets' owner, called me with the news. I was speechless, for once.

As Bart's wife, Toni, later told me, the note to Lisa was the last thing Bart wrote. I sent it on to her, so she would have it.

Sadly, Bart's short time in baseball is basically remembered for two things: suspending Pete Rose for life because he gambled on baseball and dying of a heart attack at age fifty-one, only five months after we had welcomed him as our seventh commissioner.

There's a widespread belief that stress over the Rose investigation and its ugly aftermath was what killed Bart. But that wasn't it. Bart was a chain smoker and was a little heavy. He just didn't take care of himself well. You can't live like that forever without it taking a toll.

I had realized that for myself shortly after the 1982 World Series. I quit smoking those Tiparillos and started eating better. Sue stopped smoking, too.

About two weeks before he passed, Bart and I had dinner in New York, and he ate a big Italian dinner with a lot of cream sauce. Afterwards we were walking to the Yale Club, where he was staying. He was lighting up a cigarette, and I said, you shouldn't be doing that. That was the only time he ever got mad at me.

"Toni put you up to this, didn't she?" he said.

Well, I liked Toni, but I hadn't talked to her about his smoking. It was just common sense, really.

We were all crushed when Bart died. It was a huge personal loss for everyone who had gotten to know him, and it was a blow because he had seemed the perfect leader for a tough time.

It was only two weeks later, at an Executive Council meeting in Milwaukee, that we got down to the business of finding the next commissioner. Vincent, as an extension of Giamatti, was the default option, and a lot of us were worried about the ongoing labor negotiations. I remembered how time consuming the search leading to Ueberroth had been and wasn't anxious to repeat that process, not at that point in time.

So the thought was to just give the job to Fay Vincent, though the support for Fay was hardly unanimous. Peter O'Malley was the most outspoken of the dissenters. He said, "We're rushing this." He was right, but I was head of the Executive Council and I said, let's do it. I'll take responsibility. But looking back, I was in shock over Bart's death, which had really shaken me to the core.

A short while after we named Fay as Bart's replacement, maybe five or six days later, I got a call from Bart's widow, Toni. She was stunned that we had given the commissioner's job to Fay. She said Bart had developed major differences with Fay and was even talking about firing him in the weeks before he died.

For all the time I spent on the phone, I should have made a few more phone calls before we named Fay Vincent as No. 8.

12

Not only did Pete Rose give us headlines no sport would want, but he also distracted Bart and Fay from our economic challenges, which kept growing larger. And as the 1980s drew to a close, one of the biggest issues facing the game was about television.

Few things have transformed baseball—or any sport—the way that television has. That was true in the 1950s and it was true in the 1980s, too, though by then the economics looked vastly different. Nothing encapsulated baseball's problems in the 1980s as clearly as its relationship to TV.

In December 1988, we were at another owners' meeting, beginning to discuss strategy for the next round of labor negotiations with the union, when someone burst in with the news.

Steinbrenner had signed a twelve-year, $486 million deal with the Madison Square Garden Network. Fred Wilpon didn't believe it at first.

"Don't be silly," he said.

When Wilpon found out the report was accurate, he looked like he was going to pass out. He was stunned. We all were, really. It was hard to comprehend those numbers.

The Yankees' MSG deal was going to change the economics of the sport. The Yankees were going to get $50 million before a single game was televised, and their annual local television revenues would start at $7.5 million in 1989 and rise to $29 million by 1991.

That one TV deal illustrated many of the financial problems

facing the league. The widening gap in revenues between franchises had been an irritation for a majority of teams over the previous decade, and neither Steinbrenner nor the owners of other big-market teams regarded it as a problem. They would not consider making short-term sacrifices for the good of the sport.

As news of the MSG deal landed, I couldn't help but think of an exchange years earlier. It was in 1983, when Orioles owner Edward Bennett Williams said something I never forgot. It was in a labor committee meeting, and we were talking about making some minor changes to revenue sharing. There was some thought that we had to do these during negotiations with the Players Association because of federal labor laws. It was after one of these discussions that Williams confronted Steinbrenner.

"The peasants are going to come down from the hills," Williams said.

"Peasants?" growled Steinbrenner. "Don't tell me about peasants. I know how to take care of the peasants!"

Back in 1983, we were a sport beginning to fight for its life, but by the decade's end the situation was becoming scary, and now the nuclear bomb of all local television contracts had landed square in the middle of our troubled landscape. At the time, many of the other twenty-five teams were receiving less than a million dollars a year for their TV contracts. The Brewers were getting only about twenty-five thousand dollars per game, with less than a quarter of our games televised.

This is a problem the NFL never had to confront. Their inventory of games is so small that they're all carried on national television, not local networks. Pete Rozelle had somehow convinced the teams to divide their TV pie equally, meaning that teams in cities like Green Bay and Cincinnati would get as much as the ones in New York.

There was blatant unfairness in allowing teams from the largest markets to pocket all of their local television revenue. Those contracts were created by the size of their markets, not the work ethic or ingenuity of the franchise. No matter how hard a team in a small- or medium-sized market worked, no matter how smart you were, how great was your baseball or marketing acumen, the biggest deals would go to teams in the largest cities. That's unfair. They would have a huge advantage in signing free agents and retaining their own players when they reached free agency.

We all knew the economic model had to change. The gap between small-market, middle-market, and big-market clubs was growing at an alarming rate.

We were beginning to understand what was happening, but I'm not sure any of us fully realized how the game would be changed. It added a huge amount of fuel to a smoldering fire. There was tension among the owners like there had never been before.

Perhaps that's why none of us should have been surprised when the 1990 labor negotiations ended up the same way as all the others. We were hunting big game again, with many of the owners continuing a push for a salary cap, like the ones in the NBA and the NFL. Jerry Reinsdorf owned the Chicago Bulls as well as the White Sox, and Stan Kasten had been Ted Turner's man with both the Braves and the Atlanta Hawks. While Edward Bennett Williams wasn't active in these negotiations, he understood the NFL's system because he'd been president of the Washington Redskins.

We announced that we'd lock out players from spring training camps if we didn't have a deal by February 15. The union didn't blink and talks got off to a very slow start, threatening the start of the season.

Vincent was nervous from the beginning about having a work stoppage on his watch, just as Peter Ueberroth had been in 1985 and Bowie Kuhn before him. Only two days into the lockout, Vincent interjected himself into the negotiations, essentially gutting our proposal. So much for us getting the players on the run. But even with our initial proposal highly diluted—the salary cap was pulled off the table—talks dragged like the last hour of school on a sunny day. The outcome was predictable to anyone who had followed our labor history.

We wound up with a deal that saved the season, albeit starting a week late, and we neither solved any of our problems nor introduced any changes that would help us modernize a sport that was falling farther behind all the time.

Fay worked the media like a master, especially in New York and Los Angeles, where he'd been established before being hired by Bart Giamatti. He had the high ground there, which may have caused him to begin to rule like a monarch.

He publicly backhanded George Steinbrenner for paying forty thousand dollars to a man named Howard Spira for information he could use against Dave Winfield in a contract negotiation. It was bad judgment on George's part, for sure, but he was stunned when the commissioner hit him with a two-year suspension (although in a bizarre twist, Steinbrenner negotiated a lifetime ban, which was lifted two years later).

Like the Rose camp, the Yankees felt that Vincent had been heavy-handed and unfair throughout the process. He had dragged Buck Showalter, the Yankees' manager, out of the clubhouse to a meeting across town, at MLB headquarters, before a game because he wasn't pleased with Showalter's testimony during a griev-ance hearing regarding Steve Howe.

While Steinbrenner wasn't the most popular of owners, every-one thought Fay had mishandled these two cases.

We had been studying our first expansion since 1977 for a long time, working to find two cities that could join the National League and give us fourteen teams in both leagues. We had set the expansion fee at $95 million per team, a pool of $190 million that would be shared by the teams.

This should have been very popular with everyone, but instead we wound up fighting among ourselves. We had to decide how many players teams could lose in the expansion draft and how many they could protect, and we wound up in a big fight between owners in the two leagues.

National League owners felt they deserved the full $190 mil-lion. American League owners wanted equal shares because they were going to lose players, too, along with having their slice of the national revenue pie made a little bit slimmer. Both sides were dug in, and Vincent was put into the middle of the dispute.

His ruling, revealed just before Miami and Denver were awarded teams, was a blow to the AL teams. He said they would get 22 percent of the revenue and lose three players each in the expansion draft. That was only three million dollars per team at the cost of three players. I hated the ruling, and other American League owners were livid.

I got a call from George W. Bush, the future United States president who then was running the Rangers. "You can't let this happen," Bush told me, which was interesting in that he was one of Vincent's close friends and supporters. His uncle, Bucky Bush, was a close friend of Fay's, and George was loyal to family friends.

"Buddy, we got screwed," George said.

"Yes, George, we got screwed."

This was just an ugly era for everyone in the game. The whole tone for baseball was bad coming out of the 1990 labor agreement. Small-market clubs were hurting and nobody was acknowledging it.

Doug Danforth, who had become the point person for the Pirates, was scared stiff about the future of his franchise and expressed the concern directly in a letter to Vincent.

Danforth begged the commissioner to address the concerns many clubs had. He referred to the growing economic disparities as "startling and apt to get worse if something is not done very soon." He estimated that teams on the low end were producing roughly one-third as much revenue as teams on the high end.

"Local TV and radio revenues will run from a low of about $3.5 million to a high of $50 million," Danforth wrote, saying teams in even medium-size markets would be hard pressed to survive economically while fielding competitive teams. He pleaded with Fay to consider some form of revenue sharing.

"You will get howls from six or seven owners, and applause from twenty others," he wrote. "I am sure that neither you nor I are in favor of the game of baseball becoming just a toy of the very wealthy, but I believe that's what will happen unless a new direction is sought."

Danforth eventually came to believe Fay simply wasn't the right man for the job.

I knew that, too. Fay had revealed it to me in an unexpected way one night in January 1992.

I met Fay for dinner in Arizona before spring training, and afterward, on the drive home, I talked to him about how unhappy the clubs were.

"Fay, I've run the Brewers for more than twenty years," I said. "I think I understand what's going on. It's getting tougher now. We're starting to have disparity we never dreamed about. We've got to do something about it. I know others have talked to you about it."

Fay didn't even look at me. He stared straight ahead and gave me a dismissive wave.

Huh? That wasn't what I was expecting. I pushed ahead, telling him that I had talked about this frequently with his old friend Bart Giamatti. I told him that Bart knew the economic problems and disparity had to be addressed. Then Fay said something that absolutely stunned me. It still does, really.

"Buddy, this is the best job I've ever had," he said. "I don't want Fred Wilpon and Nelson Doubleday mad at me."

He was talking about the owners of the Mets, one of the big-market teams that needed to make sacrifices for the good of the sport. I knew right then that Fay wasn't going to last. He wanted the job, but he didn't want the hard work of uniting owners to get behind changes that were imperative if we were ever going to get out of neutral.

The writing was on the wall, but no one knew exactly how Fay's time as commissioner would end. During an owners meeting in June 1992, at the Waldorf-Astoria Hotel, Fay acknowledged that "baseball may never have been in such a sad financial state." He said that one club had almost been unable to make its payroll and that clubs had been borrowing so much money that banks were constantly calling him for assurances that we could make it good if they failed. He said teams had taken loans as large as thirty-five million dollars to cover their deficits.

But Fay didn't have any solutions. He basically just told us to fix the problems. I couldn't believe he didn't see it as his role to fix the problems. He somehow thought the commissioner was above the economics of the game.

Some owners were so upset with Fay that they were again studying the Major League Basic Agreement to see if they could find grounds to fire him. The rules arguably prevented him from being fired during his term, and he fully understood that, but Jerry Reinsdorf and other owners were working to find historical precedents or other means to make a change.

As a group, we wanted Fay gone so we could get a fresh start and begin working toward curing the disease that was spreading throughout baseball. There were a lot of owners lined up against Fay, for a lot of reasons. "This guy doesn't get it," said Peter O'Malley, whose Dodgers were doing just fine economically.

I had tried to play peacemaker, taking the owners' complaints to Fay, but the reality was he'd lost my confidence with the comments he made that night in Scottsdale. But still I was reluctant to see this play out in an ugly fashion.

I'd talk on the phone with Reinsdorf all the time, and he'd say, "Buddy, how long is this going to drag out?"

While we had agreed not to discuss the Vincent situation with the media after the meeting at the Waldorf, the next day's *New York Times* had a big story in it by Murray Chass, whom we viewed as Fay's unofficial spokesman. It portrayed how Fay was fighting to preserve the commissionership from a cabal headed by Reinsdorf and Selig.

I called Fay and reminded him we didn't need the publicity.

"Buddy, I don't know how that got in the newspaper," he said.

Yeah, right. I might have been born in the morning, but it wasn't yesterday morning.

The Waldorf meeting, coincidentally enough, was the first for a trio of new owners. David Glass (Royals), Drayton McLane

(Astros), and John Ellis (Mariners) all told me later they went home wondering what they'd gotten themselves into. I'd felt the same way back in 1970, so I understood, but the issues were so much tougher now. We couldn't afford to just keep walking away from them.

More time went by without anything getting done.

Rockies CEO John Antonucci circulated a memo in which he expressed "grave concerns over certain issues facing the game, including labor relations, television, inequities between large and small markets," and concluded by writing, "We have not seen leadership exhibited by the commissioner sufficient to move the game in the required direction on these issues."

Padres owner Tom Werner wrote Vincent, telling him simply, "We feel you have lost the capacity to lead."

Doug Danforth called for a no-confidence vote on Vincent at a special meeting convened near O'Hare Airport in early September. It wasn't unanimous, but it passed 18–9 with one abstention.

The fight was out in the public now, but fortunately it didn't last much longer. Fay initially vowed to stay on in the job, knowing there would be a showdown at the scheduled quarterly owners meeting in St. Louis a week after the special meeting.

But Fay finally did the right thing for everybody. He resigned.

13

Nobody was in charge of baseball for about forty-eight hours. Nobody.

Fay was out, but nobody was in on even an acting basis for a couple of days, including me. And, to be honest, I was distracted.

After spending so much time and effort on the business side of the game, thinking about the good of the sport, I needed to take a little bit of time—a scintilla, maybe—and think about the Brewers and our No. 19, Robin Yount.

He was in his nineteenth season and pushing to become the seventeenth hitter ever to collect three thousand hits. I knew I was needed in St. Louis for the quarterly meeting, but I couldn't imagine missing Robin's milestone hit.

So I was sitting in my office at County Stadium at about five thirty when Eli Jacobs, the Orioles owner, called. He told me that I'd be the man in charge. I told him to hold on. We'd talk about it in St. Louis. He said, "No, you're the only logical guy." Later on, Fred Kuhlmann of the Cardinals and Stanton Cook of the Cubs also called. Everyone was saying I was the guy they wanted to take over. We needed a leader, and I was the guy who gave the owners the most confidence. It was as simple as that.

I was really hoping for Robin to get two hits on Monday night in Milwaukee, before I left for the meeting, but he only got No. 2,999, not the big one. So I flew to St. Louis the next morning knowing I'd be coming straight home afterward because the

Brewers were playing the Indians on Tuesday night at County Stadium.

When the Executive Council put my name in nomination to be chairman, I said, guys, shouldn't we think about this? They said, we've thought about it; you have to take over. So I did. Then we broke into our scheduled American League and National League meetings, with league presidents Bobby Brown and Bill White welcoming me to sit alongside them. This was exciting. But a part of me was like a kid on a long day at school. While I knew I was taking on the biggest responsibility of my life, all I really wanted to do was get back to Milwaukee for the baseball game.

George W. Bush is as much of a baseball fan as I am. He knew I was going back to watch Robin and asked if he could come along. Gussie Busch was having a big party at his farm, but George wanted to see baseball history, not spend another night listening to owners talk.

I've always said I'm happy in my life where I am, and I mean it. I really hadn't thought about taking on more responsibility. I know people will be cynical about it, but they're wrong. I had accepted the job as chairman of the Executive Council with the understanding that we would eventually have a search committee for a new commissioner, going through the usual process. I really did not believe I'd be the next commissioner. I loved what I was doing with the Brewers and we had begun an attempt to get a new ballpark, which I felt was vital for not just our success but our survival.

Robin Yount, a Brewer for life, made this a great night for all of us by dropping a single to right field in the seventh inning off Jose Mesa, triggering a happy celebration. Our group headed back to

St. Louis afterward, but I'll be honest: I could have floated there without the plane. This had been a day I'd never forget.

I returned to St. Louis for the second day of meetings but then came right back to Milwaukee, to my little office at County Stadium, the one I'd moved into when the Braves fled to Atlanta. I usually loved that office. But I've got to admit, the tone of the place changed overnight after I took over as chairman of the Executive Council.

Until you're in that chair, you really don't know the extent of the problems. You don't know how it will feel to be the one who has to deal with them. There was no way I could have known then that I'd be the man in charge until January 24, 2015. That's 8,174 days, and very few of them were smooth days. I remember saying at the end of that first day to my secretary, Lori Keck (who had worked for Vince Lombardi before me), "Well, this is some mess we've gotten ourselves into, isn't it?"

But never did I doubt what I was doing or why I was doing it. The sport I had fallen in love with when I was a boy dreaming about being the next Joe DiMaggio needed to change if we were going to survive, much less thrive as we had in the old days.

I was in a unique position, and I knew there was a lot of criticism early on about an owner running the sport, much less actually becoming commissioner. I got pounded quite a bit, but a lot of people didn't understand that the commissioner's office had changed. This was no longer Kenesaw Mountain Landis. This was an era that had been changed by the Players Association. One thing that Marvin used to say over and over, and Bowie had a hard time reconciling himself to—he didn't believe it; and the public didn't understand it then and there are still some people who don't understand it today—was that the union, and not management, controlled the players. I didn't often agree with Marvin Miller, but he was 100 percent right.

When I took over, it wasn't, in my mind, so much a case of an owner becoming a commissioner as much as that I knew I had received great training for more than two decades from people like Mr. Fetzer and Dan Galbreath, among others. I knew what the office was about, and that my experience helped me and it helped the sport. Bringing in an outsider often led to disaster.

Nobody loved the game more than I did. Nobody also understood the history of the commissioner's office, and had studied it, the way I had. I understood the game, the culture, the history, what went wrong, what needed to be done. I knew the people on both sides, on every side. All those years being an owner—and nobody was as active as I was—really helped me.

The world had changed, and the commissioner's job had changed with it. There was a real metamorphosis going on, and there was a lack of understanding about it. Our revenue sharing hadn't changed since the 1930s, really. Somehow the public didn't understand it, and even the parties involved didn't seem to understand it.

I did, but in those first days I didn't know how my role would evolve. I know how this sounds now, but it was true then. There was no grand plan for me to eventually become commissioner. If there was one, nobody had told me.

National television money was a great thing for everyone in baseball. Unlike the cable deals that every team had—the ones that could be huge for some teams and mean much less for teams from smaller markets—the national deals were shared evenly, so those contracts are always of huge interest to teams.

Because the NFL was running rings around us, networks had begun to take a dim view of baseball. I wanted someone to put those cards on the table and fully explain it for all the owners—another way to include everyone in our business—so I invited Dick Ebersol, the president of NBC, to speak at an owners meeting in November.

I encouraged Dick to speak bluntly, and he sure did. He said baseball is the best sport on earth and "moves people in a way that no other sport can." Our guys were smiling at that point. But then he spoke of a "cloud over baseball" that contributed to a negative public perception of the sport. There it was. We all knew it, but it was painful to hear it from someone like Ebersol.

He said that baseball had always lacked a long-term strategy, the kind that Pete Rozelle and David Stern had used for years in the NFL and NBA. He knew all about the different labor histories in the sports and pointed out that we had to put aside our ugly past and find a way to forge a partnership with the Players Association.

"There must be joint marketing of baseball," he said.

I agreed wholeheartedly and was starting my run as baseball's top man full of hope for the future. I'd always been good at looking ahead, not back, and this was one of those times.

We held our famous winter meetings at the Galt House Hotel in Louisville in December. These meetings are one thing Major League Baseball has done well throughout its history—traveling to a warm climate to discuss trades and more mundane business, generally receiving a lot of free publicity from the newspapers that covered teams.

The scope of the meetings had grown exponentially in my

years with the Brewers. Thousands of people attend every year, including a sea of job seekers looking to join the baseball industry. The meetings are part reunion, part carnival, part business conference.

Louisville was different for us. It was freezing, for one thing. We had an activity or two at Churchill Downs, which was fun, but looking back, these were among the worst meetings we'd ever had.

For starters, Carl Barger died. He was president of the Marlins and a good man. He suffered an aneurysm and collapsed. Barger had left an owners meeting, apparently headed to the restroom. Bobby Brown, the former Yankees third baseman who had become a cardiologist in Fort Worth, and Rusty Rose, one of the owners of the Rangers, were at his side within seconds. Dr. Brown and Rusty tried chest pressure and mouth-to-mouth resuscitation before the paramedics arrived but had no luck. Carl was already gone.

I wished I could immediately adjourn the meeting but after a long break to regroup we got back to work. We voted to reopen the collective bargaining agreement.

Agent Dennis Gilbert was busy closing a deal for free agent prize Barry Bonds, who had effectively priced himself out of Pittsburgh by winning his second MVP Award that season. He was like Robin Yount, a player who could have stabilized his franchise with his presence. But it had gotten tougher and tougher for teams—especially small- and medium-market teams—to keep those players.

Bonds signed a record deal in Louisville—six years, $43.75 million—with the Giants, eleven million dollars more than Cal

Ripken's contract with the Orioles, which had been the standard for guaranteed money.

Looking back now, the size of the deal seems almost quaint. But it got my attention then. So too did my first call from Congress. I'd been summoned by Ohio senator Howard Metzenbaum, who chaired the Senate's Judiciary Committee, to discuss baseball's antitrust exemption.

I traveled directly to Washington, D.C., from Louisville, accompanied by Sue and also George W. Bush, the Rangers' owner. He was on his way to visit his father in the White House but took time to help me manage the hearing. He and Sue were sitting in the back of the room when I testified.

Congressional hearings never scared me. I was never intimidated. But it was nice to have a friend like George there. Metzenbaum didn't like having an owner running baseball. He said in his opening remarks that Fay Vincent had used his independent authority to protect the public interest. Well, Fay hadn't exactly protected baseball. He'd mostly protected Fay, at least in my view. But politicians know how to work a stage, and these guys sure did that.

I looked around at one point and George W. was giving me this sign, thumbs up. Then, after the hearing, he invited Sue and me to join him at the White House. It was quite a day, I've got to admit.

We spent a lot of time and money on search committees to find a new commissioner, and it wasn't a charade. I put Bill Bartholomay in charge of the process and he really did a good job. But the timing was never right to go outside and make a hire. Owners did not want to bring in a new commissioner until we had gotten a labor deal that addressed our problems. They always felt I had the best shot to get the deal we needed, and they just didn't want to do anything that hurt our chances. They'd seen that too often in the past.

Bartholomay told owners that more than one hundred people had expressed interest in the job and that he had personally interviewed more than forty-six of them. George Steinbrenner had pushed for Harvey Schiller, the head of the U.S. Olympic Committee, and Stanton Cook had made a strong case for Arnold Weber, the retiring president of Northwestern University. But Bartholomay never made his recommendation. He was handed a letter signed by eleven low- and medium-revenue clubs stating they wouldn't vote for a new commissioner until a new collective bargaining agreement had been signed. Those eleven clubs weren't the only ones who held that view, which became clear at an owners meeting early in 1994, in Fort Lauderdale.

So I was named acting commissioner, and four years later, on July 9, 1998, officially named baseball's ninth commissioner. It was the honor of a lifetime and, while I never set out to be commissioner, in many ways the realization of a little boy's dream.

Timing is everything in life, and George W. Bush's career is a good example. Had things been different, he could have been the ninth commissioner, not me.

George was intrigued by the possibility of being commissioner. He and I talked about it. I told him at the time that I didn't want to be commissioner, and I really didn't. It wasn't until I had been in charge for a while that I began to sense that being commissioner was a real possibilitiy, and even then I had my doubts.

George would have done a great job. He had a great personality and he loved the game. He had come in as an owner with the Rangers in the mid-eighties, in a group that Reinsdorf, who was head of our ownership committee, had put together to buy out Eddie Chiles. George loves the game to this day and he was an insider.

But owners didn't want to bring anybody in until we had a labor deal, and while this was going on George had to make a decision about running for governor of Texas against Ann Richards. He ultimately chose politics instead of baseball and wound up becoming the forty-third president of the United States.

I didn't know that he had that kind of ambition, but I could tell he was bothered when his father lost his bid for reelection. I think that motivated him. But had times been different he definitely could have been commissioner. He would have been a good one, too. Sometimes people who didn't like George's politics would say it was my fault he became president. History is funny like that sometimes.

Early in my tenure I put into practice something that I've long believed critical to any leadership role: I talked to everyone. But there was something else, too. I listened.

I used to sit on the phone by the endless hour. Talking to owners, trying to convince them, persuade them. It's one thing to come to strong opinions and be right, but you have to convince your constituents that you're right. I worked hard to not interrupt the person on the other end of the phone. I know it sounds simple, but it's not. Try it sometime.

Part of being a good politician, a good leader, is the ability to listen to people. I understood my constituents. I understood what previous commissioners hadn't understood. You have to have a great majority of your constituents in your corner, and it's your job to convince them to join you there. I took them through a lot of painful subjects, a lot of change. One thing I tried to teach the owners was to learn to disagree without becoming mortal enemies, because that was the way it had been for so long and it was so unhealthy. I had only just taken over for Fay, but I had already begun to realize that in this job you can't win, so you might as well do what you think is right.

Jerome Holtzman, the great baseball historian who worked for the *Chicago Tribune,* loved to write about the Great Lakes Gang. That was the owners from the Midwest—me, Jerry Reinsdorf, Bill Bartholomay, Stanton Cook, and Carl Pohlad, mostly, sometimes some others.

But over the years there's no question that I spent a lot of time on the phone with other members of the Great Lakes Gang, Reinsdorf in particular.

In my early years in charge, there was this widely held perception that Jerry was very influential, even that he was controlling baseball through me. That was a bunch of garbage, and I can tell you exactly where it came from. It came from the union.

Don Fehr and Gene Orza talked to writers all the time, a few in particular, and I always suspected this was an idea they were selling. That something nefarious was going on in ownership because of Selig and Reinsdorf.

That was the way they worked, Orza especially. Anything they could do to cause a breach among owners, they tried. Unfortunately for them, the other owners understood what I was doing and my style of leadership—talk to everyone.

Jerry and I were indeed close. We still are. Jerry and I were never in lockstep, but in the beginning we agreed about the major issues. We knew this archaic economic system needed to be changed. He knew early on that we needed to change a lot of things. We had several disagreements, but I always knew where he was coming from. We worked together, but we did it my way.

14

Major League Baseball almost ruptured permanently in Kohler, Wisconsin, and the funny thing was, the players union wasn't even there.

The town is an hour north of Milwaukee, or about halfway to Green Bay from my perspective, and I'd brought all the owners there to the American Club, a sprawling resort and conference facility. But I wasn't trying to treat baseball owners to a good time on the golf course when I scheduled an August 1993 summit meeting. I was looking for a site with great conference facilities that was a little bit out of the way. I knew this was going to be a very sensitive meeting. I wanted both privacy and the full attention of owners so that Richard Ravitch and I could forge some consensus on revenue sharing with them. Ravitch, whom we had hired as our chief labor negotiator two years earlier, was well respected for his work running New York's Metropolitan Transportation Authority and really dug in on revenue sharing issues.

This was a step toward getting the next labor deals with the Players Association. Ravitch and I had declared at an owners meeting in February that the continued pursuit of a salary cap was tied to revenue sharing. The cap would not work without revenue sharing because the small markets couldn't afford the minimum payroll required in a cap system.

We were demonstrating to the union that we were taking steps within our ranks to solve our problems, showing them that we'd been listening when they said through the years that we should solve our own problems before coming to them for economic changes. But now we needed to convince the teams with the greatest revenue to share some of it with the teams that were hurting, like the Pirates and the Brewers.

Barry Bonds wasn't the only free agent to move from his own small-market team to a bigger club the previous off-season. Paul Molitor had left Milwaukee for Toronto, lured away as much by a bigger offer from the Blue Jays (three years, thirteen million dollars) as by the chance to try to help Toronto win a second consecutive World Series.

It was painful to see Paul leave Milwaukee after fifteen seasons. We had found ways to keep Robin Yount throughout his career and would have loved to have done the same with Paul. But there was no way we could generate the kind of revenue at County Stadium that the Blue Jays could with SkyDome, their fabulous stadium with the retractable roof, under the shadow of the CN Tower. We couldn't match the offer from Toronto. It was the same situation the Pirates were in with Bonds, except that Paul was thirty-five while Barry was only twenty-seven. Either way, whether with a franchise player in his prime or a cornerstone veteran late in his career, it was becoming impossible for a lot of teams to prevent the big clubs from picking their rosters clean through free agency.

Losing that kind of player was a dramatic manifestation of our problems. I had tried to explain it to Paul before he left and would do it again when he came to Milwaukee with the Blue Jays in late June. It was important to me that Paul understood, not just because of our personal relationship but because he was an influential member of the Players Association.

He had met with me back in 1990 during the spring training lockout, before Fay Vincent essentially opened the camps, and

I knew he'd taken my messages to Don Fehr and Gene Orza. I wanted to make sure he knew why we hadn't been able to do whatever it took to keep him in Milwaukee this time, with another round of bargaining approaching.

Paul had been candid about the downside of playing for the Brewers when he signed with the Blue Jays, saying "it doesn't breed confidence" for a player when there's uncertainty about a team's stadium and future. I knew exactly how he felt, of course. These were tough times for small-market clubs.

We talked about that in late June, before Molitor and Yount played on different teams for the first time, and Paul seemed to fully grasp the change in the game's economics and the need for revenue sharing.

The roster of owners seemed to be constantly changing, too. There was some good in that, as younger owners were more open-minded about making changes for the good of the game. But a lot of my favorite guys had left the sport.

Heading into the meeting at Kohler, I knew that we had a lot of problems. I knew that the divisions were serious. I also knew we needed revenue sharing to solve the problems.

My hope was that an honest discussion, both philosophical and pragmatic, would put us on a road to solving the problem. I hoped that once issues were out there, we would begin to structure a solution to what appeared to be problems that had existed for decades and had just gotten worse, exacerbated by the growth of local television contracts and the rising cost of salaries.

Owners on both sides of the issue were busy digging in before the meeting. Nobody said it to me, but clearly the big-market clubs were talking with each other, designing strategies to keep the small markets in their place. I had good intelligence on all sides. I had also had very good relationships with all the owners, damn good relationships. George Steinbrenner and I were close. I lifted the suspension that Fay Vincent had hit him with about the Howard Spira/Dave Winfield affair, and he was happy to be back in baseball's good graces. He and I had been close through the years, even if we were sometimes on different sides of an issue. We were certainly on different sides with this one, but we had mutual respect and I never stopped listening to George. We had very good dialogue, at least when he wasn't screaming.

In the days before the meeting I was on the phone nonstop. Much of my time was spent talking to the dissenters. Please think about the industry, not just your team. Remember what John Fetzer said, that what was good for baseball was good for the Detroit baseball club.

But I would have been naïve to expect us to make s'mores around the campfire and sing "Kumbaya" in Kohler. As an unnamed National League owner said to the *Los Angeles Times,* "We should be meeting in Madison Square Garden," because he expected a heavyweight fight over the issue.

Of course, I went in spreading hope and faith. That was my mantra for fixing the sport. We had to make changes so that fans in every city could have faith in their team and hope that it could make the postseason. I was going to sell the clubs on the relatively low amount of revenue sharing that we were trying to generate in our first deal. Less than fifty million dollars. In reality, I would have settled for quite a bit less than fifty million if we could get twenty-one of the twenty-eight owners to vote for a compromise. We needed three-quarters approval, which I could tell going in would be tough to get. The idea was to get the ball rolling.

I was preaching change, and I know that's not a popular topic anywhere. People hate change. They hate it in everything in life. They just hate change. In baseball it's particularly true. If you don't want to change, you just point to the game's great tradition. It sounds good, but it doesn't fix problems. We had problems we had to fix.

I talked about the need to find common ground. Then I turned the meeting over to Ravitch, who with his staff had spent months working on specific proposals to move money from the big-revenue clubs to the ones that needed it. While Ravitch was speaking, owners began to leave the room. One by one, the big-market owners walked out the door, trailed by their lawyers and accountants, with everyone's eyes on them.

Steinbrenner, of course. The Red Sox's John Harrington, sure. The Blue Jays' Paul Beeston, too. Then my friend Fred Wilpon, representing the Mets. And a lot of others. It's one of the ugliest spectacles I've seen, so disrespectful to me, Ravitch, and the other owners seated in the room.

If they wanted to make a point, they had sure made it. I knew we were in trouble. A lot of trouble.

For the rest of the day, the big-market clubs met in a conference room in one building and the small-market clubs stayed together in a meeting room in another building. The big-market group included the Yankees, Mets, Red Sox, Dodgers, Blue Jays, Cardinals, and Orioles (who were loving their great new park, Camden Yards). No problem there—well, unless you believed what Peter O'Malley had told the *Los Angeles Times*. He had said he was in favor of revenue sharing tied to a salary cap, but in the end the Dodgers did what was best for the Dodgers, as they'd done under Walter O'Malley.

With the perspective of history, it's surprising how some teams picked sides. The two newest National League teams, Miami and Colorado, also lined up on Steinbrenner's side. I'm not sure I saw that coming, but there it was. I guess Wayne Huizenga and

Jerry McMorris were optimists. Both Chicago teams, the White Sox and the Cubs, and the Atlanta Braves declared themselves medium-market teams. They spent their time with the teams seeking revenue sharing. The Cubs and the Braves were playing politics because they knew the owners could adjust the size of the so-called superstation tax they paid to send their games into other teams' markets.

I had a little office where I killed time when I wasn't moving between the two rooms, looking for an inch of common ground. I knew it was there, but I sure wasn't selling anyone in either of the groups. At one point George W. Bush crossed sides. He had been in the small-market caucus but someone persuaded him that he belonged in the other room. After all, he had a new stadium opening next season, one he had skillfully campaigned for against well-organized opposition. Eventually George realized he had no business with the big markets, but he stood alongside them through the meeting, which I hadn't seen coming.

The vitriol between the two groups was stunning.

Harrington got really heated a number of times, in loud arguments with small-market owners. Steinbrenner said we were all turning into socialists. Beeston said we were asking for too much.

These meetings went on into the night, with only breaks to stop by the buffet table. There were a lot of reporters there, and they were filing stories that were all over the place. Some of them were accurate, but some of them were way off with their facts. Luckily, we didn't have news and texts coming into our phones in that era, so we were able to communicate verbally, sometimes even face-to-face. I can't imagine how crazy it would be with updated technology.

At one point the small- and medium-market teams started

trying to use the only leverage they had. The National League's television agreement was expiring and some owners threatened not to sign a new one, knowing that if they didn't, they could prevent teams like the Dodgers, Mets, Cardinals, and Rockies from televising road games. That would hit them in the wallet, as they would make money only for televising home games.

This wasn't going to fly with me or anyone else, but it was a stick and they were swinging it, doing everything they could to try to get more cooperation from the more prosperous teams.

There was some movement on the second day, Thursday, thanks largely to Jerry Reinsdorf. He came up with a plan where the two Chicago teams and the Braves would join the big-market teams in paying into a fund to be shared by the small-market teams. But even with that, we were barely over thirty-five million dollars, and that wasn't acceptable to the fifteen true small- and medium-market teams, the ones like the Twins, Pirates, and Tigers, who were really hurting.

As late afternoon turned into evening on Thursday, black vans from a car service started pulling up to a side door at the American Club and groups of owners began to leave. Some owners stayed for hours after the first ones headed to the airport, but there was no breakthrough to be found, only frustration and disappointment.

I remember pulling Steinbrenner aside and telling him how costly it would be to the sport to not address our problems. "Keep this up, George, and you're going to get hurt," I said.

We were in bad shape, as Dick Ebersol had told us, and we kept making it worse.

On their way out to the vans, a few owners told their friends on the other side they were sorry for how they'd behaved. But a lot of them went away angry. It was painful to experience, especially knowing that the Players Association and others had been watching this meeting for signs of progress.

I had some explaining to do, and I knew it.

"When you're changing established patterns of life, a certain amount of trauma and a certain amount of time are needed to effect those changes," I told reporters.

Those two days in Kohler exposed all the heartache and problems we had. It was not a terrific start for me in my position, and I was bristling when I got into a car with Randy Levine, one of Steinbrenner's advisers, to drive back to Milwaukee.

"This can't go on," I said. "It can't go on. All the franchises are going to get hurt."

Kohler was a low point, make no mistake about it. We hit bottom there. I spent the next several years digging out from the bottom. Slowly but surely. One small step at a time.

I was personally shaken by the level of ugliness that erupted among people who usually liked each other and treated each other as friends. We were trying to solve the problem and we went backward. The anger toward each other was brutal. Still, we were going to have to deal with this problem, as painful as it was. It wasn't going to go away on its own. We had always been divided, but now we were more divided than ever. And I knew that nobody loved it more than Don Fehr and his people at the union. They knew that they could keep getting deals on their terms if we weren't as unified as they were, and we never were.

I knew it was going to take a while to put the pieces back together again on revenue sharing. We needed to do something that showed everybody, including us, that we could work together. If we couldn't agree on change behind the scenes and to our bottom lines, perhaps as a starting point we could find changes that everyone could see—including the fans.

One of the first things I had done as head of the Executive Council was to appoint a restructuring committee to explore basic changes in the game. We had gone to divisional play in 1969 but still had a system that rewarded only our very best teams for winning divisions. Our playoff structure was far smaller than the ones that were being used in the NFL and the NHL, and fans in too many cities were tuning out in August and September because a powerhouse team was running away with the division title.

This was happening even though we were in one of the worst eras ever for the Yankees. Despite George's spending on free agents, they went into decline after losing the 1981 World Series to the Dodgers and wouldn't get back to the postseason until '95.

With Barry Bonds leading the Pirates and Kirby Puckett in Minneapolis, we were still in an era where the little guys had chances to win. After all, from '83 through '92 there were eleven National League teams and nine American League teams in the playoffs, but the disparity in payrolls was growing at a staggering rate. Because it was becoming hard for a lot of the smaller-market cities to compete for free agency, we needed to increase the opportunity to play meaningful games in September and had a shot to increase national television revenue if we added to the inventory of games in October.

The restructuring committee suggested dividing teams into three divisions per league and letting the runner-up with the best record reach the postseason as a wild card. We'd double the number of teams in the postseason, from four to eight, and as a result add an additional best-three-of-five series before the championship series. The format was similar to the one in the NFL and, tradition aside, it was a no-brainer.

We had gone from sixteen teams in 1961 to twenty-eight

through all the rounds of expansion, so now you had twenty-four teams that missed the playoffs every season. Purists could argue that it showed the extreme value of the 162-game season—and they wouldn't be wrong—but that was a joyless argument unless your team happened to come out on top.

Given our troubles in Kohler, the timing couldn't have been better for this discussion. I switched the focus off revenue sharing and onto this restructuring as quickly as I could, adding it as an agenda item for our September meetings, which were to be held in Boston. I needed for baseball to do something that brought the clubs together, sort of as a guidepost to what needed to be done in the future. We needed to give hope and faith to more teams, not just in February and March but in July and August. We were essentially handing September over to the NFL, and why do that? It's not like Paul Tagliabue ever did anything for us.

When word got out about the wild card, there was initially a lot of negative reaction in the media and from the fans who called talk radio. I know about talk radio because I'm guilty. I listen to it. I always have and probably always will. I get stations from Chicago and the national shows, too, not just Milwaukee. It's a guilty pleasure, I guess, although in 1993 there was nothing really pleasurable about it for me.

Bob Costas led the charge for the old school. I thought he was going to have me arrested. I knew I had taken about as unpopular a position as I could have, but there was no choice. Baseball was going to be hurt badly if it didn't wake up and start moving forward.

When we went to Boston for the meeting, I was sure the votes were there to pass the changes. But for the second time that year it turned out that I didn't know the owners as well as I thought I knew them. The National League voted first and unanimously approved the concept, 14–0. Then we went to the American

League, and while I was confident, I did not think we'd get another unanimous vote.

I knew George W. Bush was against it. He is a genuine traditionalist, very conservative about matters he considered sacred in baseball, like only the very best teams advancing at the end of the 162-game season. But George had told me he'd give me his vote if we really needed it. I didn't think we would, because even Steinbrenner was in our corner on this one. He was my biggest supporter, perhaps because the Yankees were so hungry to get back to the postseason.

We took the vote and it didn't pass. It was 8–6 in favor, which was three less than we needed to pass it. I was stunned. I was furious. I called a time-out. I walked to the back of the room and used some of the worst language I've ever used. I let 'em have it, telling them that if we couldn't pass something as easy as this, we'd never get anywhere with the big issues. Never. And I wasn't even sure I wanted to keep trying if this was what it was going to be like.

"I'm not leaving here until you guys vote the right way," I said. "It is so obvious what we should do."

We took the vote again and it passed, 13–1. Only George W. Bush voted no, and that was fine with me.

While it received far less attention than the addition of the wild card, we dealt with one other order of business in Boston. We approved our new rights deal from ESPN, and it was one of those mileposts that told everyone we had hit bottom as a sport.

The ESPN deal was $255 million over six years, down from a previous deal that paid us $403 million for four years. They were reducing the games they carried from 175 per year to about seventy-five, no doubt making room for more NBA and NHL games and more of the endless hype about the NFL.

There was no getting around it—1993 was a horrible year, and the really hard work was still ahead of us.

15

You couldn't find two guys less alike on the outside than George Steinbrenner and me. But through the years we would have been an interesting study in business dynamics.

George was gigantic, bombastic New York, in all its pushy glory, and I was proud little Milwaukee, always yearning for a chance to play with the big boys. He was the towering power of the biggest franchise in baseball, and I was the head of the smallest. We argued about everything. We didn't agree on anything. Yet somehow we were the best of friends, from the start and pretty much always.

I was still a young man, only thirty-eight, in my fourth year of ownership, when George M. Steinbrenner III came barreling into baseball.

He had been a hurdler on the track team at Williams College, sports editor of the school paper, and piano player in the band. He got talked into going out for the football team in his senior year and wound up as a halfback. He went into the air force after college and then served as a graduate assistant coach for Woody Hayes at Ohio State in a season when the Buckeyes were undefeated national champions. He coached football for a while, at Northwestern and Purdue, but, like me, wound up in his family business.

George built his great-grandfather's shipping business into a giant, eventually buying American Shipbuilding Company. He never lost the passion he felt for sports, which is why he purchased the American Basketball League's Cleveland Pipers in 1960—he hired John McClendon, the first African American coach in professional basketball—and the Yankees in 1973, with a group of minority partners that included Nelson Bunker Hunt and John DeLorean.

John McMullen, who would later buy the Astros, was the partner who uttered a famous line, "There's nothing in life quite so limited as being a limited partner of George Steinbrenner." I'm sure he was right.

I welcomed George into the game. He could talk to me, and George liked to talk. But I could talk to him, too, and sometimes he even listened. Through the years, George and I would bicker and we would battle, but always about the issues. He was extremely loyal in terms of his personal life and was a very good-natured friend.

One Tuesday morning he called me at home before I headed to work. It's one hour earlier in Milwaukee, so he was in the office, but I was still at home. We were talking, and I asked him to hold on because my wife, Sue, was asking me if I had remembered to take the trash out. The trash collectors came on Tuesdays.

"Yes," I told Sue, as George listened in.

George howled at my compliance. Then he started calling me every Tuesday morning to ask if I had taken out the trash.

George would come to Milwaukee a lot when the Yankees were playing at County Stadium, and he loved that my secretary Lori had worked for Vince Lombardi. George loved Lombardi and by extension adored Lori. She could give him a harder time than just about anybody.

One time Sue and I were in New York, visiting George at Yankee Stadium, and as we walked in a woman was on her way out, sobbing. I asked George what was wrong.

"Oh, that was my assistant," he said. "I ordered a tuna sandwich and she brought me egg salad. I fired her!"

Sue was astonished. She jumped into the middle of George's business.

"You did what?" she asked, her voice rising.

"What, you think that's wrong?"

"George, that's so wrong on so many levels," Sue said. "Go fix that."

Sheepishly, George got up and went to stop the woman from cleaning out her desk. Don't underestimate Sue.

George's first reaction wasn't always the one that mattered the most. If you gave him a little time, he'd see things more clearly than he did in the moment. That was true about revenue sharing, and of course it was good for an owner to think about the game as a whole, not just his own franchise's interest.

I understood George's opposition to revenue sharing at Kohler, but I knew the sport needed it. He did, too. That's why when we took our next revenue sharing vote, at a meeting in Fort Lauderdale in January '94, it passed 28–0.

Revenue sharing was still an unpopular concept with many people, including George. But we were making our push for a salary cap with revenue sharing and eventually all the owners would see they would shoot themselves in the foot if they didn't sign off on it. The total that would move between teams was estimated at fifty-eight million dollars, with no team paying more than five million and none receiving more than nine million—not as much as I wanted, but it was a start.

What did George think? His immediate response was to stalk past reporters who were asking him why he'd gone along with it.

It took a long time for the media to realize that George had turned over a new leaf. Later on that season, with the Yankees running away with the AL East behind Red Sox turncoat Wade Boggs, headed toward their first playoff appearance in thirteen years, it had become clear that the players might go on strike rather than agree to the salary cap and our other terms.

But George Steinbrenner, bless him, had started thinking about the greater gain for our sport, not his immediate gratification.

He made that clear when reporters cornered him at Yankee Stadium on August 12, the day that the union had set for its strike.

George had made a trip into the clubhouse earlier that day, accompanied by Buck Showalter, his young manager. He asked the players not to take the dispute personally, to stay in shape in case there was a settlement, and to understand this was business.

He didn't lament the Yankees' unfortunate situation talking to reporters. "I do not intend to show any split in this group," George said. "Bud Selig is leading this ship, and I'm tired of the harpooning and hits he's taking. My interests are being represented."

For once, George was prepared to make a huge sacrifice. I'm not sure if we could have held the owners together in 1990, when Fay Vincent ordered camps to open after the spring training lockout, but by the time we got deep into '94 I knew that for once the owners were finally as united as the players.

Unfortunately for Steinbrenner and everyone else, Don Fehr and the Players Association wouldn't recognize this new solidarity between the owners until 1994 had become a blank space in the glorious history of the World Series. Chalk it up to the stubbornness on both sides—or the resolve among owners, if you want to put it in the best possible light—and the one-sided nature of baseball's labor negotiations for almost thirty years.

Yes, owners made a lot of mistakes, especially in the early years. We put the ball on the tee for Marvin Miller and he was happy to kick it through the goalposts for his team. But the Players Association had exploited our weaknesses in one labor deal after another and along the way became blind to the changing economic picture and the need for a partnership. We were still a long ways away from finding any common ground, but the time had come to make our case.

We had voted to reopen contract negotiations with the union at the winter meetings at the Galt House, back in 1992. But all we were doing then was telling Fehr and Orza what they already knew, that we weren't happy with the deal we'd had to take in '90. It would be a long time before we had our act together well enough to put a formal offer on the table.

That came in the middle of June '94. We were asking for a salary cap, of course, and proposing an even split with the players. They would get 50 percent of the game's revenues. The estimated total for salaries would be about a billion dollars, and that amount would grow as the game grew revenue. This was the NBA and NFL model, and it was accompanied by the revenue sharing agreement we'd approved in Fort Lauderdale.

I knew we were in for the fight of our lives.

I'd been telling owners that we had to be prepared to lose the season if the union went out on strike. We weren't going to lock out players, not before the next spring training, anyway, but we weren't going to fold our tent to get the players back from a strike. There was a push among owners to have a plan in place to go with replacement players to put pressure on the union. It had been done in the NFL in 1987, even in games that impacted the season's standings and helped determine who went to the Super Bowl.

That was horrible, I thought. That was a bad Packer team anyway, but it always seemed odd that replacements took over for three games early in the season, before the NFL's union caved in to the owners' demands, and the games counted in the standings.

NFL fans might not have liked it, but they didn't seem to take out their animosity on the teams or the league once the regulars got back on the field. It was almost as if nothing had happened. Still, I didn't know if that would fly in baseball.

Just like Bowie Kuhn said to me all those years earlier, baseball is always held to a higher standard than other sports. Maybe it's because we deliver a game almost every day from April through September, not just one a week. Baseball is an essential part of people's everyday lives, not a Sunday escape.

At the same time, there were some owners who wanted nothing to do with replacement players. It was a divisive issue. But we didn't have to resolve that from the start. We just had to be united in our strategy and willing to hold tight if the players went on strike.

The average player salary had climbed above one million dollars, and that was a lot of money to suddenly not be earning. Many players, like my friend Paul Molitor, had taken advantage of the system of free agency and arbitration to earn a lot more than the average. The Mets had given Bobby Bonilla a deal that paid him more than six million dollars, and Joe Carter's reward for helping the Jays to back-to-back championships was a contract paying him $5.5 million.

Molitor, who was always smart, understood the sacrifices that earlier generations of players had made when owners weren't exactly enlightened. He knew as well as anyone how Fehr, Orza, and Marvin Miller ticked. Paul hit the nail on the head in an interview with the Milwaukee *Journal Sentinel* when the Blue Jays visited County Stadium in late June, after we'd made our initial offer.

"If they're banking everything on a salary cap, then I don't think we'll see 1994 having a world champion," Molitor said. "The only optimism I can find is they've always shown they can make a deal in the 11th hour."

As I read this I thought, okay, Paul, I can see where you're coming from. We had caved every time, but that didn't mean we were going to just mark time again. The question I was asking myself was could the union make a deal? Could Fehr make a deal?

I had never thought he could. I always thought he'd rather litigate than make a deal. That was the legacy of Marvin Miller, the penance we were still paying for having played hardball with the union in its early days, when our old warhorses sought to preserve the reserve clause and fought the union constantly in lesser battles.

The history between our sides was bad, and we'd always come out on the losing side. That was what was eating at me especially after Fehr set August 12 as a strike deadline.

In trying to do business the old way, Fehr and Orza made a catastrophic miscalculation. They failed to recognize that the owners were as unified as the players, at last.

The clubs needed a new economic model; the union did not want a new economic model. The clubs were pushing for a salary cap, like in the other sports. The union leaders were not grasping that great baseball players want to win championships—and that every club should have the capacity, if well run, to compete for one. A salary cap would give all markets a chance to win.

What kind of player wants to play for a team whose economic limitations make it extremely difficult to compete for a World Series berth? The union leaders saw only dollar signs. They were always quick to call owners greedy, to say that they had endless amounts of money to spend on their teams but instead used baseball to add to their wealth. I knew firsthand that was hardly the case.

It had always been clear to me that baseball was a business. That's why I put so much of my time into running the Brewers in my early years in the sport. It took a while for that understanding to spread, but two decades later all the teams were serious about balancing expenses with revenue. These were desperate financial times for baseball, and that desperation would unite owners. We knew that business as usual—another unambiguous loss to the union in a labor negotiation—would be catastrophic. Too many teams were losing money under the antiquated system. They would go broke—maybe declare bankruptcy, maybe close their doors—if the status quo prevailed.

The folly of the union leaders' digging in their heels against change was that the sport wouldn't really start growing without a partnership between players and owners. We would eventually demonstrate to them how this could work, why it shouldn't require World War III to get a labor deal that worked for both sides. But in '94 we were still dealing with the same old trench warfare. I needed help from the Players Association to make changes to the economics of the sport, and they kept treating me like the boy who cried wolf. I wish that were true, but the truth was there was a wolf at the door.

Once the union set a strike deadline, I knew the clock was ticking on a bomb. I was as afraid as anyone about the damage we might be doing to the game I loved, but something had to change. It just had to. Unfortunately, there wasn't a lot of movement from either side before the clock struck midnight for the 1994 season.

When the last pitch was thrown on August 12, nobody knew the next time a pitcher would walk in from the bullpen to start another game. The White Sox, Expos, Yankees, and Indians were having dramatic seasons, not unlike the one my Brewers were experiencing when the fifty-day strike split the 1981 season in half. I could feel the angst of the fans, players, and management staff aligned with those teams. This was traumatic for fans everywhere, but the pain we were causing seemed personal for those in Chicago, Montreal, New York, and Cleveland.

There was a little back-and-forth between our side and the union in the weeks after August 12. But mostly the sides were dug in across from each other in trenches, only rarely getting together for unsuccessful negotiations. Peace talks, if you'd like.

The communication between me and Richard Ravitch had broken down, so I turned to Chuck O'Connor to represent us in talks with the unions. He had cut his teeth in labor battles with the Teamsters and served as outside counsel for MLB in his work for the Washington-based firm of Morgan, Lewis & Bockius.

There was no way the players were going to buy a salary cap. They did seem willing to talk about a luxury tax system, which was introduced into the talks in a meeting with O'Connor and others in our delegation about three weeks after the strike had begun. A group of players, including Orel Hershiser, joined a team of union lawyers to hand-deliver a counteroffer to MLB offices a little later.

Don Fehr was running things from his office, just as I was coordinating our strategy from my office at County Stadium. There was an interesting mix of representatives from the union, including Michael Weiner. He would become the first guy with the union who built a real line of communication with our labor guys, including Rob Manfred. Rob and I spent a lot of time together during labor negotiations. We just hit it off. He forged relationships between clubs and the union that hadn't existed before.

Rob is extremely impressive. He is smart. Very smart. He knows labor law, and he is very determined. He was a bulldog in representing our interests. I liked him both professionally and personally right from the start, and he didn't let me down.

Naturally, the union's highly public counteroffer did not include a salary cap. The talks were going nowhere. I had warned the union on September 2 that if we didn't reach a deal we would have to cancel the season within another week or so. We were running out of time because they'd triggered the strike so late in the season.

There wasn't going to be a deal. I called Steinbrenner to tell him there was no way to save the season. I felt terrible because it had been such a big year for the Yankees. I called Fehr and told him it was time to call off the season.

Too much time had passed for players to resume after only a workout or two. I had been hearing that from trainers, from some managers. They'd been gone too long to just be thrown into the fire if there was some miraculous settlement in late September.

They couldn't be ready to play in time to have a World Series. We had run out of time to have a postseason. I explained this to Don without a hint of animosity in my voice. I didn't point fingers. I just said this is where we are, this is what we have to do—make a joint announcement to tell everyone there wouldn't be a World Series this year.

Don didn't consider this for a minute. "I'm not making any announcement," he said.

Huh? His players were on strike, they'd walked out on the season, and he wasn't going to join me in taking responsibility for a regrettable situation?

A lot of owners didn't think I should announce it, since it was the players who were striking. We had not locked them out. Jackie Autry, owner of the Angels, was especially passionate. "You're going to get blamed for this," she said. "You'll get killed." She was right, of course, but what was I going to do? Put out a press release, take the phone off the hook, and lock the office door? That isn't how I operate, especially in tough times. But the union guys were burying me even before I made the announcement.

On Wednesday, September 14, I walked into the dining room at County Stadium and told America—Canada, Latin America, and Asia, for that matter—that there would be no World Series. We had already released a statement saying the season was over. It was signed by twenty-six of the twenty-eight teams—Marge Schott wanted to finish the season with replacement players; Peter Angelos didn't like the wording of the statement, thinking we were putting too much blame on the players.

Now there I was, trying to explain why there wouldn't be a World Series for the first time since 1904. I spoke about failure and pain. I stressed that this was not predetermined by anyone. This wasn't bargaining strategy. It was a legitimate failure by two sides to find common ground and make a deal.

With the benefit of 20/20 hindsight, I can see the ugliness was also unavoidable. It was the result of the dynamic that had been created over decades by the poor judgment of owners and the ability of the union to come out of every labor dispute ahead.

When Vincent resigned, I inherited a nightmare. Now the demons were coming out from under the bed, from underneath the closed closet door, and flying all around the baseball world.

On the Sunday after the announcement, I was featured on the cover of the *New York Times Magazine*. I was pictured at a table—it couldn't have been my desk, because it was clean—with my left hand on a bat and a steely look in my eyes. I would have been excited about that except for the headline: just some of the folks who ruined your summer.

It was a profile story by Pat Jordan, a former pitcher who had written some great books about both the romance and realities of baseball. He had spent a long time talking to me and other current and former owners about the baseball business and their experiences. The slant of the story was typical of the response at the time—that the problems were caused by the greed of management, by the lack of progressive thinking. I was with him on the last point, but that was about it. He at least did not get too personal, which a lot of columnists and radio/TV analysts did.

Only a small part of the media tried to really understand the issues. Most just came out criticizing owners and taking the side of the union. Maybe they did it out of habit. But the players weren't locked out; they had gone on strike.

One month after we had canceled the postseason I got a call to come to the White House and meet with President Bill Clinton. He wanted to hire this highly decorated mediator, Bill Usery, a former secretary of labor, to find a solution so that he could say his administration had ended the baseball strike.

I called David Glass of the Royals to ask what he thought. He was the chairman of Walmart, and Hillary Clinton was on Walmart's board. I also called Sue's cousin David Previant, who was a very successful labor lawyer. He knew Usery. He said he was a wonderful man, tough but fair. Everyone I asked for a scouting report said that, which was a good sign.

When I talked to the clubs, they weren't too enthusiastic. The rug had been pulled out from under us from outside before. But President Clinton called Glass and put pressure on him. David was sold. He said he thought Clinton was sincere about wanting to help us get something done, and that maybe this could be good for us. It sure wouldn't have looked good if we didn't take the president's offer, so off I went to Washington.

I got my clearance to go to the White House, with a small traveling party. I was shown into the Oval Office, where it was just President Clinton and me. He told me how he used to listen to Harry Caray growing up in Arkansas. He said that what had happened was "unfortunate." That was his word, exactly.

Unfortunate. I'd call that an understatement.

Clinton said he wanted to get involved. He said he'd like to appoint a mediator and that he would stand by whatever decision or conclusion the mediator came up with. He told me that Bill Usery had solved problems for every president since Harry Truman.

I was on board, as he knew I would be. And, yes, I felt important talking to the president one-on-one. Wouldn't you? I wished my father had been there with me just for the thrill.

I'm not sure what thrills Don Fehr. I'm not sure I've ever seen him smile. He entered the Oval Office as I was shown out, and I'm sure he and President Clinton had a similar conversation to the one we had just finished. Then President Clinton made an announcement that the sides had agreed to mediation and were committing to resolve the dispute through Usery's guidance.

Our labor committee started meeting with Usery and his staff. His right-hand man was Herb Fishgold. The discussions were thorough and they were painful. Usery never seemed to quite have the right picture, and I was constantly fighting with him about the data he was using and how he was using it. We were battling a lot with him and Fishgold.

As complicated as dealing with us must have been, Usery also had to deal with the union. Jerry Reinsdorf cautioned him that Fehr would be the most difficult person he ever encountered. I never asked Usery for confirmation, but I have to say, I doubt Jerry was wrong.

The meetings with Usery lasted for four long months, taking us to February 1995, right before spring training would normally be starting. This was very uncomfortable for both sides, owners and players, and it was horrible for baseball fans. Even though the process had run so long, I didn't know if we had gotten through to Usery. He might have been the most noncommittal person I've ever come across. I bet he was a good poker player. He would sit and listen. We would argue and debate, constructively. He was honest, fair, and decent. He was consistent in encouraging both sides to make constructive proposals.

Usery tried to get the sides to make the kinds of compromises that would lead to a deal. But along the way it became clear the parties were not going to get there with proposals and counterproposals, even under the supervision of a great mediator. Clinton took the unusual step of asking Usery to recommend the terms of a settlement.

I was summoned to Washington for a meeting at the White House on February 7. My phone rang at 7 a.m. with orders to meet Usery and Fishgold for breakfast at the Jefferson Hotel. It was some breakfast. They presented their recommendation to me, and while it wasn't everything we wanted, I thought it was fair. There were parts of it I didn't like, but we could live with it. The changes in the system he was proposing offset the pain of losing the World Series. We hadn't gotten everything we wanted, but it looked like we were going to make some progress and could get players back on the field to start a fresh season. I always loved spring training, and this one would be special.

While I left to brief the owners, Usery and Fishgold headed

out to meet with Fehr and the union officials. I think it was about eight thirty when we finished, and I waited for a call asking me to come to the White House for an announcement.

In the history of American labor relations, every time a presidentially appointed mediator made a recommendation, the president had forced that recommendation on the parties as the basis of a new deal. We didn't expect anything different this time.

I waited and waited for word from Usery and Fishgold, then waited some more. I made a round of calls to some of the people I knew on Capitol Hill: Chris Dodd, Joe Lieberman, and my old friend Herb Kohl. No one had heard a word.

I remember telling John Harrington and Reinsdorf, "Something's wrong."

It was almost 5 p.m. when we got a call to be at the White House at 7. There was a huge press contingent there.

I was shown into the Roosevelt Room, where President Clinton was standing alongside Usery and Fishgold. I knew immediately we were in trouble. Usery didn't look right. He looked distracted, almost forlorn. Uh-oh.

Al Gore, the vice president, was there. So were George Stephanopoulos, Leon Panetta, and Robert Reich. Cecil Fielder and a lot of players were standing in a group with Fehr, Orza, and the other union lawyers.

Gore, not Clinton, spoke. "The union won't accept Usery's recommendation," he said. "And we can't accept it."

Huh?

I glanced quickly at Clinton. He looked away and then ducked out of the back of the room.

I was stunned. Completely flabbergasted. I had persuaded the clubs to go through this process, putting ourselves into the hands of Usery's recommendation. It was the president's process, his mediator, and yet Bill Clinton took the unprecedented step of not supporting his own appointee.

Now we had spent four months, an enormous amount of time and money, and just like that, we were standing there with empty palms, like a schmuck left at the altar? I'm pretty sure I had never been that mad before. Nor have I ever been that mad since then.

I was left to walk around the White House feeling completely betrayed by my highest elected officials. I was astonished. I was indignant. I was very close to being out of control. I saw Usery and Fishgold. They started talking before I could even ask what happened. You could tell Usery was embarrassed.

"Harry S. Truman never did this to me," he said. "Dwight David Eisenhower never did this to me." He kept listing presidents, mentioning "JFK . . . LBJ," and then getting to a line I'd remember as about the only humor on a horrible day.

"Even that son of a bitch Richard Milhous Nixon never did this to me," Usery said.

Leon Panetta, who was Clinton's chief of staff, approached, asking me to come with him. He said the president wanted to see me.

Good, I thought. I want to see him, too.

Panetta took me into a side room that had the longest, most yellow couch I've ever seen.

"Look," President Clinton said. "I'm sorry about this, but the union is angry."

Well, I knew he was right—and later I'd hear the union guys had called Usery a "senile son of a bitch" to his face. But why did the union being upset change anything?

I was steaming, but I was respectful to Clinton. He was the president of the United States, after all. Clinton told me he and Gore were willing to come to every city and explain to fans what had happened. I don't know what that offer meant, and I didn't care. I was barely containing my fury.

"Mr. President, sir, you gave me your word on October 14," I said. "I have twenty-eight clubs. You know this. You talked to David Glass. This is not what we agreed on. What if I had been the one who didn't agree?"

The door opened and Gore, Stephanopoulos, Panetta, and Reich walked in. Clinton had to be relieved to have reinforcements, because he wasn't doing well in this conversation. Clinton said he knew he'd given me his word. I told him I'd been raised in a world where when a man gives you his word, that's it. He went quiet.

But Gore jumped in, nasty from the start.

"I'm tired of the little guys," he said, and I knew he meant the small-market clubs. "All these demands. Complaining about everything."

Well, that explained a lot.

He was uttering the union's talking points.

It was the wrong thing to say to me. Rage came pouring out of me. I exploded in his face.

"What did you just fucking say to me?" I snapped at the VP. "You're tired? You're tired? You guys gave me your word! You're tired? Because they didn't like this?"

I was just getting started.

"Well, there are a thousand fucking newspaper guys out there, and I'm going to go and tell them that, by God, this thing got worse because we agreed to this process and you backed out," I said. "Now what the fuck do you say?"

Gore turned red. And mute.

Everybody was scrambling. I got the feeling nobody stands up to these guys, no matter what they say. He did not explain himself. Nobody did. They just headed out the door, on to the next bit of business.

I went out and held a press conference, but before it started I forced myself to regroup, to get my wits about me. I tried to put the best spin possible on a horribly unproductive, disappointing process. I bit my tongue about my feelings toward Clinton and Gore.

Then I went back and tried to explain to our guys what had just happened. It was awful, truly awful. I was fuming, and maybe a little embarrassed. I had lost my temper with the leaders of the free world. But they had it coming. They had gone back on their word, and that is never okay. These guys hadn't just betrayed baseball's acting commissioner and the twenty-eight teams. They had betrayed a nation of baseball fans.

I saw President Clinton a lot after that, but we never discussed what had happened. He was there when Cal Ripken broke Lou Gehrig's iron-man record and also when we retired Jackie Robinson's number, 42, as well as at Henry Aaron's sixty-fifth birthday party.

The night of Henry's party, Clinton told Sue he spent more time with me than she did. "I like him a lot," he said.

Oh, really?

I understand that Clinton and the Democrats in office had a lot of union constituents, but baseball players should never be confused for steelworkers. We agreed to mediation in good faith. I probably wouldn't be so naïve again. I learned the hard way that political pragmatism takes over in the end, not necessarily fairness.

I guess that was the hard lesson for me to learn.

We had just lost four months, and we had accomplished absolutely nothing. Spring training was about to start. We had placed our faith and hope in the president and now a winter was gone, a season was here, and we were about to let down the entire world of baseball. Again.

We had to decide what to do about spring training. While there was a lot of reluctance from some clubs, we decided to go forward with the idea of fielding replacement teams.

A lot of us weren't crazy about it, but we were trying to figure out how we could move the sport ahead. Using replacement players was one of our options. I'll admit to you, in retrospect, that I wasn't too happy about it. But what was the choice? To have a bunch of empty fields in Arizona and Florida? To cave to the union once again, as we'd always done?

In general, the idea of using replacements went over like a lead balloon, which wasn't a surprise. Our fans were still very angry about the strike ending the 1994 season early, and this was like salt in the wound. It created chaos but was the first real standoff in the history of baseball bargaining.

But then, to the relief of almost everyone, it all ended. The Players Association had filed an unfair labor practice motion against us, and on April 1 a ruling by Sonia Sotomayor, the future Supreme Court justice who was then a federal judge in district court in Manhattan, sent the big league players back onto the field. Sotomayor did not order the players to end their strike, but she imposed an injunction that effectively killed the replacement player concept and ordered negotiations to resume in earnest, under the terms of the previous contract. The players offered to end their strike, and while we still had the right to lock them out, there was no way we were going to do that, not after the 232-day strike.

We had made the point to the Players Association that our owners were as together as their players, and everyone felt it was great to get back on the field. When Justice Sotomayor was named to the Supreme Court by Barack Obama, Fehr pointed out to the *New York Times* that while Sotomayor's ruling was limited, it came at a critical point in time for baseball.

"Her ruling did not produce an agreement, but it gave the parties time to get on with normal business and get back to the bargaining table and produce an agreement," Fehr told the *Times*. "If it hadn't ended when she ended it, it would have gone on for some time and it would have gotten uglier and uglier."

I'm sure Donald was right about that. We would take a break to let players have an abbreviated spring training and then begin a 144-game season on April 26. It would take another twenty months to negotiate a new contract.

We hired Randy Levine, who had been New York City's labor commissioner, to replace Chuck O'Connor as our lead negotiator. He had to work hard to get us a new deal that included a luxury tax (35 percent on payrolls above fifty-one million dollars, beginning in '97) and a little bit of revenue sharing.

That deal wasn't what we needed. It was helpful in a small way, but it didn't address our issues. Our problems were just getting worse, with no end in sight. In 1994 and '95, the pain definitely wasn't worth the gain.

16

In the aftermath of the strike, everyone enthusiastically returned to the game we all loved so dearly. One thing, though, was clear from the start: things were no longer the same. It's not so much that the game was permanently scarred, though there was some short-term damage done, for sure. It was more that for the first time the owners started to see that they could not rely on a union-based solution to fix the financial realities of the game. If the economics of baseball were going to be transformed, it was not going to happen through a magically elusive deal with the union; instead the owners had to pull the levers that they were in control of. The owners and the league had to look beyond the players and union for ways to increase revenue and ensure their teams' solvency. And so, that's exactly what we set about doing—and we started with stadiums.

Memorial Stadium in Baltimore was popular with Orioles fans. They loved the neighborhood feeling around the park and the history of the place, which in addition to six World Series had hosted the NFL championship game in 1959.

But while Memorial Stadium was a great home for the Orioles in the 1960s and '70s, it was a ballpark that was built for football as much as baseball. Edward Bennett Williams became interested in building a baseball-only stadium that would include suites and lots of fan amenities, allowing it to generate revenue streams that Memorial Stadium couldn't.

When Eli Jacobs bought the team from Williams's estate in

1988, he made a new stadium his top priority. In one of the most inspired series of decisions any owner ever made, he put his partner Larry Lucchino in charge of the stadium. Lucchino reached out to architect Janet Marie Smith to design the park.

They settled on a location adjacent to Baltimore's Inner Harbor, which, as a lucky coincidence, was very near Babe Ruth's birthplace. It was the perfect place for Smith to execute Lucchino's vision of a retro ballpark, bringing back touches like a brick façade on the outside and straight-line walls in the outfield, the first for a major league stadium since the Dodgers abandoned Ebbets Field. They lowered the outfield fence from the traditional ten feet to only eight in left field, which allowed athletic outfielders to show their skills night after night on ESPN.

Even with these touches, it was with some sadness that they said good-bye to Memorial Stadium. When the Orioles moved to their new stadium, Rick Dempsey, the catcher, wrote a poem as an ode to Memorial Stadium. He called it the Old Gray Lady of Thirty-third Street. Frank Robinson, the Hall of Famer, was the only player who had ever hit the ball completely out of the park. It was the home field for some of the most popular players in the Orioles' history, most notably Brooks Robinson, Jim Palmer, Eddie Murray, Boog Powell, Cal Ripken Jr., and Frank.

Despite the wistfulness, Camden Yards was a home run for Baltimore. The area where it was built was soon bursting to the seams with hotels, restaurants, and tourists. Camden Yards became the blueprint for baseball's modern ballparks in many ways, and in the aftermath of the players' strike, it showed many of the owners how a new stadium could lift up the franchise.

In truth, we were once again following the NFL's lead to a degree. The NFL made it easier for football teams to build new stadiums with a measure Paul Tagliabue put through. It is called

G-3, after the resolution that owners passed, and in essence it provided teams a $150 million grant toward the funding of a stadium. Technically, these were loans, but they were paid back in large part from seat licensing fees passed on to the public. It was a sweet deal, and it was no surprise that the NFL was a step ahead of us.

But in our 2002 labor negotiations we may have gotten something approved that is of even more benefit to teams building new stadiums. It is complicated—what isn't?—but essentially allows teams to protect local money from revenue sharing by allowing construction costs to be directly deducted against shared revenues.

Depending on the specifics of a stadium deal, this could be a bigger benefit to a team than a $150 million grant. It was a significant step in helping teams sustain the building boom that had begun with Camden Yards in 1992.

That boom would include the creation of twenty new stadiums. I'm just as proud of the work we did to help some of the greatest old parks—Fenway, Wrigley, Dodger Stadium—remain viable for future generations as I am of having played even a little role in helping Pittsburgh add the civic gem that is PNC Park or San Francisco make the absolutely vital transition from Candlestick Park to AT&T Park, where ball hawks float in kayaks in McCovey Cove.

As much as changes to the economic system and drug testing, the string of gorgeous, neighborhood-changing ballparks that opened between Camden Yards in 1992 and Atlanta's Sun-Trust Park in 2017 turned Major League Baseball into a vibrant enterprise, one that has pushed the NFL for dominance in the marketplace.

As much as I love Milwaukee's County Stadium and applaud the vision of our civic leaders, it was a lot like the multisport stadiums that were popular after World War II. County Stadium and Municipal Stadium in Cleveland were built out of steel, with crisscrossing ramps and girders everywhere. They felt more like stadiums to me than the ones that were built with more concrete in the design, like Riverfront Stadium in Cincinnati, Three Rivers Stadium in Pittsburgh, and Busch Stadium in St. Louis. All of those parks were outfitted with Astroturf, which was another strike against them. Monsanto had developed the first version of their artificial turf for the Astrodome, after it was learned the hard way that you couldn't grow grass there, but soon it became the rage all around sports. It was a better game for hitters because the ball shot through the infield, but the turf was hard on players' knees. Just ask Andre Dawson or other guys who played regularly on the turf in Montreal.

But it wasn't just the turf that was bad at those parks. Those cookie-cutter stadiums were deadly. They had no character. I do think they hurt us. I used to joke that if you had too much to drink the night before and you wound up in a ballpark in Philly, St. Louis, Pittsburgh, or Cincinnati, you wouldn't know where the hell you were. All the parks looked the same.

That's why the building of Camden Yards was really one of the most important points in baseball history. It really changed a lot of things. It also pointed out to people like me in Milwaukee why we had to build a new ballpark. It was a crucial moment. It was a good moment for baseball because it set off a wave of wonderful ballparks that represented their areas, with indigenous characteristics—whether it was Coors Field in Denver, PNC Park in Pittsburgh, or our Miller Park in Milwaukee. We went through a great renaissance in baseball, and it had a lot to do with the new ballparks.

At least at the start of the building boom, new stadiums played a major role in revitalizing struggling franchises. They generated badly needed revenues, which went into player salaries and the building of teams, helping them either reach the playoffs or at least become more competitive. Then the success built on itself. Highly competitive teams drew much more interest from fans and the media, which allowed owners to sell more season tickets and grow their franchises. They could add staff for the front offices or spend more to stockpile the minor leagues with prospects.

Once again, in all these areas, the Orioles became the blueprint for this synergy. They had been brutal in their last years at Memorial Stadium. The great Jerry Hoffberger–Hank Peters–Earl Weaver teams had been replaced by bungling ones, even with Hall of Famers like Eddie Murray and Cal Ripken Jr. on the roster. Murray was getting toward the end of his great career but Cal was in the middle of his when they went 54–107 in 1988, starting the season 0–21.

What a horrible year this was for everyone associated with the team. Cal Ripken Sr. began the season as the manager but was fired after the 0–6 start. Frank Robinson took over but would be tested like never before. And, worst of all, Edward Bennett Williams was in the last stages of his long battle with colon cancer.

It was a tribute to the Orioles' fan base that they drew 1.66 million fans that season. They would bounce back to draw around 2.5 million in the final seasons at Memorial Park, but attendance spiked at Camden Yards.

The Orioles drew almost 3.6 million in that inaugural season and would get to 3.7 million in '97, when they won the AL East for the first time since '83. Revenue generated from Camden Yards helped Pat Gillick, their Hall of Fame general manager, surround Cal Jr. and Mike Mussina with proven talents like Roberto Alomar, Harold Baines, Rafael Palmeiro, Jimmy Key, Scott Erickson, and Randy Myers.

The Indians left Cleveland Stadium for their glittering new ballpark, which was christened as Jacobs Field, in 1994. Their front office, headed by John Hart, had done a great job gathering up prospects and building a strong farm system. The Indians would have been hard pressed to hang on to their talent if it was still based at its old ballpark. But the move to Jacobs Field was perfectly timed, and the response from Cleveland fans was beyond anyone's greatest expectations.

Hart signed up many of his best players—including Sandy Alomar Jr., Carlos Baerga, Omar Vizquel, Jim Thome, Albert Belle, and Manny Ramirez—to contracts that saved the Indians money in both arbitration and free agency. Many of those players even made Cleveland their year-round home, which the fans loved.

The reward was the Indians going to the postseason six times in seven years. They just missed ending a long championship drought in the 1997 World Series, when Jose Mesa's blown save gave the Marlins an unexpected title. The franchise played 455 games before sellout home crowds from 1995 through 2001.

The Rangers won division titles for the first time in their history after moving into the Ballpark in Arlington, capturing the AL West three times in their first five years there. Previously they had built teams that could compete in short stretches but never sustained that success. The move to a beautiful ballpark with retro touches throughout allowed one of our weaker franchises to gain a toehold in NFL country.

Philadelphia experienced a huge boost when the Phillies moved from the very obsolete Veterans Stadium—one of the worst examples of a concrete cookie-cutter design—to Citizens Bank Park in 2004. They hadn't fielded a playoff team since Lenny Dykstra's team lost to the Blue Jays in the '93 World Series, but beginning

Nothing was more rewarding for me than bringing baseball back to Milwaukee after the Braves left. The Brewers lost ninety-seven games in our first season, but we were so excited for 1971 that we printed a gigantic ticket for Opening Day. *(Photo courtesy of the Milwaukee Brewers Baseball Club)*

Milwaukee is the only home I've ever had. This was my graduation photo from Washington High, before I moved on to attend the University of Wisconsin. *(Photo courtesy of the Milwaukee Brewers Baseball Club)*

County Stadium was my home away from home. I even had an office there when Milwaukee was left without a team. I loved the place. *(Photo courtesy of the Milwaukee Brewers Baseball Club)*

I was a speedy center fielder as a boy, but I was going to make my legacy running a team, not really stepping into the batter's box. I always appreciated the guys who could really hit. *(Photo courtesy of the Milwaukee Brewers Baseball Club)*

I always loved talking baseball with executives. Here, I'm standing next to Frank Lane, who was the first GM I hired for the Brewers, and Harry Dalton, who built the team that won an American League pennant in 1982. *(Photo courtesy of the Milwaukee Brewers Baseball Club)*

My office at County Stadium was tiny but it was always comfortable for me. I'd peek out its windows to look for cars entering the parking lot in the Brewers' early days. *(Photo courtesy of Wendy Selig)*

There was no fancy interview room at County Stadium. We'd just set up a podium right in a locker room when the team had news to share. *(Photo courtesy of the Milwaukee Brewers Baseball Club)*

I was blessed in having a great partner during most of my time in baseball, my wife, Sue. We married just as the Brewers were getting good, and she enjoyed the lifestyle as much as I did. Here we are enjoying an event with our friends Howard and Judy Gordon. *(Photo courtesy of the Milwaukee Brewers Baseball Club)*

I loved the time before games, swapping stories with managers, hitting coaches, and players at the batting cage. *(Photo courtesy of the Milwaukee Brewers Baseball Club)*

I received the B'nai B'rith Distinguished Humanitarian Award in 2013. But this earlier honor, in the early 1980s, might have been sweeter because I shared it with my mother, Marie, in addition to my daughters, Sari and Wendy. *(Photo courtesy of Wendy Selig)*

The Brewers' early seasons were rough, but Ed Fitzgerald, my partner, and GM Frank Lane worked to lay a strong foundation. *(Photo courtesy of the Milwaukee Brewers Baseball Club)*

We enjoyed great local support in the early years of our franchise. Milwaukee was proud of its team and showed it, like at this event, where I was seated next to Milwaukee's longest-serving mayor, Henry Maier. *(Photo courtesy of the Milwaukee Brewers Baseball Club)*

Packer legend Bart Starr, far left, was among those joining me on this occasion. I was freezing in the stands at Lambeau Field when he followed Jerry Kramer's block into the end zone in the Ice Bowl game against the Cowboys. *(Photo courtesy of the Milwaukee Brewers Baseball Club)*

I always looked at the Brewers as a business, not a toy, and that meant keeping an eye on all elements of the franchise. *(Photo courtesy of the Milwaukee Brewers Baseball Club)*

I always loved talking baseball with the people I met, and people never minded telling me what was on their minds, especially about the Brewers. *(Photo courtesy of the Milwaukee Brewers Baseball Club)*

As much as I loved County Stadium, Miller Park was essential for the long-term survival of baseball in Milwaukee. That's why I was thrilled at the groundbreaking for Miller Park in November, 1996. *(Photo courtesy of the Milwaukee Brewers Baseball Club)*

Photographers always wanted to put bats in my hands. Here's another one of those shots from County Stadium. *(Photo courtesy of the Milwaukee Brewers Baseball Club)*

The outlook for building a new stadium in Milwaukee was looking bleak in June, 1996, when I held a news conference outside County Stadium. Fans understood I was fighting to preserve the future of their team. *(Photo courtesy of the Milwaukee Brewers Baseball Club)*

My box at County Stadium was anything but fancy but it gave me a great view to so many games. Here I'm leaning on the loge outside the box, where I paced during the wild emotional swings of games. *(Photo courtesy of the Milwaukee Brewers Baseball Club)*

On the field with Paul Molitor, aka "Molly" and "The Ignitor." George Bamberger spotted his talent from his first spring training. *(Photo courtesy of the Milwaukee Brewers Baseball Club)*

When Miller Park opened on April 6, 2001, I threw out the ceremonial first pitch followed by President George W. Bush. That was quite a night. *(Photo courtesy of the Milwaukee Brewers Baseball Club)*

Milwaukee is a great baseball city. I love spending time with Brewers fans, and still find it humbling when someone wants my autograph. *(Photo courtesy of the Milwaukee Brewers Baseball Club)*

I got to talk hitting with Hall of Famer Ted Williams in the stands during the 1999 All-Star Game. I loved getting unexpected phone calls from him when I served as commissioner. *(Photo by Rich Pilling/MLB Photos)*

I believe baseball helped America get back on its feet after the 9/11 terrorist acts, which is why the 2001 World Series was a personal favorite. Here I'm presenting the Roberto Clemente Award to Curt Schilling before game 2 in Phoenix. *(Photo by Rich Pilling/MLB Photos)*

I've known Joe Torre since he was a teenager, and I was proud of the dynasty he helped put together with the Yankees. Here I'm presenting the MVP trophy to the Yankees' Scott Brosius after their sweep of San Diego in the 1998 World Series. *(Photo by Bob Rosato/MLB Photos)*

As an owner and commissioner, I prided myself on being available to reporters. Here I'm being interviewed by Fox Sports' Jeanne Zelasko after the fifth game of the 2006 World Series in St. Louis. *(Photo by Rich Pilling/MLB Photos via Getty Images)*

It was a call from Ken Griffey Jr. that prompted me to have every player wear Jackie Robinson's No. 42 on the anniversary of Jackie's first game with the Dodgers. Here I'm presenting Griffey with the Home Run Derby trophy at the 1999 All-Star Game. *(Photo by Rich Pilling/MLB Photos)*

I'll admit that my move from the County Stadium office to a thirtieth-floor commissioner's office in downtown Milwaukee was a bit of an upgrade. I was thankful the owners gave me a chance to run baseball from my hometown. *(Photo courtesy of the Milwaukee Brewers Baseball Club)*

Once we had reached labor peace with the Players Association, we began some great partnerships with players, including the World Baseball Classic. This was a great time for me and the game, as showed when I visited the interview room before a U.S.-Canada game at Chase Field in 2006. *(Photo by Jason Wise/MLB Photo via Getty Images)*

The Yankees were my favorite team growing up, and easy to root for when my friend Joe Torre managed them. Here I'm talking to Joe and comedian Billy Crystal, in Miami before a game in the 2003 World Series. *(Photo by Rich Pilling/MLB Photos)*

President Barack Obama threw out the first pitch at the 2009 MLB All-Star Game in St. Louis. We talked about his love for baseball, especially his Chicago White Sox, later that evening. *(Photo courtesy of Wendy Selig)*

Notes in hand, I was on the stage with National Baseball Hall of Fame Chairman, Jane Forbes Clark, for inductions in 2009. *(Photo by Rich Pilling/MLB Photos via Getty Images)*

My family sold the Brewers to Mark Attanasio in 2005. Mark honored me by creating The Selig Experience, a permanent exhibit at Miller Park, in 2014. I shared a lot of gratitude when that was announced. *(Photo courtesy of the Milwaukee Brewers Baseball Club)*

Vera Clemente, Roberto Clemente's widow, joins me presenting the Mets' Carlos Delgado with the Roberto Clemente Award during the 2006 World Series in St. Louis. *(Photo by Brad Mangin/ MLB Photos via Getty Images)*

Here I'm joined by Mark Attanasio, who bought the Brewers, before a game in 2010. He's done a great job with the franchise, who I cheered on in the postseason in 2018. *(Photo courtesy of the Milwaukee Brewers Baseball Club)*

Joined on the field for a ceremony by Mark Attanasio and my longtime friend, Bob Uecker. He's one of the funniest men alive and an absolutely terrific broadcaster. *(Photo courtesy of the Milwaukee Brewers Baseball Club)*

Sharing a laugh with Mariano Rivera as I presented him with the Commissioner's Historic Achievement Award during the 2013 World Series. *(Photo by Rob Tringali/ MLB Photos via Getty Images)*

I've been friends with Henry Aaron since 1958. Here I'm joining him to present the Tigers' Miguel Cabrera with the Henry Aaron Award during the 2013 World Series. *(Photo by Brad Mangin/MLB Photos via Getty Images)*

Rob Manfred, who succeeded me as commissioner in 2015, was essential to my work in finally negotiating a labor agreement without a work stoppage in 2002. He also worked in the trenches as MLB persevered to institute the toughest PED policy in professional sports. Here we're announcing a deal with the Players Association in 2011. *(Photo by Rich Pilling/MLB Photos via Getty Images)*

Celebrating my eightieth birthday with my family. *(Photo courtesy of Wendy Selig)*

Surrounded by family outside the Otesaga Hotel in Cooperstown, NY, in 2017. It was the thrill of a lifetime to be inducted into the Hall of Fame. *(Photo courtesy of Wendy Selig)*

Viewing my plaque on the wall in Cooperstown. That day was a little boy's wildest dream come true, in a way I could have never foreseen. *(Photo courtesy of Wendy Selig)*

in their fourth year in the new park they won the NL East five years in a row.

With homegrown stars Jimmy Rollins, Chase Utley, Ryan Howard, and Cole Hamels, the Phillies drew three million fans a year to Citizens Bank Park during their run, which included a World Series victory over the Rays in 2008. Philadelphia is hardly a small market, but the Phillies were being left behind at the Vet, a symbol of how baseball got it wrong for so long.

With new ballparks in cities where they were badly needed, we created a model built for the future. Seldom did they get built without controversy over financing or location, but they have been a source of civic pride for so many cities, including my Milwaukee.

San Francisco might provide the ultimate example of how a new ballpark can revitalize both a city and a franchise. I don't know if you've ever been to Candlestick Park, but I'll tell you that you didn't miss much if you weren't there. I know it carved out its niche with Giants fans, but the location, right on the water, in an area of the city that was known for cold, swirling winds, was a disaster.

Candlestick was impossible. The Giants shared Candlestick with the 49ers, and Bob Lurie was constantly trying to get a new stadium. He lost three or four stadium measures before he himself came close to selling the team to a group that was going to move it to the Tampa Bay area.

Eventually the Giants' new ownership group, headed by Peter Magowan and Larry Baer, put together a public-private partnership to build AT&T Park in an area of San Francisco known as the China Basin. It was an old area of warehouses and run-down buildings when the plans were drawn up. Now it is one of the gleaming areas in the city, not only a great place to play baseball but a hub for economic development.

That's how the recent generations of ballparks have worked. I often talk about baseball as a part of community trust, how baseball has a social responsibility. The new ballparks are a great demonstration of that.

While they benefit the clubs, for sure, they also benefit the cities. They provide jobs and stir economies. It is genuinely a great partnership and has made a life-and-death difference for a lot of franchises, including the one in Milwaukee.

Wendy, my daughter, was in charge of the Brewers while I tackled baseball's biggest challenges, but I had a deeply personal investment in the stadium situation. I knew replacing County Stadium was necessary for the survival of the franchise that had given Milwaukee a second chance at being a baseball town. Because we were the smallest market in the major leagues, we needed to maximize revenues if the Brewers were going to be competitive enough to reward fans for the passion they invested in the team.

We didn't just reach that conclusion in the 1990s, when so many other teams were opening stadiums. I had seen this coming for a long time. I loved County Stadium more than anyone in Milwaukee, but for me the need for a new stadium was like a toothache that starts long before you find yourself at the dentist. I could feel it for years before I allowed the issue to become a public matter. I knew I couldn't let an antiquated stadium become the reason that the Brewers failed, not after the heartache I experienced when the Braves moved to Atlanta. I knew I couldn't allow that to happen again. It was unthinkable.

At my urging, the Greater Milwaukee Committee—the same organization that was responsible for County Stadium forty years earlier—appointed a task force to study the issue in 1987. That was the start of an agonizingly painful process that often crawled or seemed stalled until Miller Park became a reality in 1995 and finally was ready for baseball in 2001.

I remember being in Toronto when the SkyDome opened. It had a roof to keep fans warm and dry, a hotel in left field, and the Hard Rock Cafe in right field. McDonald's ran the concessions. As much as I marveled about what the Blue Jays had accomplished with the help of financing from Toronto and the province of Ontario, I must admit I was feeling a little bit heartsick about our franchise. How could we compete with this?

It was clear we needed not only a new stadium but one with a roof, which would increase the cost of the project significantly. The journey to get our new ballpark built would be torturous and require patience over many years. The plus for me was that I was traveling it with my daughter, as Wendy was by my side every step of the way. She would step out on her own in these negotiations because I was preoccupied with the bigger issues in baseball.

When I look back on it, I still shake my head over how painful the process became. It really didn't have to be so contentious. We experienced some political defeats along the way that were crushing, especially when I compared them to the vision of the civic leaders who had built County Stadium before Milwaukee even had a team to play there. Those guys had the vision and the will to see how a stadium could draw a team in to make the whole city better. What had happened to that spirit?

We were desperately trying to stay here, to make baseball work in Milwaukee for decades to come. There was no other agenda. That's what made the opposition we faced so stunning to me. The way we were treated along the way made this the most disappointing time of my career.

We had a lot of really strong people on our side, including

Mike Grebe, an influential lawyer and civic leader who was close to Tommy Thompson, who was then the Wisconsin governor. We had Thompson's support, and I thought we would be able to count on it throughout the process, in part because of the connection with Grebe. But somewhere along the way we lost Thompson. I believe others had convinced him that supporting the stadium measure wasn't a popular position for him to take. He made a political judgment, and he was wrong. That's what I never understood. We weren't threatening to move. I never listened to overtures from other cities. Charlotte was interested, but I never talked to them.

As the person primarily responsible for bringing baseball to Milwaukee all those years earlier, it was hard not to take all this personally. Considering the unlikely way I had landed the Brewers in 1970, and again the pain I'd experienced when the Braves packed up and left Milwaukee, I simply couldn't consider abandoning my hometown. It just wasn't in my DNA, and I knew it. Everyone knew it, I think. I couldn't let the legacy of all my efforts be that the team's financial situation prevented it from staying where it belonged. Nothing over the previous three decades would have been possible if we hadn't fought so hard to make Milwaukee a baseball town. But suddenly we were faced with the prospect that it could end. If the Brewers couldn't upgrade their stadium situation, at some point the team would have to leave. What was in these rejections for Milwaukee and the state of Wisconsin? They were never going to get another team.

I'll never forget the drive home from Madison after one setback. It felt like a nail in our coffin, and the mood on the way back to Milwaukee was gloomy. This was probably the lowest point for me. Wendy and the other people in the car asked what we were going to do. I said we would keep trying. I think they thought I was crazy. They certainly couldn't believe I was going to go on.

What else was I going to do? Of course I was going to go on. We were going to get this done. I would have liked to have told those people to go take a hike, believe me. I'd like to have done that, but that wouldn't help me get a new stadium. We couldn't survive without the stadium and I wasn't going to let Milwaukee lose its baseball team, the team I'd worked so hard to bring to the city all those years ago. Not on my watch.

We regrouped and, in the end, we won. That's *we* as in all of us in Milwaukee and Wisconsin. I am so proud of how Wendy problem-solved and persevered through some angry and ugly confrontations with politicians and produced a state-of-the-art ballpark that has allowed the franchise to draw more than three million fans in three different seasons.

The Brewers have played there for eighteen seasons now, with the annual average attendance about 2.7 million. Milwaukee is the smallest market in the majors but finished tenth in attendance in 2018 and is likely to do even better in '19. That's pretty spectacular, if you ask me. Thank goodness Wendy persevered.

She had a lot of help along the way. From the start, Wendy put together a group of community leaders who were dedicated to the cause. We were so thankful for the work of Jim Keyes of Johnson Controls; Jack McDonough, the chairman and CEO of Miller Brewing; Jack McKeithan, a former chairman of Schlitz Brewing; Jim Ericson of Northwestern Mutual; Bob Kahlor, chairman and CEO of Journal Communications; Roger Fitzsimonds of First Wisconsin; Frank Busalacchi of the Teamsters; and Tim Sheehy of the Metropolitan Milwaukee Association of Commerce. State assemblyman David Prosser and Milwaukee County Executive Tom Ament were helpful from the start.

Wendy was a warrior in the fights at city hall and at the state-house. She was involved not only in the grueling political aspects but also in the design and construction that have made Miller Park a prototype for other new ballparks, especially those with retractable roofs.

I witnessed some of the worst, most Machiavellian behavior you can imagine. I had politicians—including our governor at the time, Thompson, and our mayor, John Norquist—routinely say one thing to my face and do the opposite behind my back.

We eventually got it done with a public-private partnership, with dozens of people working tirelessly behind the scenes—even Henry Aaron stepped up to help—and with committed people who believed that, in the end, Miller Park would be good for the city. They believed, correctly, that it would not only be good from a financial standpoint—studies show it adds $330 million a year to the Wisconsin economy—but have a sociological benefit.

I'll never forget the sacrifice made by George Petak, a state legislator from Racine. He helped us get across the finish line because he knew it was good for his home state even if public funding was a divisive issue. George was convinced Milwaukee would lose the Brewers without a new stadium. He was subsequently voted out of office by residents of his county but went out as one of my heroes for how he helped make Miller Park a reality. He was like me. He understood the impact baseball can have on a community.

When the project was in trouble, we received a huge late lift from Michael Joyce, president of the Bradley Foundation, one of the biggest and most respected foundations in the country. His support, along with Tim Sheehy's, rallied other local business leaders who were supportive of the stadium effort.

We got Miller Park built because, truly, our fans wanted it, and ultimately, our fans demanded it. I knew what we needed was a midwestern version of SkyDome, but that didn't exactly fit in the Brewers' budget. The challenge was how to build a partnership with local governments to help finance it. We had many tough days, many painful days, many days when there just didn't seem to be a way out. Yet we pressed on. That's the way I had achieved every victory in my career—with perseverance in the face of skepticism.

Miller Park opened on April 6, 2001, with the Reds back in town. Wendy and her husband, Laurel Prieb, had added so many wonderful touches to the ballpark, from an innovative kids' zone to décor that only people who really loved the game could have imagined. But Bernie Brewer still had his slide.

My friend George W. Bush came through for me. He told me he'd be honored to throw out a ceremonial first pitch for our first game, and I was honored to have him in town. I was going to throw out a first pitch, too. Yount warmed me up in our new batting cages beforehand. President Bush warmed up, too, but not quite enough, as it turned out. He bounced a ball to the plate, perhaps because he was wearing a bulletproof vest underneath his shirt.

I thought of a million different things that night, including Wendy's tenacity and the sacrifice of George Petak. I thought a lot about three construction workers who were killed in a horrible crane accident during construction and the thousands of other workers who could point with pride to the bricks they laid, the grass they planted, the signs they hung. I was so very grateful to so many people.

Without new ballparks, along with changes in baseball's anti-quated economic systems, a lot of teams would have been out of business. Maybe ten teams, maybe twelve teams. All the small markets. I know critics dismiss this reality, but that's how truly desperate these times were.

Bringing stadiums into the modern era was a huge step forward for baseball.

Stadiums weren't the only area in which we were taking action to modernize baseball as we tried to get beyond the pain everyone experienced in 1994–95.

Interleague play was the oldest "new" idea in baseball. Some point to talks taking place to have regular-season games between our two leagues as far back as the 1930s. I can't swear to that, but I was privy to a push for it in 1973, when Bowie Kuhn was the commissioner. I know that Hank Greenberg, the Hall of Fame first baseman of the Tigers, had been an advocate. So too was Bill Veeck, who never really had the influence to pull it off. There was talk about it in '73, when we adopted the designated hitter rule, but the two leagues weren't capable of working together.

I was actually on the committee that discussed interleague play in '73, working with Frank Dale of the Cincinnati Reds. We came up with a plan. We'd have a six-game interleague schedule running into the All-Star break every year, with the opponents switching around annually. I pitched it to American League owners and they were sold. But we needed the National League's approval, and I don't think it got out of the gate with them. Walter O'Malley was against it, and everyone generally followed his lead.

The rivalry between leagues was good on one level but turned into an impediment to progress. I don't want to put this too strongly, but there were times the leagues despised each other. You would think people would have understood we were in this business together, but for too much of our history it was the opposite.

The game was still stuck in neutral in so many ways, and, like adding the wild card, I thought interleague play was an idea we could use to build some momentum and get back on solid footing.

For a while after we got back on the field in '95 I brought interleague play up at every meeting. We formed a committee to study it. We were also studying expansion, from twenty-eight teams to thirty.

We were adding teams in Phoenix and Tampa Bay. Even though Arizona was going to the NL and Tampa Bay to the AL, we needed one team to change leagues. It didn't work to have fifteen teams in both leagues unless you were going to have interleague play every day, and we were only pushing for it on a limited basis, at least at the start.

That meant we needed a team to change leagues. My daughter Wendy, who had done such a great job on the stadium effort in Milwaukee, immediately saw the wisdom of moving from the AL to the NL, which would help the Brewers travel and create a major rivalry with the Cubs. But I was focused on the Royals, pitching David Glass on the idea of having rivalry games with the Cardinals as well as the Cubs. He wasn't sold, so I told him to take his time.

It was one of the few times that Wendy Selig was miffed at the commissioner.

"You gave him four to six months to think about it?" she asked me. "You never gave me four to six months to think about anything."

Well, she may have had a point. But in the end Glass did not want to switch leagues. There was no better option than Milwaukee. We vetted the issue at an owners meeting, with an abundance of caution. No one objected to the Brewers joining the NL Central.

The Brewers' move worked out well, as has interleague play. Traditionalists complained that interleague play would water down the All-Star Game or even the World Series, but I knew from the start the positives were much greater than the perceived negatives. We should have added interleague play much earlier than we did, and when we did it was like the wild card—a common sense move that demonstrated baseball had moved into a new era.

The first interleague game was played in Arlington on June 12, with Barry Bonds's Giants beating Ivan Rodriguez's Rangers. But the series that were the most fun were played a little later in the season, when the Mets visited Yankee Stadium, the Cubs played on the South Side of Chicago, and the A's crossed the Bay Bridge to play the Giants. There's such anticipation for games between crosstown rivals, even when the teams aren't strong. It just makes sense to schedule games that fans want to see. Interleague play was a smart idea, and it hasn't hurt the World Series or the All-Star Game one iota.

The best idea we had in that era was the simplest one.

We decided to honor the fiftieth anniversary of Jackie Robinson's breaking the color barrier by retiring his number, 42, on April 15.

I'm so proud of my predecessors in baseball for opening the doors to Jackie in 1947. It was a terrific message to signal to America—that color didn't matter. It didn't matter then and it never should have mattered. But progress came slowly in many parts of our society.

Branch Rickey signed Jackie in 1945. He played minor league baseball in Montreal in '46 and then was at Ebbets Field in '47. You can't overstate the kind of a pioneer you got with Robinson.

This was more than a year before President Truman desegregated the United States Army. It was seven years before the Supreme Court's landmark ruling in *Brown v. Board of Education*. It was seventeen years before the Civil Rights Act.

Baseball was leading the nation, and Robinson was the right man for the job.

"What if Jackie hadn't come along?" Henry Aaron has often asked me.

Len Coleman, who was the National League president, played a key role in our deciding to retire Robinson's No. 42 all across baseball. There was unanimous support for it throughout baseball. We planned the announcement for Shea Stadium in New York. I had lunch with Rachel Robinson, Jackie's widow, at the Plaza hotel that afternoon. I could have listened to her stories all afternoon.

She told me how Hank Greenberg encouraged Jackie, with an unusual perspective. Greenberg was playing for the Pirates then but had spent most of his career in Detroit, where he took a lot of abuse for being Jewish. He weathered it and over time became a revered player, both in Detroit and everywhere else.

When Robinson reached first base in a game in Pittsburgh, Greenberg told him he was doing great. "Don't let 'em get to you, kid," Greenberg told Robinson. "You're going to be all right."

Robinson never forgot that support.

President Clinton attended the Robinson dedication ceremony at Shea Stadium. It was a much more joyous occasion than the time we'd spent together in Washington a few winters earlier.

There were thirteen players wearing No. 42 on those 1997 rosters, and we agreed they could wear them the rest of their careers, if they decided. It was fitting that the last 42 in the game was

Mariano Rivera, a great pitcher and every bit as dignified as Jackie and Rachel Robinson.

I think our understanding of who Jackie was and what he meant has grown a lot since his number was retired. I think it means a lot to players, especially African American players, to walk in Jackie's spikes one day a season.

The Dodgers asked if all their players could wear 42 on that day, and of course we gave them permission. Credit Ken Griffey Jr. for the players on every team wearing 42 on April 15 these days. Junior called me at my home in Phoenix in early April 2006 and told me he had an idea.

"I was talking to the guys, and I know the Dodgers all wear 42 on Jackie Robinson Day," Griffey said. "What about the rest of us? I'd like to wear 42. What if everybody wears 42 on April 15?"

What a great idea. I told him I'd think about it overnight and get back to him, but I was sold from the time I hung up the phone.

I've really valued my friendship with Rachel Robinson through the years.

Once we talked about Dixie Walker. I had read that Walker had refused to play with Jackie back in 1947 and been traded to Pittsburgh by the Dodgers.

I told Rachel that I broached that subject with Walker in 1964, when he was batting coach for the Milwaukee Braves. We were at dinner and Dixie was raving about Hank Aaron.

I don't know how I got up the nerve—remember, I was only a thirty-year-old kid then—but I asked him if he'd ever been sorry about how he acted with Jackie Robinson.

He gave me an amazing answer. He said that yes, as a matter of fact, he did regret it. He was ashamed.

But Walker went on to explain that he'd been raised in a

redneck environment in Birmingham, Alabama, with almost no interaction with blacks. He said that years later he wrote a letter to Jackie, telling him he was sorry, and that Jackie had replied, saying they should get together the next time Dixie was in New York.

"That's absolutely true," Rachel said.

She said that Dixie came and visited, and that Jack—as she calls the man we all called Jackie—appreciated it.

Ignorance has so much to do with the difficulties between races and different groups of people. But there's no excuse for racism or to treat anybody badly based on any prejudice.

Imagine how difficult it was for Jackie when Branch Rickey instructed him to turn the other cheek to the vile slurs that came his way on a daily basis. That was not his nature, you know, but his brave, bold wife, Rachel, helped get him through that.

Society resists change; social institutions are very slow to change. But here was Jackie Robinson, change personified.

Jackie's last public appearance was the 1972 World Series, honoring the twenty-fifth anniversary of his taking the field in Brooklyn. He was in failing health, but he still looked handsome and strong, his wife and children by his side.

He was pushing for change even till the end.

"I'm extremely proud and pleased to be here this afternoon," Robinson said, thanking Bowie Kuhn for the invitation. "But I must admit, I'm going to be tremendously more pleased and more proud when I look at that third-base coaching line one day and see a black face managing in baseball."

Jackie died nine days later.

Frank Robinson was hired to manage the Indians in 1975, and there have been some terrific African American and Latino managers since then. Cito Gaston guided the Blue Jays to back-to-back titles. Dusty Baker, Ron Washington, and Dave Roberts have reached the World Series with their teams and Alex Cora, a Puerto Rican, led the Red Sox to a championship in his first year as a manager.

But you can't take opportunity for granted.

That's why I sent a memo to clubs in 1999 that requires them to consider minority candidates "for all general manager, assistant general manager, field manager, director of player development and director of scouting positions." I asked to be included in the loop on their openings and their candidates, and pushed for candidates when it was appropriate.

It's not a perfect process, of course, but I'm proud that it's known as the Selig Rule. I was also tremendously proud when Dr. Richard Lapchick, who has long conducted the most prominent study of diversity in sports, praised me for helping "make MLB's central and team front offices look like America."

17

Henry Aaron broke Babe Ruth's record by staying healthy and being incredibly consistent. He never hit more than forty-seven homers in a season. Think about that.

This was the kind of home run production I was used to from watching baseball from an up-close-and-personal viewpoint for almost three decades. Fifty homers in a season was magical. When Cecil Fielder hit fifty-one for the Tigers in 1990, it marked the first time anyone reached that milestone since George Foster's fifty-two-homer season for the 1977 Reds. So when balls started flying out of ballparks at unprecedented rates in the nineties, it represented a significant trend in how the game was being played and how games were being decided.

Of course, you can look back now and say baseball was entering the steroid age, but that was not so obvious at the time. It wouldn't be until the end of the 1990s that I really understood what a huge threat steroid use posed for our sport.

Looking back now, the first signs of what we were up against presented themselves back in the late eighties. It was 1988 when Oakland's Bash Brothers team, with Jose Canseco and Mark Mc-Gwire, played the Red Sox at Fenway Park. The *Washington Post*'s Tom Boswell, who has written about baseball reverently, had reported that Canseco was using steroids.

The Boston fans, always on the cutting edge in riding the Red Sox's opponents, serenaded Canseco in the American League

Championship Series. Fans in the right-field corner at Fenway were hooting at Canseco, then started a singsong chant.

"Ster-oids! Ster-oids! Ster-oids! Ster-oids!"

Canseco responded by flexing his oversized biceps at the fans, then led the A's to a sweep of Boston.

As we got into the mid-nineties, no one was putting up obscene home run totals, but scoring was up all around baseball. There were fewer 2–1 games, more 10–9 games. There was a trend. There were about a third more home runs in '93 than in '92, but the high was forty-six, from the Rangers' Juan Gonzalez and Barry Bonds, who was in his first season with the Giants. Five players hit forty-plus home runs in '93, and twenty-two hit at least thirty. The numbers were changing, but the history of baseball's stats has always been about the game's cycles. There are always different factors at play, different eras and different players.

It's easy in hindsight to say that more of our players were taking steroids and other performance-enhancing drugs. There was no way for us to know that at the time because we couldn't test the players. Ever since our attempt to drug-test the players following the cocaine scandal in the eighties, the Players Association had stonewalled us. We certainly didn't understand the scope of the problem.

Still, it wasn't as though steroids were legal in baseball. In fact, they weren't legal anywhere. In 1990, there was enough concern about the increasing use of steroids in athletics in all American sports that Congress passed the Anabolic Steroids Control Act, making it illegal to possess steroids without a prescription from a doctor. That made them against baseball's rules as well, on the banned substance list just like cocaine and other so-called recreational drugs.

But it wasn't just that they were now illegal. Fay Vincent sent out a memo in 1991 serving notice to teams and players that we wanted steroids out of the game.

I'll be honest, though. Fay's memo went nowhere because we still had no way to test the players. Remember, drug testing was a subject of collective bargaining. It's not something a commissioner can unilaterally implement. The union, both privately and very publicly, was absolutely, unalterably opposed.

So Fay put out a memo and we notified the union we'd seek testing in the next labor negotiations, which we did.

We put a provision for testing into our collective bargaining agreement proposal in 1994. Canadian sprinter Ben Johnson had been stripped of his Olympic gold medal in 1988 after a positive test for a performance-enhancing drug. NFL star Lyle Alzado had blamed steroid use for his brain tumors before he died in 1992. We didn't see steroids as a baseball drug because our sport is more about skill and hand-eye coordination than strength or sheer speed, but we wanted to do our due diligence.

Rob Manfred was then with the Washington law firm of Morgan, Lewis & Bockius. He was outside counsel to MLB. I had him draft a revised drug proposal to include in the '94 talks.

It was detailed, twelve pages' worth. It cited marijuana, cocaine, opiates, phencyclidine, and amphetamines, as well as "steroids or prescription drugs which the player uses or possesses without a valid prescription."

We were offering treatment for the first violation, followed by a sixty-day suspension, then a twelve-month suspension, and for the fourth offense, a lifetime ban. We didn't know then how big a problem steroids were, but I remember Rob saying "it's better to be ahead of the curve." He was right, but the union ignored our proposal.

We first informed the union of our interest in random testing for performance-enhancing drugs in the early stages of negotiations in 1994, but it was immediately clear our choice was either to go to war over that topic or table it. We had no idea at that time how widespread steroid use would become, so we kept our focus on the lack of real revenue sharing and the owners' desire to put a salary cap in place.

Given all that we were up against during the strike in '94, you wouldn't be wrong if you said our focus was on the economic problems in the game, not how some of our players were circumventing our rules for their own gain. In truth, there was as small a chance of Don Fehr and Gene Orza accepting PED testing as there was of a salary cap, so to get a deal we pulled it off the table.

Bob Nightengale, then with the *Los Angeles Times,* wrote a story that has gotten a lot of attention in hindsight. This was 1995—three years before the great home run race—and he quoted one of our general managers, Randy Smith of the Padres, as saying that 10 to 20 percent of major league players were using steroids. He quoted an unnamed GM saying the total could be as high as 30 percent.

It was a sensational story but there was no follow-up on it, even by Nightengale. At the time, the feeling throughout the game was that steroids were not making a major impact on players or their performance. If more and more players were beginning to use steroids, they kept it to themselves. Once I did bring up the question of steroids at a major league meeting. The silence was deafening. Nobody knew. I didn't know.

I called a lot of my players who I had great relationships with—Robin Yount, Paul Molitor, Cecil Cooper, other guys, too. I asked them if we had a big problem.

Robin had the best answer. He said he didn't know of anybody on his teams doing it. He said everybody knew Canseco did it, but everybody hated Canseco. That was his direct line. He didn't think Canseco would be lining up players to follow his example.

There was no sign of the trend stopping, however. In 1996, six players actually matched or beat Henry Aaron's season high for home runs—Mark McGwire with fifty-two, Brady Anderson with fifty, Ken Griffey Jr. with forty-nine, Albert Belle with forty-eight, Andres Galarraga and Juan Gonzalez with forty-seven. That year there were forty-three players who hit at least thirty homers.

It was a staggering amount of home runs. There were only thirteen who hit thirty in 1986, a decade earlier.

Something was going on, for sure. But we didn't know what it was. Nobody really did. Players were spending unprecedented amounts of time in the weight rooms. That's what I was told when I asked some of our best baseball men—John Schuerholz and Andy MacPhail, to name a couple—what they thought was happening. They could see the sizes of guys. But they saw them working out on all the new weight equipment that teams had installed, trying to build teams that would match up physically with the Canseco-McGwire Oakland team, which had gone to the World Series three years in a row. In hindsight, sure, you can point to steroids, but I'd asked players who had been in clubhouses as well as owners and nobody said they knew we had a big problem.

Early in the 1997 season, I did something nobody remembers me doing. Maybe I didn't pound my chest enough for doing it. Maybe I knew that it was largely like Fay's memo in 1991, well intentioned but lacking teeth.

You've got to remember that I like baseball players. I like baseball players a lot. And the Alzado story shook me. I worried about our players making decisions that came with health risks, as Alzado felt he had done.

That's why on May 15, 1997, I sent out the following memo to our thirty clubs:

Baseball's Drug Policy and Prevention Program
INTRODUCTION

This memorandum sets forth Baseball's drug policy and the principal components of our drug abuse program. As in the past, the health and the welfare of those who work in Baseball will continue to be our paramount concern. No less compelling, however, is the need to maintain the integrity of the game. Drug involvement or the suspicion of drug involvement is inconsistent with maintaining these objectives.

The basic drug policy for the game is simply stated: There is no place for illegal drug use in Baseball. The use of illegal drugs by players, umpires, owners, front office, League or Commissioner's office personnel, trainers or anyone else involved in the game cannot be condoned or tolerated. Illegal drug use can cause injuries on the field, diminished job performance or alienation of those on whom the game's success depends—baseball fans. Baseball players and personnel cannot be permitted to give even the slightest suggestion that illegal drug use is either acceptable or safe. It is the responsibility of all Baseball players and personnel to see that the use of illegal drugs does not occur, or if it does to put a stop to it by the most effective means possible.

MAJOR LEAGUE BASEBALL'S DRUG POLICY

The possession, sale or use of any illegal drug or controlled substance by Major League players and personnel is strictly prohibited. Major League players or personnel involved in the possession, sale or use of any illegal drug or controlled substance are subject to discipline by the Commissioner and risk permanent expulsion from the game. In addition to any discipline this office may impose, a club may also take action under applicable provisions of and special covenants to the Uniform Players Contract.

This prohibition applies to all illegal drugs and controlled substances, including steroids or prescription drugs for which the individual in possession of the drug does not have a prescription. Clubs will dispense prescription drugs only under the direction of the team physician and appropriate records of such distribution and use will be maintained. All drugs on Club premises will be kept under lock and key. For their own protections, players who are taking a prescription drug under the direction of a physician other than the team physician must notify the team physician of this fact and of the drug(s) prescribed.

Major League Baseball recognizes that illegal drug use has become a national problem, and that some players and Baseball personnel may fall victim to drugs. In such circumstances, Baseball will attempt to treat and rehabilitate individuals with a drug problem through a Club's Employee Assistance Program (EAP) or through resources identified by the Commissioner's Office. Baseball will approach its treatment and rehabilitation efforts with the welfare of both the individual and the game foremost in mind. However, Baseball will not hesitate to permanently remove from the game those players and personnel who, despite our efforts to treat and rehabilitate, refuse to accept responsibility for the problem and continue to use illegal drugs. Finally, the concern of an individual Club about a player's availability to that Club will not be a meaningful consideration in determining the course to be followed. If any Club covers up or otherwise fails to disclose to this office any information concerning drug use by a player, that Club will be fined $250,000, the highest allowable amount under the Major League Agreement.

In that memo I mentioned steroids specifically and raised my concerns for the integrity of the game. But in '97 we didn't understand the issue. I wasn't yet worried enough about steroid use to publicly campaign to get them out of the game. I didn't make a big deal about the memo. I probably should have made more noise at the time. In hindsight, it might have saved me some headaches from critics who have said I was secretly happy about the steroid use because home runs were packing stadiums. That's a great theory, sure, and if I heard it on one talk-radio show I heard it on ten thousand talk-radio shows, but it couldn't have been more wrong.

Ultimately, it probably wouldn't have mattered how much I publicly pushed this memo; without testing we had no way to enforce any policy we set, dealing only with players who got arrested or publicly exposed by law enforcement.

It was against this backdrop of increasing home run totals and the absence of testing that we entered the 1998 season. Few baseball seasons have ever been as memorable or as surprising. We'd never seen anything like what happened that summer in St. Louis, Chicago, and ballparks all over the United States and Canada.

McGwire, who had followed Tony La Russa to the Cardinals in a midseason trade the year before, had pretty much crushed the ball his whole career, including a forty-nine-homer season as a rookie in 1987. I liked Mark personally. He was from a strong family. His father was a dentist. He himself seemed to be a good father. He was quiet. I found him to be very nice, very thoughtful. He hadn't been blessed with good health, battling plantar fasciitis in his feet, but once he regained his health in the mid-nineties he was the picture of a slugger. Mark had big home run seasons in '96 and '97. He hit fifty-two while playing only 130 games in the first of those, then stayed on the field and hit fifty-eight the next year. He hit the ground mashing the ball in the spring of '98.

McGwire homered in each of the first four games, including shots off Ramon Martinez (on Opening Day) and Mark Langston. He finished April with eleven homers and then went on a tear in May, running his total to twenty-seven in the Cardinals' first fifty-three games.

By the time we reached Memorial Day, sportswriters and fans were saying he had a shot to break Roger Maris's record, the sacred sixty-one. There really hadn't been that talk before. He'd missed most of April in '96 and in '97 had been only at forty-three after August, turning it on at the end to move into Maris's neighborhood.

The script was different this time. It changed in a major way in June, when Sammy Sosa seemed to hit every other pitch out of Wrigley Field. That's hyperbole, but not by much. I had gotten to know Sammy a little bit through the years and, like almost everybody else, I liked him a lot. He had a big smile and played the game with a joy that came from appreciating the opportunities baseball had given him. Sammy had thirteen homers at the end of

May, less than half of Mark's total. But he hit twenty home runs in only 114 at-bats in June. It was crazy what he was doing.

These homers weren't coming entirely out of nowhere for Sammy, either. Like McGwire, Sosa had foreshadowed '98 in '96, when he hit forty homers before the Marlins' Mark Hutton broke his right wrist with a pitch on August 20. He'd never had a fifty-homer season before '98 but probably would have if he'd gotten out of the way of that pitch.

McGwire and Sosa weren't the only guys who showed this could be a historic season for sluggers. Ken Griffey Jr., one of the unquestioned really good guys, had thirty-three homers for the Mariners by the end of June. He had hit fifty-six homers the year before, so with the All-Star Game approaching we had three guys—not two—positioned to make a run at Maris.

In truth, I didn't really start focusing on the home run race until after the All-Star break. As usual, I'd been centered on the business of the game, identifying changes we needed to make and trying to build consensus to execute them. As always, I was looking for ways to increase revenue sharing. I was beginning to build a consensus for eliminating the two league offices and separate umpire staffs. That was the way baseball had always been run, but it really didn't make sense anymore.

When I talked on the phone to the owners about the need to modernize the sport, they returned the favor by saying I needed to take the word *acting* out of my title and step into the commissioner's job permanently. It was a chorus I heard all the time, and finally we made it official in a meeting at Chicago's O'Hare Hilton on July 9, with a unanimous vote.

We had hired the Blue Jays' architect Paul Beeston as MLB's chief operating officer in 1997. I beefed up our staff by hiring Bob DuPuy and Rob Manfred away from their law firms and adding

Sandy Alderson, a Vietnam War vet who had put together the Oakland team that went to the World Series three years in a row. These moves were all well thought out and would put baseball in a position to reassert its position in the American landscape. We had made some progress—revenues were up to $2.5 billion a year, about double what they'd been when I stepped in for Fay Vincent in 1992—and owners were beginning to benefit.

At the meeting in Chicago, I told the owners that I was going to continue to work to build hope and faith for every team, and I vowed to help them grow their franchises. At the end of the day, I told them, judge me on the value of your franchise. The Dodgers had recently been purchased by Fox Entertainment Group from the O'Malleys for $314 million and the Rangers had been bought from George W. Bush's group for $250 million. I can guarantee you none of the other baseball commissioners I dealt with ever would have used that as a yardstick, but I knew as an owner that the growth of franchise values was what teams wanted.

That day in Chicago I wasn't just surrounded by the owners who had become my longtime friends; I was humbled by the sight of the beautiful family that had supported me through my early years in baseball.

In the heat of the summer, Griffey slipped into the shadows of the home run race. Even though he'd wind up leading the AL with fifty-six homers, the same as the year before, he couldn't keep up with Sammy and Mark. They blew the doors off in August, entering September tied with fifty-five apiece. This really was crazy.

Let me make a confession here. Down the stretch, I was just as captivated by the saga as was the rest of America—not because it was "saving baseball" but because it was unbelievable theater.

As for anyone who looks back and says anything that happened in 1998 saved baseball, shame on them. Baseball didn't need to be saved. It is and was too strong for that. We still were hurting, yes. Attendance had been down since the strike wiped out the World Series in '94. Players and owners alike knew the strike had damaged the trust that the public placed in MLB, and we were eager to get it back. But things had been trending in the right direction for a while. Long before Sosa-McGwire, we had celebrated Cal Ripken Jr.'s breaking Lou Gehrig's iron-man streak.

I couldn't imagine anyone playing more than 2,130 consecutive games. Gehrig did that and his record stood for fifty-six years. Ripken was cut from the same cloth as Gehrig—a super-talented player with a blue-collar work ethic.

The Baltimore shortstop had played 2,009 games in a row when players went on strike in 1994. He resumed his march toward Gehrig's record when we got back on the field in '95, and passed him on September 6, to the delight of fans everywhere.

Cal was magnificent in his role as a baseball treasure. He took time for the fans every day he was at the ballpark, and I have to say most of our players got a lot better at that following the strike. Ripken allowed us to regain a measure of goodwill with fans, who were reminded of how they loved the way our guys played the game. Thanks to Cal and a great, seven-game World Series between the Cinderella Marlins and the powerful Indians, we were well on our way to recovery before the McGwire-Sosa home run race.

Financially, we had to make changes to get the game back on solid ground, that's true. But it's beyond preposterous to think that we were somehow orchestrating these developments to increase attendance and ratings.

That's just not true. Not a bit of a chance.

What did get my attention, and the attention of a lot of people, was a story by Associated Press reporter Steve Wilstein. This was late August, in a piece Wilstein was doing as an overview on the home run race. Mark had homered in both games of a doubleheader at Shea Stadium on August 20—his fiftieth and fifty-first—and while Wilstein was in the visiting clubhouse, he checked out what was in McGwire's locker. He wrote about packs of sugarless gum, a can of Popeye spinach, and "a brown bottle labeled Androstenedione."

Androstenedione. What the hell is that?

That was Wilstein's reaction, and it was certainly my reaction.

Andro has steroidlike qualities, helping to raise testosterone levels, and was already banned by the NFL, the NCAA, and the Olympics. Yet you could buy it over the counter.

I know because I went to my pharmacy the day after the AP story ran. The pharmacist, whom I had known for years, knew why I was there. "It's right over there," he said, and pointed me to the shelf of supplements to build strength and stamina.

I knew we had to do something to address the issue. There was an almost immediate dialogue with Don Fehr and the union staff about how to approach this unwelcome development.

We held a joint news conference on August 26, announcing we would hire Harvard researchers to study whether androstenedione works like an anabolic steroid and whether it presented a health issue to players. The union wouldn't even concede that these substances enhanced the performance of players. They wanted the researchers to conduct an extensive study to establish the basics.

Of course, we had no idea at the time that results of that study would not be completed until the 2000 season, more than a year and a half later. But that's the pace the union was allowing us to move on steroids.

When Mark hit his sixty-first and sixty-second home runs—in

a series against Sammy and the Cubs, no less—on September 7 and 8, I was there to watch. In fact, I was seated in a box down the first-base line, which I shared with Roger Maris's children and Bob Costas.

I like Bob. I always have, I always will. How can you not like Bob? But he was like so many of the reporters in that era. While the home run race was going on, he was enjoying it like a kid. Years later he'd insist he knew it was fueled by steroids all along.

At the time, Costas wasn't peppering me with questions about the acne on McGwire's back or if I really believed Sammy took "Flintstone vitamins," as he often said when asked about steroids. Nonetheless, he was loving every minute of this American drama, which was casting baseball in the light it had been in when we were all kids. It was a great story and we were all enjoying it. That wasn't against the law.

McGwire, of course, admitted his use later on when he became a hitting coach for the Cardinals and then the Dodgers. Sosa has always denied using illegal substances. But in the moment, none of that really mattered. Outside of linking McGwire to andro, we didn't know anything else was going on, and without testing we couldn't know anything. Not for sure, anyway.

After McGwire sailed No. 62 over the left-field fence off Cubs pitcher Steve Trachsel, I went on the field and presented McGwire a foot-tall trophy with a sterling silver baseball mounted on the top. It was the first Commissioner's Historic Achievement Award, which I'd later present to a cast of players, many of which I still greatly admire and a few others whose careers were later tainted by links to PEDs. I didn't think twice before honoring McGwire or later honoring Sosa. There was no one on either of those clubs who said to me, "I think we've got a problem." They celebrated it. They celebrated it in Chicago, and they celebrated it in St. Louis.

Here's an amazing fact about McGwire's '98 season: he was walked 162 times in 681 plate appearances—almost once every four times he left the on-deck circle and walked to the plate. Tony La Russa said in September that Mark would hit eighty homers if they pitched to him, and he wasn't wrong.

In the end, after a crazy last weekend in which Sammy briefly took the lead (66–65), McGwire finished the season with seventy homers, Sammy with sixty-six. We were all out of breath.

In hindsight, it's surprising that the steroid story largely moved into the background after that season, but that's what happened. The focus was still on McGwire and Sosa in 1999, along with the rising offensive totals in general, but nobody within the game— nor in the media or among the fan base—seemed alarmed by what was happening.

I did wonder if the data told us anything. I had recently hired Jerome Holtzman, the highly respected baseball writer who had retired from the *Chicago Tribune,* to serve as the game's official historian. Jerome was really smart and had covered the game since the 1940s. At home, he had his own baseball library, including every issue ever put out of *The Sporting News.* He was a real treasure and we'd been friendly for years.

Jerome had covered the founding of the Players Association and was one of the first reporters to see a baseball strike coming after Marvin Miller united players. He knew the landscape, for sure. So as one of Jerome's first projects as baseball historian, I asked him for a report on the spike in offensive numbers—what did they say about the integrity of the game and, specifically, did they indicate widespread steroid use? He knew how worried I was, but he didn't think anything was happening that was out of whack with the history of baseball. He said, "I can tell you right now how this is going to come out, but I'm going to look up the history and write you a report." He said he knew it would show that anyone pointing toward steroids was "making way too much of it."

So Jerome did the research and wrote a long, detailed report. It said that in every decade since the twenties there were always certain conditions or factors that affected the game, whatever they were, and what was happening now was no different.

Holtzman, whom the other writers called "The Dean," went through the report with me, but mostly it was stuff I knew—how Babe Ruth's style changed the approach of hitters; how a livelier ball was introduced at one point and how the ball had been changed in World War II, when the talent pool also was thinner than normal; how the talent base increased through integration and the arrival of Latin Americans; how expansion, Astroturf, and the designated hitter rule factored in. He went over everything and said the run-scoring in the nineties was just another trend and not anything to get worked up about.

I asked him what I should say to people criticizing baseball about the suspicion of steroid use. I can remember his answer word for word: "Fuck those assholes!" That was Jerome for you.

We had no choice but to wait for the results from the joint study of andro to come in. Given that the union leaders couldn't accept what "performance enhancing" even meant, I knew this conversation wasn't going to result in drug testing for a long time.

But I didn't take Jerome's advice on how to address criticism. I began to press the union for testing every chance I got. I would be open when the subject was raised in interviews, saying I felt we should be able to test players to understand the issue and to minimize the impact of performance-enhancing drugs. It was a huge health issue, for sure, and that really worried me.

I was consulting a lot with team doctors and professional athletic trainers. They were very concerned. But not that many other people were concerned in those days, certainly not the union.

This became clearer to me after a conversation I had with Don Fehr around that time. His parents lived near my house in Arizona. I would bump into him from time to time. One day I was out walking and crossed paths with him. I didn't recognize him at first, but he said hello, so we stopped to talk. We got around to talking about steroids and the conversations I was having with the doctors, and I said:

"What do we say when someday, when you and I don't have our jobs anymore, we're retired, a widow of one of these players comes to us and says you guys knew the risks and you didn't do anything about it?"

He shrugged his shoulders and said, "We just can't let you start testing. We can't do that." So there we were—facing a major problem and knowing our hands were tied. But whenever I got a chance to talk on the subject, I made it clear we wanted testing.

I'm not exactly sure when it started, but the *New York Times'* Murray Chass started referring to me as the Evangelist because I was preaching on the issue. Murray didn't mean it as a compliment, I'm sure, but that's the way I took it. And all this time the problems—along with some of the game's best players—were getting bigger.

Barry Bonds, who I still thought of as a tremendous hitter who was built like a wide receiver, was feeling overlooked. He had won the MVP award three times already. In the 1998 season he hit .303 with thirty-seven home runs, 122 RBIs, twenty-eight stolen bases, and 120 runs scored for the Giants, and he felt like nobody noticed.

Bonds finished eighth in the baseball writers' voting for MVP that season. The spotlight had been taken from him, and we would soon see the price he was willing to pay to get it back.

18

Every now and then during my tenure, things would happen to remind me of the unique role baseball plays in American life. For all the change we had weathered inside the game, sometimes there were events outside the game that reminded all of us about the power of the game. Such was the case in the aftermath of September 11, 2001.

Most of my mornings start with a one-hour workout, either at home or in the fitness room of a hotel. The routine is the same either way—stretch for seven minutes and then ride an exercise bike for fifty-three minutes.

Our quarterly meetings for September 2001 were at the Pfister Hotel, in Milwaukee. I was doing my workout before driving downtown, watching the *Today* show, as always. Suddenly, Katie Couric came in with a report of an airplane hitting one of the towers at the World Trade Center.

Wow. That's odd, I thought. I kept watching and then came the report of the second plane hitting another tower. Sue came down the stairs and asked, "What the hell is going on?"

I didn't know what to say. I was stunned. She was stunned. Everyone in America was stunned.

We kept watching the coverage and then there was a report of a plane crash in Pennsylvania and of another plane hitting the Pentagon. We watched people running down the smoky streets of New York City. The White House was being evacuated.

The president, my friend George W. Bush, was speaking at an

elementary school in Florida, but then he was whisked into the sky on the way to an underground command area. Oh, my God. What a frightening time. I still get chills when I think back on it.

It was the most surreal day of my life.

I got dressed and drove to the Pfister, where the owners had either stayed overnight or were arriving for our meetings. We just wandered around the lobby, not knowing what to do or think. We knew we needed to grasp the magnitude of what we were dealing with, as it was happening, but how could we?

One thing that became clear quickly was that we were not going to hold our meeting. That was obvious. But the owners who were in Wisconsin had no way to get home, because airports were closed.

Everybody scrambled to rent a car to get home. But the rental cars went fast and when the Mariners owners—John Ellis, Chuck Armstrong, and Kevin Mather—were unable to get one they bought a car in Milwaukee and then drove to Seattle.

As they headed out of town, I walked over to my office, just a couple of blocks away from the Pfister. My office was on the thirtieth floor, and there were people in the lobby who didn't feel safe in the tallest building in Milwaukee. People told me not to come upstairs, but I needed to be near my phones, so of course I got on the elevator and rode upstairs.

I checked on the safety of the White Sox, who were in New York to play the Yankees, and checked with our staff about all our people based in New York. I canceled our games that day, a Tuesday, which was obvious. But it was clear that it was going to be a while before we and the country got back to normal, so I canceled them through Friday, leaving open the possibility we might be back on the field Saturday. But I didn't know, of course.

This was an unprecedented tragedy. Everyone in the country

was grieving and all the focus was on the victims, their families, and the heroic efforts of the police, firefighters, EMS personnel, and other courageous people who came together to deal with this horrific attack.

At about four I called Sue and told her I was coming home. We spent the rest of the day and that night watching television. I wondered what had happened to our country, to our world. You had to wonder.

There was no real clarity the next day, just more questions. I went to the office to try to unravel what baseball could do to help, what would be appropriate. September is one of our biggest months, with playoff races getting hot, but I could barely tell you who was in first place and who was in last place as my thoughts raced.

Talking on the phone calmed me down a little bit, as it always has, for whatever reason. Clubs were in disarray, with the teams that were on the road still having trouble finding their way back home. Some had taken trains, many had rented buses and made long drives. The airways weren't going to return to normal anytime soon.

There really wasn't anything to be done on Wednesday. I was just trying to absorb the events and begin to think about a response.

I began making phone calls to other sports leaders on Thursday. I would have daily talks with NFL commissioner Paul Tagliabue as we discussed the weekend ahead. I also talked to Jim Delany, the Big Ten commissioner, and to University of Wisconsin athletic director Pat Richter. We were all facing similar questions and none of us had any answers. But I know it helped me to talk to other leaders who like me wanted to do what was best for the country.

There was one guy I could probably call that they couldn't: George W. Bush. So I called him at a number he'd given me and, almost to my surprise, he came on the phone.

Same old George, even as he dealt with the greatest crisis America had faced since 1941. I told George that I respected what he was doing for America, and that was true. I got chills when I saw him at Ground Zero, with that bullhorn in his hand. He was so strong, at least on the surface, but I couldn't imagine he wasn't at least as shaken as we all were. He was just another guy in our group when we gathered in Kohler to fight about revenue sharing; now he was in charge of responding to an unspeakable act of terrorism.

I'll admit that I thought about how there was a time he had wanted my job.

Watching him in a much bigger job, I was really glad that the times had unfolded the way they had. It was remarkable to see George out front.

I understood the pressure he was under, or at least tried to understand, and wanted to make sure any decisions I made about baseball were viewed as appropriate with our nation's response and recovery.

I told him we'd do anything he wanted us to do. He told me he'd back whatever I did.

"I know that you'll do what is thoughtful," President Bush told me.

History guides you at times like these, maybe even more when you've studied it.

I knew about the memo that FDR, my favorite president, had sent Judge Landis in January 1942, the one that's called the Green Light Letter. It's on display at Cooperstown, and I always try to find it when I'm there.

Roosevelt told Landis that he wanted the major leagues on the field for spring training in '42, even though the nation had gone to war since the Yankees beat the Dodgers in the World Series.

"I honestly feel that it would be best for the country to keep baseball going," Roosevelt wrote Landis in a letter on White House stationery. "There will be fewer people unemployed and everybody will work longer hours and harder than ever before. And that means that they ought to have a chance for recreation and for taking their minds off work even more than before."

I had gone to watch the Packers on the weekend after John F. Kennedy was assassinated, and I remember how horrible I felt being there. People just stood there when the National Anthem played. We were numb. It was a horrible feeling. I wished I hadn't gone to the game.

Upon reflection, I decided we couldn't play that weekend, even if our teams could travel to their destinations. It was just too soon. I consulted with our MLB Executive Council as well as with every owner. I was on the phone around the clock, it seemed.

I decided we should resume on Monday, and called the White House to tell them before making an announcement. I was nervous and knew that I could always announce another postponement if anything happened over the weekend to make Monday seem unrealistic or insensitive.

I was on edge all weekend, and again on Monday. All the games were night games, so I spent the longest afternoon waiting to see what baseball would look like after the national nightmare that was becoming known as 9/11.

After dinner Monday, I went upstairs at home to watch games with my eight-year-old granddaughter, Marissa. I loved watching games with her.

The games started and I was switching the channel like crazy, trying to take it all in. Of course I settled in on the game in St. Louis, as the Cardinals were hosting the Brewers.

There was the Cardinals' iconic announcer, Jack Buck, reading a poem on the air.

He had written the poem himself and was standing on the field at Busch Stadium, wearing a red jacket with an American flag lapel pin. I'll never forget the presence he gave off, almost like George W. Bush with his bullhorn.

Buck started reading his poem to the crowd in the stands and those of us watching on TV and, oh my gosh, he nailed it. An absolute home run. A great moment for baseball and for America.

The poem goes:

Since this nation was founded under God,
more than 200 years ago,
We have been the bastion of freedom,
the light that keeps the free world aglow.
We do not covet the possessions of others;
We are blessed with the bounty we share.
We have rushed to help other nations;
anything . . . anytime . . . anywhere.
War is just not our nature,
We won't start but we will end the fight.
If we are involved,
We shall be resolved,
To protect what we know is right.
We have been challenged by a cowardly foe,
Who strikes and then hides from our view.
With one voice we say,
"We have no choice today,
There is only one thing to do."

Everyone is saying the same thing and praying,
That we end these senseless moments we are living.
As our fathers did before,
We shall win this unwanted war,
And our children will enjoy the future we'll be giving.

Buck paused a few seconds after the end, then looked to the crowd.

"Should we be here tonight?" he asked.

The crowd roared, "Yes!" I don't think I needed my television to hear that crowd. I think I could have just opened my windows and heard that crowd. They stood and cheered and they just kept standing, kept cheering.

I started to cry, not for the first time in that horrible period. Marissa didn't understand.

"Why are you crying?" she asked.

How do you explain all those feelings—ones of horror and fear but also pride and hope—to an eight-year-old?

I had to wrestle with that, just as parents and grandparents around the country tried to explain the horrible, unnecessary loss of life in New York, Pennsylvania, and the Pentagon to children around America.

I probably should say around the world, really, because the world was on our side in that time period.

That night I also watched the Mets play at Shea Stadium, which had been used as a staging area for getting supplies to Ground Zero. Bobby Valentine, the Mets' manager, and his players had organized a hands-on relief effort that was exactly the right thing for Americans to be doing at that hour. I was so very proud of them. I still am.

So when Liza Minnelli sang "New York, New York" during

the seventh-inning stretch, I cried again. I'll tell you I wasn't unhappy when the Mets' hero, Mike Piazza, hit a home run to win that game, the first one played in New York after the attacks. Those were the loudest, greatest cheers any New York players ever heard, and that covers a treasure trove of baseball history.

For some reason I had the number of the great young announcer in the Buck family, Joe Buck, but not his father's phone number. So on Tuesday morning I called Joe to tell him how moved I was by his father's poem. He suggested I call and tell him myself and passed along Jack's number.

He picked up immediately when I called.

"I want you to know you made my night," I said. "I just called to say a sincere thank-you."

He told me he had written the poem at three o'clock Monday afternoon, on a piece of cardboard. He asked if I'd like to have it. You bet I would. I still have it, and I treasure it.

Jack told me that baseball would help America heal. And I know that can sound corny and like we're patting ourselves on the back, but when I look back I think he was right. Baseball played a role, even if it was a very minor role, and I'm proud we did.

I'm also proud that we were still able to complete the 162-game schedule. It took some juggling and some crossed fingers about the weather in late October and early November, but we pulled it off.

One of the major stories that season was Lou Piniella's Mariners, who were on a record pace for wins despite having just lost Alex Rodriguez to free agency. They had signed Ichiro Suzuki, a six-time batting champ from Japan, and he wound up being the American League's Rookie of the Year and MVP, collecting 242 hits and stealing fifty-six bases.

Those Mariners—the ones without A-Rod—were a throwback team to an earlier era.

They had also recently lost their ace, Randy Johnson, whom they traded before he could get to free agency because they knew they couldn't afford to keep him, yet still had a deep rotation. It was built around Freddy Garcia, whom they got from Houston in the Johnson trade, and crafty veteran Jamie Moyer, who was then thirty-eight but would pitch until he was forty-nine, just missing making it to fifty. True professional, and a great competitor.

I loved how those post–Alex Rodriguez Mariners were built by future Hall of Famer Pat Gillick but, like everyone else, I couldn't get my head around how they kept winning and winning. They seemed almost unbeatable down the stretch, with players like Mark McLemore, David Bell, and Mike Cameron making big contributions every night.

Of course, there was also a surprising home run hitter involved in that success. Bret Boone, a five-foot-ten-inch second baseman who had generally been good for about fifteen homers a season, hit thirty-seven that year and led the AL with 141 RBIs. Eyebrows were raised, as was always the case when power came from a surprising hitter, but with no testing there was no way to know one way or another.

Boone would deny suspicions about steroid use years later—in a book he wrote he said he didn't try steroids "not because I was holier than thou, but because I was scared to get caught"—but by 2001 the scandal had begun to diminish great performances.

Boone wasn't the story of the Mariners; it was about a great team effort. It was really intriguing, really exciting, and it didn't hurt my appreciation that this was only the second full season the Mariners played in Safeco Field, their gorgeous stadium with a retractable roof, a short walk from Seattle's Pike Place Market and the original Starbucks.

Now I'll make a confession that Mariners fans won't like: I was rooting for the Yankees that October more than I had since Mickey Mantle was their center fielder. You can't really root for one team over another as commissioner. I'd have sworn to my objectivity even if the Brewers were involved. But of course I had teams that I hoped would win at times, either because of the people involved or the impact on the sport.

It just seemed right to have a New York team in the postseason in 2001, even though the city was still in the early stages of digging out at the World Trade Center. We had to be sensitive to the work going on, the grieving that was still on every corner in the city, but holding a big event like the World Series would be a way of announcing publicly that New York was back in business, that the evil men in the airplanes—and the network of terrorists that sponsored them—hadn't beaten us.

Not only was the timing right but George Steinbrenner, Brian Cashman, and my old friend Joe Torre had built a Yankees team that was easy to root for. Their best players—Derek Jeter, Bernie Williams, Jorge Posada, Mariano Rivera, Mike Mussina, Roger Clemens, and Paul O'Neill—weren't just the kind of players who would be in Hall of Fame discussions one day; they were all easy to like that fall.

Torre, the kid I had watched over that one summer in Milwaukee, is just the best guy and a really good friend. He'd had chances as a manager with the Mets, Braves, and Cardinals, but he wasn't with any of those teams at the right time. He was the perfect guy in the perfect spot when the Yankees gave him another chance—much to the chagrin of the New York media and fans, who weren't sold on him as Buck Showalter's replacement—and proved that by presiding over five World Series–winning teams in an eight-year run.

This would be one of the years they didn't win, but I believe the 2001 World Series between the Yankees and the Diamondbacks— won by Arizona in the ninth inning of game 7 on Luis Gonzalez's single off Rivera—was my favorite World Series in my years as commissioner.

Curt Schilling and Randy Johnson won the first two games in Arizona, to the delight of really loud crowds in Arizona. But there was a kindness shown to the Yankees that I'd never seen outside of New York. Fans had signs supporting New York, and the Yankees got an extra loud hand when they were introduced.

America was pulling for New York, and you could tell that even in downtown Phoenix. But of course Arizona fans wanted their team to win, and they should have. You never know when you'll get another chance.

Much of my time at the start of the Series was spent coordinating and signing off on security and other logistics for the upcoming games at Yankee Stadium. We had heard from my old friend George W. Bush, who said he wanted to be there for game 3. I was so happy, but I'll admit I was a little scared, too.

How can you guarantee safety in a big public place at a time like that?

Major League Baseball worked with the Secret Service, the New York police force, and other groups to set up a coverage plan that would prevent incidents. I felt very good about the assurances I was getting, and I admired and appreciated President Bush for wanting to be there.

On the morning of game 3, Sue and I went down to Ground Zero. I'm not sure what I expected, but it was a stunning experience. We had wonderful guides, a young policewoman and a firefighter. They obviously had lost friends in the effort to save lives after the planes hit. They had to have been tired from working long hours and doing a job we couldn't even have imagined.

Yet they were resolved to get New York back to normal and were very patient letting Sue and me get our brains around all of this unnecessary heartbreak. Those two young people made us feel so proud of our country and its strength.

There was a grayness that hung over the site, the dust still in the air almost a month later. There was a smell to the site, too. Nothing really prepared you for what you were experiencing. How could it?

There were thousands of flowers and cards—photos of office workers who had ridden an elevator to work and never come down again, photos of first responders who had sacrificed their lives to try to save others. We stopped and read some of the cards and letters.

Survivors were writing to their parents and brothers and sisters, who had been here one day and were gone the next. I don't have the words to describe the love that was in those letters, the grief, too. It was one of the most emotional experiences of my life.

As we wrapped up the tour, I invited our two guides to join us at game 3 that night. I'm happy to say they accepted the offer and joined Sue and me as we saw the Yankees beat the Diamondbacks 2–1, with Scott Brosius putting the Yankees ahead and Clemens getting the win.

What a night.

I've never spent a night in a ballpark that felt as special as the night of game 3 in New York, not even watching Jackie Robinson for the first time at Wrigley Field or seeing Henry Aaron wrap up a pennant in Milwaukee. This surpassed those cherished memories.

You could feel something special was about to happen when you walked into Yankee Stadium, which was ringed by military vehicles in every direction. The police presence itself was different than anything we'd experienced, but that was the world we were living in that fall—one where it was no longer unusual to see officers with machine guns at airports and train stations, even sometimes on street corners.

The word was out that President Bush was going to participate and you could feel the tension and expectation in the ballpark. I went looking for George after I had Sue and our guests seated in our box. I found him in the batting cage, loosening up his right arm. I'm not sure if I needled him or not—hopefully I didn't, given the strain on him at that time—but I was remembering how he'd bounced his ceremonial first pitch at Miller Park that April.

Derek Jeter stopped by to say hi.

"Don't bounce it tonight, Mr. President," Jeter said. "You'll get booed."

That broke the tension, at least a little bit. I wanted George to know how much it meant to baseball to have him there, but this was bigger than baseball. Way bigger.

We knew that when he walked out from the dugout to take the mound. Yankee Stadium went nuts, absolutely nuts. The crowd started chanting.

"USA! USA! USA!"

It was terrific.

Regardless of your politics, if you had voted for President Bush or not, that vision of the president of the United States right there, in front of the whole world, while the heinous villain on the other side hid in the mountains somewhere, if that didn't make you proud to be an American, I don't know what will.

I watched from George Steinbrenner's box upstairs and got such chills that I had to hold on to something. It was overpowering.

I've watched too much baseball to believe in karma and intangibles, but there was no way the Yankees were not going to win that game 3. When Brosius got a hit to put the Yankees ahead, there was an unbelievable roar. It was the same thing when Arizona was batting in the ninth—a huge roar for every out Mariano Rivera produced. The great old ballpark just rocked and rocked.

The Yankees won all three games in New York, putting them within one victory of what would have been their fourth consecutive championship. But it wasn't a fait accompli, not with the Diamondbacks' duo of Johnson and Schilling set for the last two games.

Arizona pounded the Yankees in game 6, forcing a game 7. I'm biased, but I don't think there's anything better in sports than game 7 of the World Series. I was delighted that this great series was going the distance, but I couldn't show it the next day, a Sunday. Sue and I had Steinbrenner over to our house for lunch.

He wasn't happy. He let me have it for our guys getting the Yankees' clubhouse ready for a possible celebration once they went out on the field to start the game. He thought we'd jinxed the Yankees. That's George.

George had become a Tampa Bay Bucs fan living in Tampa. We watched the Bucs play the Packers while we had lunch. He was very quiet during that lunch, no doubt worrying about game 7.

It turned out he had something to worry about, all right. The Diamondbacks pitched both Schilling and Johnson in a game 7 that was worthy of a great World Series.

Rivera was a future Hall of Famer and arguably the greatest postseason relief pitcher there ever will be. When he retired at age forty-three, after the 2013 season, the quiet man from Panama had somehow pitched in ninety-six playoff games, including twenty-four in the World Series. He had piled up forty-two postseason saves, including eleven in the World Series.

But in game 7 he was handed a 2–1 lead in the eighth inning and it got away. The Diamondbacks scored twice in the ninth inning, when an exhausted Rivera faced six batters and retired only one of them, on a bunt.

It was a surprise ending and without question the greatest game ever played on November 4. It was a dramatic manifestation of how good baseball can be.

Had baseball solved all the world's problems? Of course not.

But had baseball helped this great country begin to heal?

I think it did, and that makes me proud.

19

Nothing I ever did in baseball would have been a success if the labor negotiations in 2002 had gone sideways. Everything I had done led to this point in time, toward getting a peacefully negotiated—if also extremely tense and contentious—labor deal. It was my most crucial work as commissioner.

I don't like to deal in hypotheticals, so don't ask me what would have happened if we had failed. But I knew that failure wasn't an option for me and the thirty clubs at that point in time. It just wasn't. We had to get a deal that would help us in every area.

And as always, we knew we'd have to do it without the support of the media. The union had great relationships with the press, especially Murray Chass of the *New York Times*. He was very influential in those years and he was no friend of owners, for whatever reason.

I had a good relationship with him, but it didn't matter. He would echo what the union said to him. He trusted them, he didn't trust us.

He would say, "The union never lies to me; the owners always lie to me." We talked a lot. We argued a lot. He had my number at home and he used it so much that Sue recognized his voice. He'd say, "Hello, Sue," and she'd say, "Hi, Murray."

One day I asked him a question.

"Murray, when did I ever lie to you? I want you to tell me."

Of course, he couldn't.

"Well, I don't mean you," he said. "I mean the owners."

I thought that was so funny. When he wanted to he'd see me as the commissioner. Other times I was just the guy from Milwaukee who owned the Brewers. Whatever fit the narrative.

Whenever we talked about being in tough financial shape, Don Fehr would say there's nothing older than owners telling you they're losing money. Except we were losing money. We were losing a lot of money, and we were piling up huge debts with the banks. Huge.

I remember asking Don how he'd like to run the Brewers franchise and compete with the Yankees. He didn't have an answer, but he'd say disparity wasn't a problem. The union didn't want us to do anything that would affect the teams that were spending the most on players. He was all in favor of disparity if the Yankees and Red Sox were winning with huge payrolls. He would tell you the industry was just fine as it was, but it was anything but fine.

In the period since our labor agreement in 1996 and these negotiations, we were losing at least $175 million a year and we were projecting to lose $500 million in 2002 because player payrolls were taking up nearly two-thirds of our total revenue.

Pete Rozelle had been so good at telling the NFL's story. We needed to get aggressive about telling our story. I got some of our people on board to go around and talk to editorial boards— Larry Lucchino, Sandy Alderson, Andy MacPhail, some others. I wanted some from big markets and some from small markets. We got some favorable editorials as a result, and more important than that, we showed that we weren't trying to hide anything.

We acknowledged that we had made mistake after mistake to get in this position, all the way back to Curt Flood and the reserve clause. We said we all knew how badly our labor history had hurt us and that all we wanted was a chance to make a mutually beneficial deal with the union. But we needed change and we needed it soon.

I borrowed another idea from Rozelle. He had always done a big interview with the press the week of the Super Bowl. It began to get bigger and bigger coverage and was very popular with the writers. I talked to my friends with the baseball writers association about finding a time to do something similar, and we agreed on the day before the All-Star Game.

That's when the writers held one of their annual meetings, and I began attending and doing a wide-open interview, every year. I loved the newspaper writers. I always had, starting with the years I'd walk into the County Stadium press box to give Bud Lea grief about the Packers. I think it was a good idea to be open to them in a setting like their All-Star Game meeting, and I do think it was productive.

I'd read *Sports Illustrated* through the years, of course, and got a kick out of when the magazine chose to write about me. Ron Fimrite had come to Milwaukee in 1979 for a story about George Bamberger, and the magazine put it on the cover. It was a thrill to read that story.

But in 2002, I was the focus of a long story in the magazine. I spent a lot of time with Frank Deford, one of my absolute favorite writers. When the story came out, I was almost afraid to read it. Just the headline scared me: suicide squeeze—bud selig has put his legacy on the line by tightening the screws on the players union. if there's a strike this season, he'll be the one to take the fall.

Well, I knew Frank was right. That was exactly the pressure I was feeling. I had spent the last decade bringing the owners together. I had studied past negotiations and tried to help the owners understand why we hadn't been successful with the union. I had worked with Rob Manfred, Frank Coonelly (initially outside counsel from Morgan, Lewis & Bockius, we hired him full-time in 1998 to assist Manfred; he would leave to become president of the Pirates), and other lawyers to try to find ways to build off the deal we had wound up with in 1996, after the horrible strike that wiped out the World Series.

Whether the press was on our side or not, we needed economic relief, we needed to address the growing disparity between clubs that was leading to problems with competitive balance, and we absolutely had to have a testing program for performance-enhancing drugs. We were the only major sport that couldn't test our players, and the integrity of our competition—and our records—was an open question.

These were crucial times for baseball, and while I rarely stepped back to look at my own situation, they were vital for me, too. Still, there was one thing I knew would not be in a new deal—a salary cap. I'd heard too many diatribes about the free market and seen how the union wanted to keep the teams with the most money—the Yankees, mainly—free to sign players for whatever amount they wanted, the rest of the teams be damned. I knew that we were never going to get a salary cap and had been explaining that to owners for years.

We had to solve our problems, but we had to be ingenious as hell in the way we did it.

One small step toward solving our problems came, once again, by pulling the levers of change that we had at our disposal that did not require help from the Players Association. A couple of years earlier, we did one such thing that would put baseball at the forefront of innovation and ahead of all the other sports—including, for once, the NFL. We tapped the power of the Internet in a major way, building a new division within MLB called Baseball Advanced Media, or BAM.

There's an obvious irony here. I'm not exactly a technological innovator myself. The truth is I still don't do anything online— not e-mails, not banking, not even setting up a DVR to record the Brewers or the Packers. I just never bothered to have a hands-on relationship with the digital world, if that's the right way to describe it. Now, my personal assistants and the staff around me? They're very technologically savvy. But I never have been, and somehow I've survived.

Maybe BAM was a makeup call for us, after we had the opportunity to buy controlling interest in ESPN in the early eighties and Bowie Kuhn passed. It was one of the best ideas we've had.

It was the result of a dinner in New York between Jerry Reinsdorf, Paul Beeston, and Bob DuPuy.

Al Gore had been in the news talking about the Internet as the information superhighway. Not many people knew what he was really talking about, including Reinsdorf, Beeston, and DuPuy, but they came to the conclusion that it had the potential to be something really big.

After that dinner, those guys came to me. They said we had to capture this.

They said that we could create a bigger pie by having the league run all the teams' Web sites instead of every team having its own. They also had the idea that however big we could grow the pie, we could cut it up equally among the teams, so it would be a form of revenue sharing. It was a brilliant concept, especially from a bunch of men who didn't understand technology.

I jumped on it, creating a committee to explore how to start it, how to staff it, and how to draw up the contractual language we needed to make it work.

Arizona's Jerry Colangelo was in that group. He and DuPuy were the guys who recommended Bob Bowman to run it for us. We had headhunters bring us some candidates with the skills to make it successful, and DuPuy was really the one who believed in Bowman. That would prove to be another great choice.

Teams each agreed to contribute one million dollars a year for four years—$120 million total—for the start-up costs. Almost everybody was enthusiastic from the start, but it took some work to get Steinbrenner and the Yankees to sign off on it.

Sue and I went to dinner with George the night before we were going to take a vote. I was studying the menu when Sue got right to business.

"So, George, how are you going to vote tomorrow?" she asked, smiling because she knew the answer was going to be good. I braced myself.

"You know, these damned socialists, they would have done well under Stalin!" George bellowed. "These little guys. . . . It's communism! Besides, Buddy, you got all those nitwits in line; what do you need me for?"

I explained to him I wouldn't do the deal if it was 29–1. I'd kill it until we could get a unanimous vote. The last thing I wanted was for Steinbrenner to sue baseball. He was always threatening to turn Roy Cohn loose on us, even after Cohn passed away.

George continued to mumble and grumble. "You can't tell me Kansas City's Internet site is as valuable as the New York Yankees'," he said.

I knew what John Fetzer would tell him, so I reminded him. "George, you've been in the game a long time," I told him. "You know that what's good for baseball will be good for the New York Yankees."

I really didn't know if I had George's vote the next day, when

Tom Ostertag, one of our longtime attorneys, began calling out each club's name. We had nothing but yes votes when we got to the Yankees.

They were normally called last because we went alphabetically, but I told Tom to move the Yankees into the middle of the vote this time because I couldn't take the suspense.

So Tom surprised everyone when he called for the Yankees vote after somebody like the Marlins or the Mariners. There was silence.

He repeated, "New. York. Yankees!"

More silence.

Then we heard this utterance, a rumbling sound, from Steinbrenner's direction. It started as a growl and it turned into an agonized concession for the good of the game. "I don't know why," George started, then changed directions. "Aw, the hell with it, I'll vote yes."

Everyone clapped. We had our 30–0 vote, and it was one of the best ones we ever took.

When I met the media that day, I said I thought this would be as important in baseball history, and sports history, as the day in 1961 when a thirty-three-year-old commissioner got the NFL to share national television revenue. But it was much bigger for us than any of us knew it would be.

Bowman grew BAM beyond our wildest imaginations. We started with Web sites, but we wound up as pioneers of streaming sports through the Internet.

Bowman found innovative tech guys who kept us at the leading edge in being able to provide live content on first computers and then tablets and phones. It made it so much easier for our fans to watch our teams play.

Once it got really established, we were so good at what we did that other people would pay us to provide the technology. HBO became one of our clients in the second year of their show *Game of Thrones*. It was so popular, HBO couldn't keep up with the demand. Its computer servers crashed because so many people were trying to access it at the same time.

Bowman's people thought they could handle it, and it turned out they could. So HBO became a huge client, and so did ESPN and many, many others. We wound up creating a new division of the company called BAM Tech. When I was no longer the commissioner, MLB would sell controlling interest in it to Disney for about $2.6 billion.

Pretty good return for an investment of $4 million per team, if you ask me.

Of course, we wouldn't reap the profit on that investment for years to come, but it demonstrated that we were willing to innovate with new ideas to try to solve problems ourselves.

Another step the owners took heading into the 2002 negotiations that would prove crucial down the line: the clubs had given me powers that no other commissioner had ever had, strengthening me for the battle ahead.

In a quarterly meeting at the Ritz-Carlton in Phoenix in January 2000, the owners approved a measure that gave me discretion to use the best interests power to address problems caused by economic disparity and competitive imbalance. I could reroute money from the central fund (television money, mostly) headed to the Yankees or Red Sox—to name two teams—and send it to the lowest-revenue teams if I deemed a situation dire enough.

You wouldn't be wrong if you said George Steinbrenner had problems with this, but George knew what we were doing and, believe it or not, had started to understand that he'd have problems if the overall picture of the sport didn't improve.

I was also given authority to fine a team as much as two million dollars and an executive five hundred thousand dollars if they weren't acting in the best interests of baseball. This was a bigger hammer than any commissioner had ever had in dealing with clubs, but I didn't plan on swinging it. I had built strong relationships so I could get the results I needed, with everyone on the same page.

This added authority strengthened the hand I had to play with the owners during the negotiations in 2002, even if I never ended up having to use it. The challenge of these negotiations was to find a variety of ways to get the changes we needed without forcing a salary cap or another heavy-handed mechanism on the union. We had to find mutually acceptable ways to attack our issues, and there was little common ground in the history of baseball labor relations. We had to find ways to create some out of the animosity and the chaos of the past.

I knew it wasn't going to be easy. That's why we started talks privately long before anybody knew we were doing so.

The 1996 agreement ran through the 2001 season, seemingly setting up talks during the season in '01. There was no doubt this was going to come down to me and my guys—Rob Manfred, Frank Coonelly, Paul Beeston, Bob DuPuy—negotiating with Donald Fehr, Gene Orza, Michael Weiner, and Steve Fehr, Donald's younger brother who was considered a calm negotiator and steadying influence.

Early in 2000, I assigned Beeston and Manfred to begin having preliminary talks with the union about the collective bargaining agreement. We didn't announce what we were doing and neither side leaked the meetings to the press. That was a great sign in and of itself. The public nature of our talks had never been good for the sport, with the union essentially authoring the narrative. I was thrilled that Paul and Rob were establishing a strong dialogue with the union out of sight of reporters. The talks quietly ran for more than a year, with Beeston building his relationship with the Fehr brothers and Orza and Manfred gaining more and more respect for Weiner.

We were using the luxury tax system that was included in the '96 deal—known as the competitive balance tax—as a starting point for these talks. But even then, even without mentioning the dreaded words *salary cap*, we were getting the familiar pushback from the union.

By June 2001, Beeston was excited by the little bit of movement we'd gotten from them. But Manfred knew this wasn't the framework for a deal that the clubs would authorize. We needed a lot more than they were offering. So I thanked Paul and Rob for what they'd been doing but told them it was time for us to try something different. Those talks were dead.

We pulled back from talks and got to work internally to try to devise ways that we could build an economic system that worked for us and was acceptable to the union. For Manfred and the staff that helped support him, the mission was clear. We had to be creative.

One of the ideas we had was to create a rule requiring clubs to generate enough cash from operations to service their debt. It's a sound principle of business—any business—and wasn't exactly a new concept to MLB. As far back as when Bowie Kuhn had been commissioner, I worked with William Williams, a co-owner of the Reds, on a finance committee that recommended a rule that required clubs to maintain assets-to-liabilities ratios of sixty/forty. We had put it in place but it had never been enforced or included in a CBA. This was the time to put financial stability rules in place, as debt in baseball was soaring. We had $2.1 billion in debt on the books in 1999, and it had grown to $3.1 billion two years later.

It was common sense to have this rule on the books—and to enforce it—but we had to convince the union we didn't intend to use it as a drag on overall salaries, just a check on any clubs that were acting irresponsibly.

We had also begun to discuss the possibility of relocating some struggling franchises—the Expos were dying on the vine in Montreal, without any hope of a new stadium to save them—or maybe even eliminating some franchises as a means of making the sport stronger as a whole. This was a concept that got labeled *contraction.*

One of Fehr's battle cries had always been that owners wanted the players to solve the owners' problems. We were showing them we were serious about taking strong steps to clean up our own house. But, yes, contraction wasn't just an issue for us. It would mean a loss of jobs for players, reversing a trend by which the industry had grown from 16 to 30 clubs since 1961. It wasn't popular with fans, either, as a bad team was a lot better for a city than no team.

Fehr seemed outraged over the talk about contraction. I'd guess his players really were alarmed about the possibility of lost jobs.

There was some thought that the union might interpret our pulling the plug on talks in June as a sign of a split within ownership. That was the farthest thing from the truth, but the clubs awarded me a three-year extension as commissioner in late November, just to make it clear that we were still planning to go full speed ahead in the talks.

This was a strong statement of support as the deal I was given in 1998 ran through July 2003. The extension would take it through July 2006. We were finally in position to give ourselves

the best chance we'd ever had at making a deal—a real deal—
with the Players Association.

In early December 2001, just before everyone headed to Boston
for the winter meetings, I invited the union leaders to Milwaukee
to talk about restarting negotiations. Beeston and I met with the
Fehr brothers—Don and Steve—and I presented an outline of
terms that would work for a short-term agreement, say two or
three years.

Because there were radical changes in the proposal, it made
sense for both sides that we put it in place and then go back and
address it after we had seen it in effect. But it was clear the union
was, as always, committed to maintaining a status quo that was
the result of dysfunctional negotiations on the owners' side allowing the pendulum to swing too far to the players' side. I can't say
I was shocked.

In mid-January, we met with the union at the Arizona Bilt-
more. While Manfred was going to head the talks—this time
with DuPuy as his second, not Beeston—I attended the meeting
so that I would have a firsthand feel for the tone of the discussions. I needed to have my finger on the pulse.

I also wanted to be available for interaction with Fehr, Orza,
and the players who accompanied them, a group that included
longtime Brewer Mark Loretta and then–Tigers first baseman
Tony Clark, a rising star in the union (he would become the first
former player to head the union after Weiner's death from cancer
in 2013). The one thing that was troubling to everyone was that
the union—at least publicly—continued to reject our notion that
teams were losing money. They would always say we were using
accounting tricks, like audited financial reports.

There were owners who felt we should lock out the players to put pressure on them. But I knew we could not take another work stoppage. I would hope everybody knew it, but there were always some who didn't seem to understand that we weren't talking about short-term damage anymore.

The All-Star Game was scheduled to be played in Milwaukee, allowing Wendy and everyone associated with the Brewers to show off Miller Park, the beautiful stadium that still had that new-car smell. You could say I wasn't shocked when there were published reports that the union was considering a boycott of the All-Star Game.

This was classic saber-rattling, and you could see it coming from a million miles away. But look: The All-Star Game largely funds the players' pension fund, and it showcases the game's greatest players. They might complain from time to time about missing out on time off over the All-Star break, but believe me, those players like to be All-Stars.

I was unhappy when I read the threats. It's not the type of publicity you would want. Instead of solving problems, this was the kind of thing the union was doing. My answer back to Don Fehr was how about working together to solve these things?

I really wasn't stressed. I had learned not to take these things too personally. It turned out I was right not to get caught up in this threat.

Talks restarted in earnest in March, with Manfred and DuPuy holding a series of meetings with the union staff in New York. Among the issues Rob was including was testing for steroids, which had to be in any deal we negotiated. We expressed that quite clearly to the union.

There were no dramatic developments until June, when owners and the union were summoned to Washington for a hearing before a Senate Commerce subcommittee. The subject, of course, was steroids.

In the years since the McGwire-Sosa home run race, speculation about players abusing steroids had only gotten louder and harder to ignore.

One of my first steps after the Steve Wilstein story linking McGwire to androstenedione had been to hold a summit of team doctors, trainers, and outside medical experts on the impact and use of steroids. We recognized the potential danger to the players and to the sport, but there was too much we really didn't know. One thing we agreed was that we needed to gather as much information as we could.

Of course, we also joined the union in commissioning the joint study on andro, but it was a slow process. Andro was already banned by other sports, but the union challenged us to show it was really a performance-enhancing drug. We waited until February 2000 to get the report back from Joel S. Finkelstein and Benjamin Z. Leder of Massachusetts General Hospital. Their findings showed that test subjects given one hundred milligrams for seven days experienced no change in testosterone levels. But those given three-hundred-milligram doses increased their testosterone levels by 34 percent.

In the aftermath, we couldn't even agree what those results meant. All the union would concede was that the study showed we should have more studies. That's what we were up against.

We were beginning to have major public relations problems and damage to the credibility of our competition, and it was coming from the players themselves. There were two sensational stories in the media in May 2002.

Ken Caminiti told *Sports Illustrated* he had been taking steroids when he won the National League MVP Award in 1996.

He estimated that half of players were using PEDs and didn't apologize for his use. "I've made a ton of mistakes," Caminiti told *SI*. "I don't think using steroids is one of them."

Jose Canseco kept getting attention, too. He told Fox Sports Net that 85 percent of players were taking steroids. "There would be no baseball left if you drug-tested everyone today," Canseco said.

These stories caught everyone's attention, including our elected representatives in Washington. For me and others in MLB, it was maddening to read them and listen to all the conversations they produced. We had kept trying to get our arms around the issue, and a lot of people—including baseball executives and many in the media—felt there were other reasons for the spike in home runs.

Call us naïve if you want—you wouldn't be wrong—but that's the truth about what was happening. Sandy Alderson, one of the smartest executives I've known, was working for Major League Baseball, and God bless him, he spent hundreds of hours in 1999 and 2000 studying all the possible factors—the balls, the bats, the smaller size of ballparks, the dilution of the pitching pool through continued expansion. We were looking for every reason in the book, including steroids, but Sandy really thought there was something to the bat and the ball.

It's likely that all of those factors played a role, of course, but in the end—because it had taken so long to get there—we had to be hit over the head with the biggest reason.

And meanwhile, records were continuing to fall. Barry Bonds had broken Mark McGwire's single-season home run record in 2001, blasting seventy-three home runs while essentially being almost impossible for pitchers to get out. He was combining artificially generated power with his best-in-the-game hitting skills, and ended the '01 season with the following stats: .328 batting average, .515 on-base percentage, and .863 slugging average.

Bonds walked 177 times, but opponents probably would have been better off if they'd intentionally walked him every time he came to the plate. He was the type of hitter that nobody could have ever imagined when his godfather, Willie Mays, or his father, Bobby Bonds, were in their primes.

Bonds always denied using steroids, but the Caminiti and Canseco stories early in the 2002 season made it tougher to believe anyone's denials.

Caminiti said that at first he'd felt guilty when he started injecting steroids in 1996, but that he "looked around, and everybody was doing it." He was playing for the Padres that season and would cross the border to Mexico to get steroids, he said, but six years later it was everywhere. Maybe it was, but by then everyone knew we wanted to get steroids out of baseball. I had implemented testing for minor league players before the 2001 season. I could do it unilaterally because they weren't protected by the union (although the most advanced minor leaguers, those on forty-man rosters, were in the union and exempt from testing). I just hadn't convinced the union to allow us to test major league players.

Minor league testing might have seemed like a small thing because these were largely eighteen- and nineteen-year-olds nobody knew and older players—some in their thirties—who were chasing a dream. These weren't the guys who were role models for children. But I was making a statement that performance-enhancing drugs have no place in baseball.

Following the Caminiti and Canseco stories, John McCain, the Arizona senator who had been a POW in Vietnam, exploded. He had voted to deregulate the supplement industry in the nineties, which now made it easier for athletes to use dangerous products, and he was angry. He called for the Senate Commerce subcommittee to hold hearings, and they were quickly scheduled.

For once I did not go to Washington. I assigned Manfred to represent Major League Baseball, while Don Fehr represented the union, at the hearing on June 18.

Manfred told the Commerce subcommittee that testing was a priority for owners in the ongoing negotiations. Every chance he got, he would emphasize that we had previously asked for testing in contract talks but had been stonewalled by the union.

Fehr told the committee exactly what he always told us—that testing was an invasion of privacy and personal freedom, that players shouldn't be subject to testing any more than anyone in any profession.

McCain asked Fehr if players understood that the credibility of their sport was at stake. Fehr replied that they didn't live in a bubble. They heard the talk in public, they understood the suspicion and the cynicism that existed with fans. Other senators jumped in, threatening action by Congress if baseball did not regulate itself. There was a lot of angry rhetoric, and Rob represented us very well. I can't say the same for Fehr on behalf of the union.

Byron Dorgan, a senator from North Dakota who chaired the subcommittee, said he didn't want baseball to become a sport where players had to use PEDs to "make it." Fehr took the exact same position he and Marvin Miller had taken with our cocaine problems in the 1980s.

"The Players Association has always believed that one should not invade the privacy of an individual without cause related to conduct merely because of his status as a baseball player," Fehr told the senators. He would not commit to even being open to testing in the ongoing negotiations.

While the hearing did little to resolve the issues of steroids, in hindsight it became something of a crucial first step in things to come. With the senators' public grilling of Fehr and his evasive, sometimes combative responses, it seemed like he and the union hierarchy were willing to protect cheaters at the expense of the honest players' reputations. I was told that a lot of players wanted to know why the union was protecting players who would use steroids or other banned substances.

In my earlier years in baseball, revenue disparity had divided owners, who could never stand together against the Players Association in negotiations. But finally we were seeing the union breaking, and that break had very little to do with us. It was all about leadership continuing to protect cheaters when a majority of players wanted a clean game and a level playing field.

I didn't know this at the time, but a segment of players had quietly been pushing for testing for years. In his book *The Game*, author Jon Pessah reported that Rick Helling, a pitcher for the Texas Rangers, had told Fehr he was underestimating the scope of the problem at the union's executive board meeting in December 1998.

"It's a bigger problem than you think," Helling said. "You don't see what the players see. There are guys feeling pressure to use drugs to keep their jobs. I think it's something we need to look into."

Fehr turned a deaf ear to that segment of players, but by 2002 more and more of them were speaking up. The union leaders had been meeting with teams when they visited New York, holding informal sessions in the afternoon before games at Yankee Stadium and Shea Stadium. Fehr would sometimes travel to meet with teams, keeping them apprised on labor talks, but it seemed that more and more he was listening while players took the floor and asked him hard questions about testing. The tone of talks continued to change after baseball's latest trip to Capitol Hill.

On July 8, the day before the All-Star Game, *USA Today* published a Gallup poll it had conducted with CNN, asking fans about steroid use. It showed 86 percent of fans supported testing for players and 80 percent felt steroids were a factor in so many of our once sacred records being broken in recent years. *USA Today* also released its own survey of players that same day, and it was devastating for the union's leaders who had been opposing testing. It showed that 79 percent favored testing. The story that ran with the survey quoted Derek Jeter, probably the most popular player in the game, saying he was in favor of testing.

I knew that was the case because of a chance encounter with Derek during one of my visits to New York. He had been there for some promotional work and then asked if he could see me. I always liked to talk to players.

He told me he was troubled that so many television and newspaper reporters had been talking about baseball being in "the steroid age." He said it wasn't fair to players who were accomplishing what they set out to do without steroids. He pointed to his Yankee teammates Bernie Williams, Jorge Posada, and Mariano Rivera, along with himself.

"We haven't done what we've done because of steroids," Jeter said that day. "It's not fair to call this the steroid age, because a lot of players are doing great things and wouldn't touch steroids."

It was one thing for Jeter to tell me in private, and another for him to say it in *USA Today,* in a piece asking his union to implement steroid testing. For the first time that I could remember, the union was advocating a position that seemed at odds with the will of the majority of its members. The union was divided and its leadership was slow to react. For the first time ever, we were the side that was united during a labor negotiation. This would prove to be a major factor as we worked to put aside our past animosity and enter into a true partnership with our players. One era was ending, and one I had envisioned was looking more and more realistic all the time. Who would have thought that would be the one real benefit for Major League Baseball from our struggle to get players to submit to testing?

Negotiations were heating up. The Players Association held a meeting near O'Hare Airport on the day before the All-Star Game, when players were working out and holding the Home Run Derby at Miller Park. Then it absolutely poured that night, an epic downpour that at an indoor-outdoor gala held at the Milwaukee Art Museum ruined gowns and hairdos that had been planned for weeks. Noah would have been proud. We had everything except an ark.

On the day of the game, Manfred and DuPuy held a meeting with Michael Weiner and Steve Fehr at the Milwaukee law office of Foley & Lardner, just down the street from the Pfister and the Marriott, where they were staying. The press didn't know about the meeting because Don Fehr and Gene Orza were at Miller Park, taking questions from reporters in a casual setting while also spending time with All-Stars.

And how did the game go, you ask?

I'm guessing you probably remember. We wound up with a 7-7 tie when I stopped play after eleven innings because the two managers, Bob Brenly and my old friend Joe Torre, had run out of players. The managers wanted to get all their players into the game, but a lot of players didn't want to do more than make a quick cameo, which illustrated a fundamental problem that had developed.

For a variety of reasons, the All-Star Game had become an afterthought for the players, hardly the way it had been through its history. We had added the Home Run Derby as an attraction for television and fans at the Metrodome in 1985, and it just kept gaining in popularity, perhaps at the expense of the game itself.

With more players traveling on their own chartered flights, it became common for starting players to grab a quick shower and head to the airport before the game had ended. The clubhouse was clearing out as quickly as the bullpens in 2002.

There were long lines of limos parked nearby, waiting to take players and their families to the airport the moment they came out of the game. We were concerned before the tie.

Years before, I remember Ron Santo calling to say he was upset about what was happening to the All-Star Game. "When I was young, we loved the game," he said. "It was an honor."

Henry Aaron had said the same thing.

"When I played, Willie, Roberto, and I played nine innings," he said. "Now guys are heading out."

I'll never forget attending the 1950 All-Star Game at Comiskey Park. Ted Williams shattered his left elbow crashing into the left-field wall to take an extra-base hit away from Ralph Kiner in the first inning but played until the top of the ninth. That's how much those guys loved the All-Star Game.

But it was so different in Milwaukee, when I was hosting as commissioner. I had first become concerned about the supply of pitching when Joe used Oakland's great starting pitcher Barry Zito for only one batter in the sixth inning. I told Sue, "I hope Joe knows what he's doing." Sandy Alderson was sitting near me and he was also getting nervous. Bobby Melvin, who had worked in the Brewers' front office and now was Brenly's bench coach in Arizona, was sitting at the end of the dugout, near us. He told me he was getting worried.

This was playing out in slow motion. You kept hoping somebody would get a big hit and end the game, but they didn't—just the opposite, actually. Shawn Green reached second base for the home team, the National League, with one out in the tenth. But Freddy Garcia struck out Andruw Jones and got Jose Hernandez to hit a grounder to Tony Batista, getting out of that jam.

In the eleventh, Omar Vizquel drew a leadoff walk from Vicente Padilla but advanced no farther (in part because Torre had emptied his bench and had to let Garcia hit for himself). The NL threatened seriously in the bottom of the eleventh, with Mike Lowell reaching second with one out. But as my insides turned, Garcia struck out Padilla (also hitting for himself, with no reserves available) and Benito Santiago.

What are you going to do? That's baseball. You almost never get the result that you want. The sportswriters call it Koppett's Law, after late *New York Times* sportswriter Len Koppett—whatever creates the greatest inconvenience for the most people must happen.

Understandably, stopping the game angered the fans. It was an ugly scene, with beer bottles flying onto the field and fans going home angry. I understood the emotion but we couldn't risk players getting hurt by having position players pitch or any of the other ideas that were floated.

I took the hit, which was okay. But the next day I got phone calls from both Joe Torre and Bob Brenly apologizing for what had happened. There was an embarrassing element to this, no question. It wasn't the way I wanted the game to play out, but I did one interview after another, taking responsibility and saying we had to make changes to the game so it didn't happen again. One thing I made sure to do was protect the managers. I wasn't going to nail Torre and Brenly. I wouldn't and I didn't.

I did get off one good line the next morning: Did the fate of Western civilization change with a tie game?

Still, I meant it when I said we could never let this happen again, and we made the game competitive again by declaring that the winner would get home-field advantage in the World Series. There's a misperception about why we made the change. People think it was the tie game. It wasn't the tie game—or at least it wasn't just the tie game. It was about the line of limos parked outside the clubhouse in the early innings as much as anything else. I hated the perception that represented, and so did our television partner, Fox, which wanted the game to be as compelling as possible.

Too many players simply didn't respect the importance of the game to our fans. They loved elements of the event, especially getting to have their children on the field in front of the dugout for the Home Run Derby, and all the parties and rewards that came with being an All-Star. But they weren't focused on the game itself, and it was showing. There were some serendipitous moments, like Pedro Martinez striking out the side at Fenway Park and forty-year-old Cal Ripken Jr. hitting a homer in his final season, but too many of the games dragged. Television ratings had dropped 33 percent in a decade, falling below 10 in 2002 from a high of 28.5 in 1970 (ratings points represent the percentage of television homes watching a show).

We weighed a series of ideas for how to revitalize the game following the Miller Park disappointment and settled on using the outcome to decide home field for the World Series. We had never had a great system for that, merely rotating between leagues on an annual basis. A lot of people ridiculed that idea, because the All-Star Game has always been an exhibition, but I was delighted watching the next year at U.S. Cellular Field in Chicago, where the leagues played a highly competitive game with managers Dusty Baker and Mike Scioscia grinding away trying to win. What's wrong with that?

We were sitting right next to the dugout in Chicago, and the atmosphere on the field was completely different than it had been in Milwaukee, night-and-day different. Players on both teams were out on the steps of the dugout, into the game, just the opposite of what it had been.

I felt like I had done something for the legacy of All-Stars from earlier eras. When I told Santo and Henry that we were going to put home-field advantage for the World Series on the game, they were thrilled.

The morning after the All-Star Game, a number of reporters visited me in my office. They were there to talk about the labor negotiations, not the eleventh-inning tie.

I was more candid than normal in these situations. I told them that debt was no longer an abstract concept for troubled teams. One, I said, might be forced out of business in the near future because it can't meet its payroll, and another could join it after the season, if we can't get a better way of doing business.

"That's it," I said. "I'm done. Major League Baseball's credit lines are at the maximum. We've done everything we can to help people by arranging credit lines. Frankly, at this point we don't have that luxury anymore. If a club can't make it, I have to let 'em go."

This was hard for me to even discuss, but teams were really hurting. I was running out of ways to use the strength of the industry to prop up franchises that weren't producing enough local revenue to build competitive teams, the kind that would put fans in the stands to grow revenue.

Teams like the Marlins and the Diamondbacks could build championship clubs through free agency but couldn't produce the revenue to keep their roster intact and sustain their success. So not even winning satisfied fans for long, because teams couldn't afford their star players. It was a sad cycle we had to break.

There were no breakthroughs in negotiations in July and early August, and we knew it was only a matter of time until the union played its usual card, setting a strike deadline. That happened on August 16, when Fehr announced that players would walk on August 30, a Friday, if we didn't have a deal.

There were still two central issues—PED testing and how a luxury tax would work. We thought we could get agreement on everything else, but these two worried me. For at least the third time in these talks, I brought in new faces to sit across the table from the union leaders. I reached out to Cubs president Andy MacPhail, a third-generation baseball man whose father, Lee MacPhail, had been the AL president (and played a central role resolving the short strike in 1985) and Peter Angelos, the Orioles owner who had historically worked well with unions.

I was in Milwaukee while talks were taking place in New York, but I'd get calls all the time and relay them to all the owners. The one guy I talked to most was Rob Manfred. I'll bet I talked to Rob twenty times a day as we went down the stretch to get a deal. Nobody was sleeping much. We were working as hard as we had ever worked to find ways to get an agreement.

One thing I liked about having Angelos involved is that he

was sort of an outsider as far as the union was concerned, but I knew he was angry. He saw where the sport was heading and was working to help. He was great. He never missed a labor session once I asked him to be involved. Neither did Andy. Those guys were great.

Andy called me one night.

"I wish you were here today," MacPhail said. "It was worth the price of admission. Angelos and Orza were screaming about steroids. They just kept getting madder and madder. Peter got right in his face. It was great. You would have loved it."

Orza and Fehr had held the line on testing as long as they could. It was becoming more and more clear that the players had seized momentum on the issue from their longtime leaders. They were telling the union executives they wanted testing, too. The players understood the risks steroids posed to the game, even if the players union was more focused on the privacy rights of players. Not all the players would have said it, but enough did that finally the union presented us with a proposal—survey testing.

The plan would work like this: We'd mutually agree on a threshold that would demonstrate steroids had become enough of a problem to require mandatory testing, then test every player anonymously and if there was enough use to reach the agreed-upon level we'd begin random testing with consequences for players who tested positive. If the survey testing showed a smaller percentage using PEDs, we'd continue to play without testing.

This wasn't what I wanted, but it was something. I knew it was a major personal concession for Don and Gene because they both knew they were going to catch hell from Marvin Miller. He was always in the wings and he remained very influential. He would say later that if he were still in charge nobody would be peeing in a bottle. He was smart, but he was out of touch with the times.

Manfred and others convinced me survey testing could work, that we would get what we wanted if we were only patient a little while longer. This wasn't overnight change; it was incremental change. But it was change, and that was huge for baseball.

We first had to argue about where to set the bar. We eventually settled on 5 percent. The union wanted the number to be higher, we wanted it to be lower, but 5 percent would prove to meet our needs.

Talks went down to the wire, the way they always do. I headed to New York for the final few days, but Manfred remained in charge, with MacPhail and Angelos playing big roles. I remember the last issue being the survey testing level required to trigger real testing, but others say it was the specifics of the luxury tax structure.

As confusing as these deals always get when it comes to crunch time, who can really say?

I do remember the last night before the strike. There was to be a day game in Chicago on Friday, the day of the deadline—Cardinals at Cubs—and the Cards had already flown there from Cincinnati. They'd be ready to play a game if we reached a deal. The Red Sox were the question. They were at home on Thursday and had a game scheduled at Cleveland on Friday.

Tony Clark, who had switched teams from the Tigers to the Red Sox, prevailed on the Boston players not to travel to Cleveland on Thursday, which had been a scheduled day off. Instead the team booked its charter for Friday morning, to take off only if we had a deal.

I didn't know which way it was going to go. Honestly, I didn't. I was hopeful, but we had our horrible history and this time we weren't going to sign off on a weakened deal that didn't address our issues. We'd done that too many times.

Late Thursday night, very late, about 3 a.m., I left MLB's headquarters to walk back to the Regency Hotel, where I was staying. I didn't know if I could sleep, but I was going to get a little rest. I walked up Park Avenue to the hotel and about the time I walked in the phone was ringing. Rob said I'd better come back.

"What the hell?" I asked.

He told me Tom Glavine, Al Leiter, and some other players had shown up in New York, and the tenor of the talks had changed. Glavine and his cohorts showed amazing common sense, the kind that had so often been lacking in negotiations. Michael Weiner had called Manfred and said they were coming over to the MLB offices. I hoped that would mean we could make a deal, and sure enough, we did.

The Red Sox got word in time to catch their flight to Cleveland, so every game that was scheduled on Friday was going to be played. It was anything but another weekend of games in baseball. It was the start of a whole new era.

20

Everyone says baseball should have acted quicker on steroids. But I stand by my position that we moved as quickly as we could have, given the complicated realities of the situation.

In the end, it didn't matter who was at fault. Our image suffered. We paid a terribly high price.

Even after we had convinced the Players Association to accept testing, the story just seemed to grow and grow. It had a life of its own, forcing us to spend years trying to control the damage that steroids and cheating players did to baseball.

It was great to know that we had the support of so many players.

In the spring of 2003, when testers came around to camps to collect samples, there were many players who wanted to refuse testing—not because they had something to hide but because a non-test counted as a positive test—and the players themselves (many of them, anyway) were hoping we'd get beyond the 5 percent threshold to trigger a full-blown program in which there was regular testing and discipline for cheaters.

One heartening story played out in the White Sox camp. Pretty much their whole team was refusing to take tests when the testers showed up. I don't know if it was Frank Thomas's influence or somebody else's, but the whole team wanted to go down as positives. I don't think the union was too happy with those guys, and after a fair amount of arm-twisting they did agree to be tested.

But the message was being sent loud and clear—baseball players, like management, wanted a clean game.

Results from the survey testing wouldn't be released until after the 2003 season. About twelve hundred players were tested—the forty-man rosters of thirty clubs—so we needed sixty positive tests to get the program we wanted.

The initial report received in November showed 104 positives, far more than we needed. There was the usual disagreement with the union about the results, but whether the total was 83, 96, or 104 it was clearly more than 5 percent, so the survey testing had worked, just as Rob Manfred said it would.

When I announced the results, I might have had my chest puffed up a little too much.

"Hopefully this will, over time, allow us to completely eradicate the use of performance-enhancing substances in baseball," I said.

Through the ensuing years, I've learned it's impossible to eradicate PEDs from sports. But we did a pretty good job limiting them. We went from being the last sport to have a testing program to having a program that even our very strong critics at the World Anti-Doping Association and the United States Anti-Doping Association say has become the best in professional sports.

None of us knew it at the time, but while we were working on survey testing, our biggest steroid scandal was about to happen, thanks to Barry Bonds and the work of a determined federal agent named Jeff Novitzky.

On September 4, two months before the survey testing results were released, the feds raided the Bay Area Laboratory Co-operative facility, near the San Francisco airport. Like you, I had never heard of it until the *San Francisco Chronicle* began reporting on the raid and the company's ties to athletes, including Bonds and other baseball players.

Suddenly BALCO became a part of the lexicon of sports

speech, even if it was an unwelcome part for so many of us. I honestly don't remember the first time I heard BALCO mentioned, but I do know that mention of a link between Bonds and steroids caught my attention.

Let me say this about Novitzky as well as the work of the *Chronicle* reporters Mark Fainaru-Wada and Lance Williams. They nailed the story. So too would T. J. Quinn of the New York *Daily News* as the story grew.

I never traveled to BALCO myself. I never met Victor Conte, the guy who ran BALCO. I never met Greg Anderson, Bonds's trainer, who was linked to the steroid regimen that was detailed clearly in the *Chronicle* and the book *Game of Shadows,* which would be released four years later. But that business and those people sure impacted my life.

That's putting it mildly. The reality is this was an ongoing nightmare for me.

So was Barry Bonds, who wasn't the most likable player I ever met.

Peter Magowan, the Giants' owner, used to call me from time to time about things involving Barry. I'd go see him, usually in spring training, when I was in Arizona anyway. Barry and I had a good relationship for a long time.

But I think Barry is one of those guys who just don't get it, who don't know when to quit. He can be his own worst enemy, in ways he never really understands.

At some point in time after the BALCO story broke, I sought out Barry for a straightforward conversation. I wanted to ask him if all the stories were true, if he had used a regimen of PEDs while he was en route to his seventy-three home runs in 2001 (by the way, the only year he ever hit more than forty-nine).

I don't know what I could have done to help Barry at that

point, but my instinct has always been to help players. So I told him that if he was cheating, he should tell me, and that I'd do the best I could to help him manage the fallout that seemed to be everywhere. He looked me in my eyes and denied everything.

While I was there in Scottsdale, we had a pleasant talk about other topics. He stopped me as I was walking away and said his godfather, Willie Mays, had told him something that surprised him. He said he had just found out Henry Aaron and I had been close friends for fifty or sixty years.

I said that was true. He said he'd been trying to get Henry on the phone but he hadn't been returning the call. There was some business deal Barry wanted to talk to Henry about.

"Oh, yeah?" I said.

He asked if I'd call Henry and ask him to take his call since I talked to him all the time anyway.

"Do you want the commissioner to help you—one individual player in a sport with thousands of players—in a business deal?"

He looked at me funny for a moment or two, and said, "I guess I do."

"Barry, the commissioner can't be a go-between in a business deal. I can't use my office and my friend to help you make money. That's not appropriate."

That was when the dealings I had with Barry turned tough. I guess he didn't like me anymore, and he was doing things that I certainly didn't like.

We were working hard to get ahead of the story on PEDs, but it was like we were running on a treadmill that just kept turning at higher and higher speeds. It never stopped. We could never catch our breath, let alone actually catch up.

With BALCO still in the headlines and Bonds in the middle of a run in which he would win the MVP Award four seasons in a row—delighting the Giants' owners but absolutely no one else in baseball—Bonds became a target for public skewering.

Representative John Sweeney, a New York Republican, authored a bill to toughen steroid legislation. He called for an asterisk to be added to all of Bonds's records.

Reggie Jackson went on an unusually candid rant talking to the *Atlanta Journal-Constitution*.

"You're going to tell me [Bonds] is a better hitter than Henry Aaron?" he asked. "Bonds hit 73 and he would have hit 100 if they would have pitched to him. I mean, come on, now. There is no way you can outperform Aaron and Ruth and Mays at that level."

Reggie was right. The math didn't add up. Our all-time greats were having their careers diminished by the soaring offensive totals. We had put a testing program in place, but it would be years before we began to undo the damage to our sport and again be perceived by the media and fans like the sports that had drawn a line on steroids earlier than we did.

McCain called another set of hearings on the subject of PEDs. He summoned officials from all across sports, including NFL commissioner Paul Tagliabue and Gene Upshaw, head of the football union, but they must have wondered why they were there. They got about as many questions as the security personnel ringing the room. This was about baseball, not the broader context of sports, and McCain was livid. He said the sport he loved was on the verge of "becoming a fraud."

I was aware he had a relationship with Don Fehr from the Olympic Committee. He'd clearly heard a lot from Don about the owners, but as this hearing played out I noticed he was really listening when I spoke about how the union had obstructed our desire to get a testing program. He didn't seem quite as friendly toward the union as he had in the past.

McCain threatened that Congress would take action that would force us to clean up baseball, whether either of us liked it or not. Then Don made a mistake. He turned the tables on Mc-Cain, pointing out how Congress had deregulated supplements, at least partially opening the door for the problems we were facing. I can't say Don was wrong, but I don't think it's smart to say that in an open session of Congress, with television cameras in the room. I wasn't going there. I did tell Senator McCain we wanted a tougher deal than we got in the 2002 labor agreement and that we were already working to strengthen it.

Baseball had been criticized by Congress through the years, with the union always wearing the white hat, but we'd finally reached a point where that wasn't the case anymore. Over the years, with the media friendlier to the union than the owners, we'd never been able to effectively wage a successful PR campaign about any of our disputes with the union. Now, because of these hearings and the union's largely indefensible position, the tables were shifting a bit. The union was feeling the pain, too, and soon enough, it showed.

After that hearing, I wrote Fehr seeking to reopen the CBA to toughen the penalties for steroids. It would take a while to pull it off, but there was momentum from the start.

Still, the bad news kept coming. We got our next black eye after the 2004 season, when the *San Francisco Chronicle* published leaked testimony to a BALCO grand jury from Jason Giambi and Bonds. Giambi admitted his use while Barry denied his, against all plausibility. He would wind up getting charged with perjury down the road, keeping the story alive far beyond when it could have been contained if he had been a little bit sorry for what he was doing.

From what I could tell, he sure wasn't sorry.

My friend President Bush issued a statement urging baseball to deal with steroids and other PEDs immediately. McCain threatened to introduce legislation. But we were working hard on this before the latest governmental nudge, and we got the union to agree to unannounced, year-round random testing and a stronger schedule of discipline.

During spring training in 2005, Congress came calling again. This time the House Government Reform Committee didn't just want Fehr and me to come talk to them. They wanted a lot of our players to interrupt their training to go to Washington for hearings, and showed how seriously they were taking it by issuing subpoenas to a number of players.

These would be the most famous of all hearings. They received enormous coverage in the press because of the players who were there—Sosa, McGwire, Rafael Palmeiro, Roger Clemens, and Curt Schilling, with Frank Thomas appearing via a tele-link from Arizona.

I was busy behind the scenes doing the best I could to contain the damage we would experience in those hearings. I worked closely with Tom Davis, a Republican from Virginia who was chairman of the committee, and Henry Waxman, a representative from California who was the ranking Democrat on the committee.

I went to see the players before the hearing. I had a great relationship with McGwire, but that day I could tell he was embarrassed. He was with his lawyer, and if he could have made himself invisible he probably would have.

The New York *Daily News* reported a steroid story on March

13, a few days before the hearings, which no doubt made Mark even more uncomfortable heading into the hearings.

FBI sources told the *Daily News*'s investigative reporters that McGwire's name had come up several times during Operation Equine, a landmark anabolic steroids investigation that had led to seventy trafficking convictions in the early 1990s.

Two dealers caught in the case named a trainer who had provided McGwire, Canseco, and others with a variety of performance-enhancing drugs, injecting McGwire at his Southern California gym on multiple occasions. It was one more black eye for baseball, and it came just as the spotlight was about to be shined on all of us. Not great.

After meeting with Davis, I approached Mark the day before the hearing. I told him I wanted to talk to him. I really did want to pass along some advice I felt might be helpful. But he told me he couldn't say anything. I knew he was in terrible shape for that hearing, and it turned out he damaged his name by being concerned about steroid use in a broad perspective but evasive about his own use of steroids.

He kept saying he wasn't there to talk about the past, which just sounded terrible. Sammy Sosa was just as bad. He suddenly forgot how to speak English. That seemed odd, since he and I had talked many times, almost always having pleasant conversations, and always in English. But this time he was lawyered up, like a criminal. It was horrible to see.

Palmeiro would come off the worst, in hindsight. He wagged his finger at Congress and said he'd never cheated, never done anything wrong.

Then, before the season was over, he'd test positive for stanoz-olol, one of the most high-powered steroids, and become only the sixth player suspended for PED use. The first was Alex Sanchez, an undersized outfielder with the Tampa Bay Devil Rays.

Like Sanchez, Palmeiro did not look like a bodybuilder. He was a ballplayer with a beautiful swing. It's true he piled up home runs in the second half of his career, but he did it with grace, not brute strength. Palmeiro would insist he'd never deliberately taken steroids. He blamed one of his Baltimore teammates for giving him a vial that he thought contained vitamin B12, not a steroid. But rules were rules, and whether you were a guy with Hall of Fame credentials, like Palmeiro (3,020 hits, 569 home runs, 1,835 RBIs), or a journeyman like Sanchez, we enforced the rules without picking and choosing who would be penalized.

Make no mistake, the hearing that discredited McGwire, Sosa, and Palmeiro wasn't a fact-finding mission. It was a shameless bit of politics, designed so politicians could show their constituents how tough they were. The demagoguery would have made Huey Long blush.

We were easy targets, and they laid into us. It probably made captivating television, but it was a nightmare for all of us involved. There were only so many times that I could say, "We would have a much tougher program if the union would agree."

That hearing displayed the game's failings on this issue for all to see. Still, there was a silver lining in my eyes. As painful as it was, we didn't run from the headlines when our star players were involved. That's one of the things that make me proud.

The hearing was also powerful for me for reasons that escaped almost everyone who wasn't in the room. There was testimony from two families that had lost young men—Rob Garibaldi and Taylor Hooton—to suicides while they were using steroids. Their parents spoke and the testimony was heartbreaking.

They wanted to be baseball players, and they looked up to major league players. I thought about how I would have felt if these young men had been my children. I so admired the parents for telling their story, but I was haunted. I got on my plane to go back to Milwaukee that night and I cried. I couldn't sleep when I crawled into my bed. So the next morning I called Don Hooton, Taylor's father.

The first time I called and identified myself, he hung up. Hopefully he thought it was a crank call.

I called again and left a message, asking him to call me at my office number. He did, and we had a good talk. I asked him to help and he said he would. He created a foundation in his son's name and has done great work speaking about the dangers of steroid use. Don Hooton created an advisory board of active big-leaguers that has helped his foundation work with major- and minor leaguers, reaching out to teenage athletes like his late son, Taylor. I'm proud that Major League Baseball has been a partner to the Hooton Foundation.

Later I would ask Don Fehr why I was concerned about the health of his union members while he wasn't. I never really got an answer.

But I got an earful from the Hall of Famers when I went to Cooperstown that July. I always loved going to induction weekend, for a lot of reasons, but my favorite part was that as commissioner I had a standing invitation to join them on Sunday night for a dinner that was exclusively for the Hall of Famers, including the newcomers who had just been honored.

You should hear the stories at those dinners. But the subject of the day in 2005—after Ryne Sandberg and Wade Boggs had been inducted—was steroids.

The Hall of Famers were outspoken on the subject, and mad.

In particular, the older players—guys like Bob Feller, George Kell, and others from an earlier era—were furious about what was happening to the game they loved.

I left Cooperstown extremely worried about our image. On the flight home to Milwaukee that night I got an idea—the next time McCain calls, I'm going to bring some guys. I knew there was going to be another hearing. He had told me that.

Sure enough, the very next morning, the phone rang.

"You won't believe this," Lori Keck said. "John McCain's on the phone, himself."

Well, that was certainly good timing, wasn't it?

We had a great conversation. I told him what the Hall of Famers had said in Cooperstown, and I asked him if I could bring five or six of them to the hearing.

"Oh, my goodness," Senator McCain said. "Can I ask who you'd bring?"

I started with Henry Aaron, who I knew would agree to go. Senator McCain respected Aaron so much, I don't think I needed to add anyone else, but I mentioned Robin Roberts, Lou Brock, and Sandberg, who had just taken a shot at steroid users in his induction speech.

He was thrilled with the idea. I asked him to listen to what the Hall of Famers said, telling him he'd see that I wasn't his problem. I told him we were busy at that time trying to toughen up the program again and were getting the usual pushback from the union.

When the hearing rolled around in September, I showed up accompanied by Aaron, Roberts, Brock, Sandberg, and Phil Niekro. We all went to an Italian restaurant for dinner the night before.

I had wanted to talk to them about what we wanted to accomplish at the hearing, but it was quickly obvious I didn't need to say anything. These men were as ready for the hearing as they'd been for the biggest games in their lives.

Henry and I walked the streets of Washington after that dinner, talking about our relationship and the unexpected roads we'd traveled since we first met when Henry was a Milwaukee Brave.

I'll never forget we stopped under this old-fashioned streetlight on one corner. Henry said to me, "Who would have believed when we met that one day I'd break the most famous record of all time and you'd be the commissioner of baseball?" We were two kids back then, twenty-three, twenty-four years old. Hank was already a hell of a player but a long way from what he became, and I didn't even have a dream about getting into baseball. We had the best kind of friendship, the kind where we could always count on each other. It was a moment I'll never forget.

Rob Manfred and Peter Angelos joined me and the group of Hall of Famers at the hearing. Henry had the committee enthralled when he spoke. I swear, it was like he was the voice of God.

Gene Orza was furious. He was so angry about having to sit apart from a group of great ballplayers, and there was an irony in Roberts being on the owners' side. He was one of the founders of the union, after all. But these times were so different than the 1960s, when the owners refused to bring baseball into the modern age. Now it was the union with its head in the sand, and these hearings went a long way toward demonstrating that.

McCain asked me what I would do, if I could.

I told him I wanted maximum penalties.

He asked Don Fehr what he'd do.

"Well, we'll take a look . . ." Don said.

I believe that was the moment where we knew we had gained the high ground.

"We're at the end of the line, Mr. Fehr," McCain said. "We're at the end of the line here. How many more Rafael Palmieros are there going to be? . . . We need an agreement and we need it soon. It's not complicated. All sports fans understand it. . . . I suggest you act, and act soon."

Other senators followed McCain, calling out the union leaders for impeding progress. It was a great day for us, a horrible one for them, and before the year was over we had a much tougher program.

I was devoting my life to this issue, and so were Rob and our other top guys. They were talking to the union directly, and the union still wasn't very helpful, not even by this point in time. Earlier that year, we had held a meeting with the union in Arizona to talk about increasing the penalties for a positive test. Rob was going to start the meeting without me, but I planned to join it later.

When I got to the hotel, it was only Rob and our people. "Where's Don?" I asked. Rob just shrugged and gestured with his hands. He'd gotten so mad, he'd left. He'd stormed out. Rob said, "Buddy, he doesn't want to talk to us anymore about it." That's how it was.

We finally got the discipline increased after the 2005 season ended. I had wanted one hundred games for a first offense, up from ten, and the union agreed to fifty. It was another huge step in the right direction.

One side benefit was that I developed a strong relationship with John McCain. I respected him as a man of principles and a great leader. He was a true American hero, and I was so sad when cancer claimed him in 2018.

We exchanged letters shortly before he died, through a mutual friend in Arizona. I told him how much I appreciated his looking at our situation in baseball with an open mind and how helpful he'd been to our process. I told him how much all of us in America had benefited from his service and his character. He was such a good man, with a real sense of integrity. His death was a huge loss.

Steroids were back in the news at the start of 2006, too. Fainaru-Wada and Williams, the two *San Francisco Chronicle* reporters who had broken all the BALCO stories, were publishing a book called *Game of Shadows,* and *Sports Illustrated* was running excerpts during spring training.

With everything we had done, we still didn't know if we had gotten our arms around the full depth of our problems. Heck, we couldn't even get our arms around Barry Bonds. We had been using Tom Carlucci, managing partner of Foley & Lardner's San Francisco office, to be our eyes and ears out there, but there was only so much he could do.

When *Game of Shadows* came out, I thought we should do our own investigation of Bonds—but not just Bonds. We couldn't target one player. We had to do a thorough, independent study that would fully investigate baseball's steroid problem. I knew we were making progress, but we were still getting killed by the press and everyone else. I finally said to myself, we don't have anything to hide, but maybe there are things we should know that we don't know. People kept accusing us of cover-ups and everything else. So, okay, let's find out. Once and for all.

It was in Phoenix in spring training. I was there with my staff—Rob, DuPuy, everybody. They all looked at me like I was crazy when I proposed it. They said don't do it—the union's going to be mad, players are going to be mad. I knew they were right about that, but I was convinced it was the right thing to do.

It was unprecedented, but we needed to do everything we could to restore our credibility, to show that we were motivated to protect the integrity of the game. I knew we could do that if we could find the right person to lead the study.

I kept telling myself that no commissioner has ever gone outside his sport to conduct an investigation like this. I understood the negatives, but it didn't bother me. The more I thought about it, the more I wanted to do it. I wanted somebody with an impeccable reputation to lead this investigation, which is why I kept coming back to George Mitchell.

He was chairman of Disney when I reached out to him. I had first met George in the late eighties or early nineties, when he was Senate majority leader. He was very close to Haywood Sullivan of the Red Sox. If I hadn't become commissioner he would have been a very serious candidate for the job. That was how highly I thought of him.

When I spoke to him about the prospect of the steroids report, I said, George, we don't have anything to hide. I need somebody to do a thorough examination. I'll turn over everything we have and so will all the clubs. They did, too, to their ever-lasting credit.

One thing George insisted on was complete independence. He wanted to hire his staff and do his work with total autonomy. He wanted free rein to follow the investigation wherever it took him. That was a given, as far as I was concerned. He was going to get no interference from the commissioner's office.

George did have a tie to baseball and personal ties to me. He was on the board of the Red Sox, and he was a friend of mine. There were some people who took umbrage at that. But George also had a good relationship with Don Fehr. They were on the U.S. Olympic Committee together. Don always told me how much he liked him, and you can't help but like him. He is a very classy man.

I said to all the clubs that George and his law partners were going to do a lot of looking, talking, examining—so the clubs should turn over anything they want. I was unaware of what they were going to find out. I didn't know what players did. We had a good idea on some, but it was just an idea.

I hired him amid protests from both sides. I knew I had done something right because both sides were mad. But I didn't really care at that point. I sure didn't care that my peers in charge of the NFL and the NBA thought I was crazy. They weren't in my shoes. I had reached a point where I didn't care what it looked like or what anybody thought.

I really don't know how much money we spent on what came to be known as the Mitchell Report, but it was a figure well into the millions. I formally commissioned the report on March 3, 2006, and he made his report December 13, 2007.

I wasn't the least bit surprised how long it took. I thought George and his people did a good job of reining it in, so to speak. They interviewed nineteen hundred people. They looked into everything. Yeah, there were some clubs that grumbled. They had to produce many, many documents. I remember talking about it once at a major league meeting. But really, the clubs were great. They indulged me.

Mitchell wound up working closely with Jeff Novitsky and the BALCO investigators. Mitchell gained access to Kirk Radomski, a former batboy and clubhouse kid of the Mets who had grown up to become a supplier of steroids to ballplayers. He had pleaded guilty to distributing steroids and money laundering and agreed to cooperate with our investigation.

That was a good break for Mitchell and a very bad one for a long list of ballplayers. They would be named in the Mitchell Report when it was released to a ballroom full of reporters at the Grand Hyatt in New York. It identified eighty-nine current and former players who were linked to steroids. The list included a guy who had the same kind of unquestionable Hall of Fame credentials as Bonds—Roger Clemens.

Radomski had told investigators about selling steroids to a trainer named Brian McNamee, who worked with Clemens when he was pitching for the Toronto Blue Jays, after he'd left Boston as a free agent, and continued to work for him after the Blue Jays traded him to the Yankees. I had been tipped off about Clemens being in the Mitchell Report two days before by Bob DuPuy, who had met with Mitchell and his staff to discuss how we would present the findings. I should have been shocked, right?

But we weren't back in 1998 anymore. There had been so much scandal already that I'm not sure I could use the word *shock*. But was I disappointed? Yeah. I was disappointed. I was sad. He had been a very good soldier for baseball, and a great pitcher. One of the best ever. But I was philosophical at that point because I meant what I'd said to Senator Mitchell: We have nothing to hide. Go do what you have to do. I wasn't going to stop anybody.

Mitchell made twenty recommendations about how baseball could improve its operation regarding PEDs, including the creation of our own investigative staff. We did that, and it wouldn't be all that long until that investigative group turned up results of its own regarding a lab known as Biogenesis, in South Florida.

While it was sad that players were still tempted to use PEDs, I felt that the Mitchell Report really helped us completely develop our protocol for dealing with cheaters. I think the report showed the public that we were going to lengths no league had gone to before.

In the years since then, you would have thought that players would be scared away from steroids, that we'd never have another scandal as bad as BALCO. They should have learned some hard lessons by the time we had our testing program up and running. But again, I was naïve.

First there was Ryan Braun, a much-beloved player in Milwaukee. This hit home, of course. While my daughter Wendy had orchestrated a sale of the Brewers to Mark Attanasio for me in 2004, I remained close to the franchise. Braun was a franchise icon. We all knew him, of course, and I'd be lying if I said I didn't like him a lot.

He was Attanasio's initial first-round pick and would win the National League MVP award in 2011, when the Brewers won the Central and reached the NL Championship Series. He was so valued by Attanasio that he handed him a five-year contract extension that season, even though he was still five years away from free agency.

An owner only does that with a player he trusts. That's why the events that transpired in the off-season of 2011–12 were stunning for me and troubling for Milwaukee fans.

Rob Manfred didn't always call me when positive results came in on a drug test, but with Braun he gave me the courtesy of a heads-up.

"Do what you have to do," I told him.

Braun had been tested after a postseason game against the Diamondbacks on Saturday, October 1. The sample was sealed and boxed according to protocol. The tester would normally send it to the lab the same day, via Federal Express. This time, however, FedEx was closed by the time the sample was ready to be sent.

The tester followed protocol, protecting the sealed sample in a cool, secure place under his care until Monday morning, when he shipped it. The test came back positive for synthetic testosterone, at a high level some reports said were unprecedented.

Ryan appealed the decision. His lawyers argued that because the cool place where the tester stored the sample over the weekend was in his home refrigerator, such handling was questionable. Even though the sealed layers showed no evidence of having been tampered with, arbitrator Shyam Das ruled in favor of Braun. It marked the first time in our program when a player's positive drug test was overturned.

Manfred vehemently disagreed with the arbitrator's judgment. That's probably not putting it strongly enough. Rob was pissed, and so was everyone at MLB.

Ryan held court in Arizona shamelessly. "It is the first step in restoring my good name and reputation," he said. "We were able to get through this because I am innocent and truth is on our side."

We'd soon find out differently, to the embarrassment of all.

Not even a year later we got blindsided with another calculated effort by players to use some of the most hard-core steroids available. The source was the Biogenesis clinic in Coral Gables, Florida, operating essentially for clients seeking help with weight loss and aging. But the operator of the clinic, Anthony Bosch, was supplying steroids to baseball players, including Braun and—oh boy—Alex Rodriguez.

Again, I was long past being shocked, but you wouldn't be wrong if you said I was horrified reading the report in the *Miami New Times,* which had gotten records from a disgruntled employee of the clinic. Clearly Braun was not the guy he'd appeared, and A-Rod had not learned his lesson, either.

One untidy bit of business from the survey testing in 2003 was that the union had failed to promptly take all the procedural steps necessary to destroy the samples and records linked to individual players. We had promised the players anonymity and, believe me, I wanted them to be anonymous. It did baseball no good for those names to get out, and it was extremely unfair to the players.

But with the BALCO investigation going full tilt at that time, the government had issued injunctions to keep the samples from being destroyed. Then it seemed like the names of players testing positive dripped out batch by batch over time, with Rodriguez, a three-time AL MVP, being named by *Sports Illustrated* in early 2009. Alex quickly arranged to do an interview with Peter Gammons on ESPN and in it came off quite contrite—a posture that was working for lots of other players.

He actually tried to shed some light on the motivation for players, saying he had used steroids only after he had left Seattle for Texas, getting that mind-boggling contract from Tom Hicks.

"I felt like I had all the weight of the world on top of me, and I needed to perform, and perform at a high level every day," Rodriguez told Gammons. "Back then, [baseball] was a different culture—it was very loose. I was young. I was stupid. I was naïve. . . . I did take a banned substance, and for that I am very sorry and deeply regretful."

Sounds good, right? But A-Rod was about as sincere as a snake-oil salesman. He was one of Bosch's best clients, along with Braun and Nelson Cruz.

For a variety of reasons, the Biogenesis investigation became very complicated. A-Rod was mad at everybody and lashing out. He would even sue the players union before everything played out.

While the union was fully on board supporting the work we were doing to promote an even playing field, individual players were being creative in their defenses. Melky Cabrera and his agents had tried to pull a fast one when he was suspended for amphetamine use. A-Rod was doing everything he could to block our work on Biogenesis.

That's why, in the end, I handed down the longest suspension I'd ever given—211 games. That was the end of the 2013 season and the entire '14 season.

Alex, who was then thirty-seven, was allowed to play while he appealed the suspension. He would eventually get arbitrator Fredric Horowitz to reduce the suspension to 162 games, but that was a hollow victory, as he was still forced to miss the entire 2014 season.

There is no question it was the right thing to do—and the only thing to do.

Suspending a player for such a long time may be one of the most painful judgments a commissioner can make. Here is a pleasant, personable human being with such enormous talent who had all the makings of being one of the greatest players in the history of baseball. Yet, regrettably, he compounded his mistakes.

It's remarkable to me that Alex not only sued MLB but also sued the Players Association. Think about that. Think of where Alex Rodriguez would have been without his union in the first place.

I believe Alex received very poor advice from people with whom he never should have associated in the first place. Alex paid his penalty, sat out the '14 season, and made a concerted effort to be a good teammate when he returned in '15, for what everyone figured would be his last season. Rodriguez did so well that season, he was back in '16, and that's a credit to his work ethic and talent. Few players could have missed a full season in their late thirties and been productive again. He did.

I harbor no anger at Alex. He made terrible mistakes that cost him his good name. His mistakes cost his teammates and his franchise even more success. I'm sad about that, and for him.

I also respect how prepared he was when he began his second career as a broadcaster in 2017. He rehabbed his image in ways guys like Bonds, Clemens, and Sosa never could. He did some TV work for Fox, mostly working a studio in the postseason, but ESPN named him to its highly successful Sunday Night Baseball booth in 2018.

Alex Rodriguez, Ryan Braun, and the other stars who hurt their names also hurt their innocent teammates. There were so many players who privately wanted tougher penalties and more testing, but most of them were nervous about talking publicly.

When history looks back on this period, I hope there will be a full understanding that many of our players—including some of baseball's biggest stars—were not involved in illegalities and were not enmeshed in scandal.

In retrospect, there was a real shift in the dynamics of dealing with the union after we got the labor deal in 2002, which included the first provisions for testing. One part of that was a change in the leadership of the union, as Rob Manfred had forged a terrific relationship with Michael Weiner, who in 2009 replaced Don Fehr as executive director.

But it was also true that union leadership miscalculated how strongly—and for how long—to fight against testing. It became out of step with its membership, just as so many of baseball's commissioners and their labor lawyers had been out of step with the needs and desires of major league owners.

There were a total of forty-four PED and amphetamine suspensions on my watch by the time I retired as commissioner in 2015. It's fitting the list includes one (reliever J. C. Romero) for the substance that really started us on this journey, androstenedione. Senator Mitchell advised us against suspending players whose use was revealed by his report; otherwise the list would have been longer.

Bonds was never suspended. Ditto Clemens, Jason Giambi, Jose Canseco, Lenny Dykstra, Andy Pettitte, Gary Sheffield, Kevin Brown, Juan Gonzalez, and dozens of other well-known players who were linked by the Mitchell investigation to banned substances, including human growth hormone (which we began doing in-season blood testing to detect in 2013).

I wouldn't have minded hitting those players with suspensions. I felt strongly that what they had done was an affront to baseball. But Senator Mitchell, Rob Manfred, and others persuaded me that it would be sufficient punishment merely to identify the players who had cut corners and beat the system.

When you look at how poorly Bonds, Clemens, Palmeiro, Ramirez, McGwire, and Sosa have done in Hall of Fame voting conducted by the baseball writers, it's clear that damage to their reputations wasn't a small price for them to pay.

By the way, I agree with the writers. I do not believe players who are known to have used steroids should go into the Hall of Fame. I hear the argument about there being others already in the Hall who aren't necessarily of the highest character, and I'll grant you that's true. I also understand it's impossible for voters to know who did and who didn't do anything.

Suspicion isn't enough to keep a player out. Who can honestly say about players from this era? But when we do know that a player used steroids to make himself a better player, making it easier for him to compete against his peers, we shouldn't ignore it.

The integrity of the game is serious. Those players who took PEDs hurt the game. I don't see how anyone can argue the other side on this one.

21

While we continued to deal with the fallout from the steroid issue, I had many good days after the 2002 labor deal. It served all the purposes that I hoped it would, making life better for teams that had been hurting financially and showing fans they could trust us to be responsible stewards of their interest.

It was a huge development to negotiate a deal without a work stoppage—something that hadn't happened since the Players Association was established. We set a foundation to peacefully negotiate the next three labor agreements, more often working with the union instead of constantly being in conflict with the players.

With our labor issues no longer center stage every year, we began to grow baseball in ways we had never been able to before. We had finally become true partners with the players, which opened doors that we couldn't have opened by ourselves.

This was a vision I'd had for decades, not years. It was so rewarding to see it play out.

One of the best examples was the World Baseball Classic.

It makes so much sense to have an event where players represent their nations, as soccer players do in the World Cup. Baseball may not quite be the same kind of global game, but it has grown internationally in a major way, especially in Asia and Latin America.

More and more major leaguers have come from the Dominican Republic, Venezuela, Puerto Rico, Cuba, and even Japan and Canada during my time in baseball. The passion for baseball in these places is apparent when you watch the game played in those countries.

It was a natural for us to tap into, and we did.

We began discussing our desire to hold a baseball version of the World Cup shortly after the ink dried on the 2002 agreement. But this event was different than any others we had ever held. It was a 50/50 partnership with the Players Association, and that was true from the planning stages.

We knew we needed a dramatic event, and the union helped us create one. I'll give Gene Orza credit. The union was very cooperative. Our guys were great, but Gene was great working with our people. We couldn't have gotten this done without labor peace.

We held the first WBC in 2006, with teams representing sixteen countries, including Cuba. It took a lot of work to coordinate the Cubans' appearance in the event, but it would have weakened it a lot if they weren't there. The Cubans had been a huge power in international tournaments, and lots of people thought they'd be tough to beat in this one, especially the Cubans themselves.

That first year we played WBC games in Tokyo, Puerto Rico, Arizona, Florida, and two different sites in California, Angel Stadium in Anaheim and Petco Park in San Diego. We've played the event three other times since then (2009, '13, and '17) and gone to South Korea, Taiwan, Mexico, and Canada.

We've seen so many great stories. The first year of the WBC we had an all-Asian semifinal in San Diego between Japan and South Korea, and the enthusiasm of the crowds was unbelievable. Japan beat Cuba in the championship game, and the atmosphere at Petco Park was electric.

I wish I had been at Marlins Park for a first-round pool in 2017 because I would have loved it. The Dominican Republic team was there, and their fans might be unparalleled in terms of making noise. They beat a United States team managed by Jim Leyland. It was such great theater—exactly as we thought it could be when the event was just a vision.

We invited sixteen teams for the first two events but added a qualifying round in 2013, and that provided a pathway for Spain, Brazil, Israel, and Colombia to get teams into the tournament. Nine other countries have fielded teams that haven't yet qualified for the tournament. That list reads like roll call at the United Nations— Pakistan, Nicaragua, Germany, the Czech Republic, the United Kingdom, France, New Zealand, Thailand, and the Philippines.

If I had to pick one country that I've most enjoyed watching, I'd probably say the Netherlands. Its WBC teams are a fascinating mix of veterans from its own thriving league, which has been around since the 1920s, and professionals from its Caribbean island territories, especially Curaçao.

The Dutch pulled off one of the greatest upsets in the WBC in 2009, eliminating a powerful team from the Dominican Republic. The catcher on that team was Kenley Jansen, who would become the Dodgers' closer in the next decade. The 2017 Netherlands team went all the way to the semifinals before losing to Puerto Rico.

One of the best things about the WBC is that it allows our fans their first look at international players who will find their way to the major leagues, like Jansen. That was certainly true for Japan's Daisuke Matsuzaka, a pitcher who was MVP of the first two WBCs. The list of others includes Aroldis Chapman, Jose Abreu, Yoenis Céspedes, and Kenta Maeda.

I think the WBC has great significance. It took our game to places it had never been, and that will be more true as the game goes on. It's a dramatic manifestation of what we're trying to do internationally.

People always ask why we can't send major leaguers to the Olympics. We've sent teams of minor leaguers, but from a pragmatic standpoint it doesn't work with major leaguers.

What could we do? Just stop playing in August? Tell our fans we'll see you in three or four weeks? I don't think so. And there's no way we could keep playing while many of our best players are representing their Olympic teams. We'd have serious integrity issues. You'd be punishing teams for having the players that the Olympic team wants. From a matter of sheer pragmatism, it's not possible.

We spent a lot of time studying different ways to do the WBC and never found a way that worked better than holding it in March, when teams are in spring training. There's always some pushback from major league teams that worry about players being hurt, but to me that's silly. Players get hurt in spring training games, too. Players have always gotten hurt.

It's not surprising the WBC is more popular internationally than with our fans here. We knew it would be a harder sell in the United States because we have so much baseball here when the season starts and fans are accustomed to rooting for teams like the Dodgers, Yankees, and Red Sox, not their national team.

It was great for the event when Leyland's U.S. team won the championship in 2017, beating Puerto Rico at Dodger Stadium. One of the great plays that season was made in the second-round pool, when Adam Jones sailed over the center-field fence at Petco Park to take a home run away from Manny Machado (his Orioles teammate, playing for the Dominican Republic) in a game that sent the U.S. to Dodger Stadium for championship-round games against Japan and Puerto Rico.

Leyland was great. He was as nervous as he'd ever been managing the Tigers or the Pirates, maybe even more nervous, if that's possible. He was chain-smoking and sweating out every detail and, in the end, as proud of his WBC gold medal as anything he'd achieved in baseball. The only thing he had on the line was his pride, but he'd tell you representing his country was the ultimate. I was really proud of him and that U.S. team.

There's no doubt in my mind the WBC is going to grow in a major way in future years. It shows what happens when baseball's management truly works side by side with players. We just had to stop fighting each other and work for the same goals. It's so rewarding to see how productive the relationship can be.

Pete Rose is never far from the minds of the media and baseball fans. The question of whether he might one day be reinstated from the permanently banned list was one of the constants in my years as commissioner.

No one takes any pleasure in seeing a guy who was a great player limit himself with a seemingly never-ending run of bad judgment. Pete is never far from a microphone, either, so he's made a cottage industry not just out of being the Hit King but also of criticizing me and everyone else in baseball. It's sad.

When Rose was suspended, Bart Giamatti left provisions for him to apply for reinstatement. The commissioner is judge and jury in that process, so I've always had Rose's backers trying to persuade me to his side, saying he's paid a high enough price for ignoring the cardinal rule of not betting on baseball.

The first time I was ever in a major league clubhouse was in May 1958, and I can still remember that right by the door was a huge sign, signed by Ford C. Frick. It said if you gamble you're suspended for life. You grew up understanding that was a no-no.

Most people understand. Even when I've been in Cincinnati,

there were more people than you'd think who understood. But some people say he bet on his team to win, what's wrong with that?

What about the days he didn't? Did he try as hard to win those games as the games he bet on? You can't rationalize that kind of behavior. If we lose our integrity we have nothing left, and I knew that.

People said I wasn't open to reinstating Rose because I was so close to Bart. Well, I was close to Bart. Close enough to remember Bart telling Pete to reconfigure his life.

Has he ever reconfigured his life? I'll ask you.

Rose knew I was close to Robin Yount, so after I took over for Fay Vincent he was always calling Robin to ask him if he could help him with me. But it was another group of Hall of Famers who tried the hardest to help Rose.

Mike Schmidt, Joe Morgan, and Johnny Bench were all former teammates of Pete's and at least somewhat sympathetic to him. They asked if they could bring him to Milwaukee to meet with me. Of course they could.

I didn't feel any pressure from them when they came to Milwaukee in December 2002. They were his teammates. They just felt they wanted to bring him and I was to make my own judgment.

Schmidt seemed the most interested in helping Pete, based on my conversations with him. Morgan felt sorry for Pete and wanted to help him. I had the idea that Bench could barely be in a room with him, but this time he came along as a favor to Schmidt as much as anything.

They got to my office and those three guys were dressed beautifully. Then there was Pete, and he wasn't dressed well at all. He was wearing one of those sweatsuits you'd always see him in, looking like he was about to go to the gym, not an important meeting.

We talked, all of us, and then the other three left the room. It was just Pete and me.

He told me how unfair his suspension was. He was very nice, not nasty. He was trying to put his best foot forward. I explained my position, and he kept telling me how close I was to Bart. Well, I was, but that was irrelevant at this point.

Then he told me he never gambled on baseball. Remember, I had read the Dowd report, which contained betting slips with his name on them. Now he was telling me a different story, not to be confused with the facts. It was a full denial.

Huh? Not even his best friends thought he was really rail-roaded out of baseball. He was just a compulsive liar, his own worst enemy.

I didn't like his presentation, so it sure didn't make me more inclined to let him back into baseball. As it turns out, things he later admitted to he didn't admit to that day. I always had the uncomfortable feeling that whatever you did with Pete, the truth would ultimately come out and you'd be embarrassed.

That was the only time I met with Pete as commissioner. I was never close to reinstating him. Some people thought I was at different points in time, but that's not right.

I'll admit I was annoyed when Rose released a book on the same day that Paul Molitor and Dennis Eckersley were elected into the Hall of Fame by the baseball writers. That book contained the first admissions from Pete that he had bet on baseball—not very long after he'd denied it to my face. The Rose story stole headlines from Molitor and Eckersley, who deserved the spotlight.

What a bad sense of timing. That wasn't real smart. But look, he wasn't going to get reinstated either way.

He was a great player, make no mistake about it. He gave you everything he had, obviously. There was a reason they called him Charlie Hustle. I had great respect for him as a player.

But baseball is a social institution. It brings certain responsibilities for those who work in it, and Rose didn't fulfill those responsibilities. He thrilled us as a player but then he hurt the game.

Bart was right. It was a stain on baseball.

Strong ownership is essential to the success of all professional sports, so it is not only appropriate but imperative for a commissioner to try to facilitate the best possible transfer of franchises. I had seen for myself the impact of weak and erratic owners and likewise the difference that can be made when the right person owns a team.

Through my years in charge, I was personally involved in most of the ownership transfers in baseball, to one degree or another. Sometimes a commissioner has to be very creative to save a team. That's how Peter Ueberroth used Jerry Reinsdorf and the ownership committee to get George W. Bush involved in baseball. Eddie Chiles couldn't find an acceptable buyer for the Rangers, so Reinsdorf worked hard to combine several smaller groups into one strong group, bringing together Rusty Rose, Tom Schieffer, Roland Betts, Richard Rainwater, and Bush, who then was known only as one of President George H. W. Bush's sons. The success of the Rangers deep in the heart of football country is rooted in the ownership group Reinsdorf put together in the late-eighties.

I helped usher Drayton McLane into baseball in 1993. His family had been in trucking and had gotten itself a pretty good contract. It handled the shipping for Walmart. Drayton became close to Sam Walton, and in 1990 essentially sold his trucking business for stock in Walmart. He bought the Astros from John McMullen, who had purchased the team from its founder, Judge Roy Hofheinz, in 1979.

McLane was a strong owner. He got things done in Houston, including the construction of a new downtown stadium, now known as Minute Maid Park. It was a huge boost to that long-neglected area, which now is home to a gigantic civic center and the Houston Rockets' arena. Drayton also guided the Astros to their first pennant, in 2005, which brought him great pride.

Through Drayton I got to know David Glass, another top Walmart executive. He would purchase a downtrodden Royals franchise from the estate of Ewing Kauffman in 2000 and patiently lead it to back-to-back World Series in 2014 and '15, with the Royals losing a dramatic seven-game series to the Giants and then beating the Mets to trigger a parade that was one of the most joyous days ever for Kansas City. The Royals weren't much when Glass took over. They had been a model franchise in the eighties but lost that luster when future Hall of Famer John Schuerholz was lured to Atlanta in 1990. Glass was committed to building a winner and in the end did it the right way, with scouting and player development.

One of the most controversial ownership situations I resolved was also one of the best decisions I ever made, even if it is still a sore subject to fans in Montreal. I loved Charles Bronfman, who owned the Expos when I got into baseball. But it was a bad sign for the future of the franchise when he decided he couldn't operate the team during baseball's economic downturn.

The Expos had produced great young players in large batches, including future Hall of Famers Andre Dawson, Tim Raines, Vladimir Guerrero, and Gary Carter. They had exciting teams but reached a point where their revenues wouldn't allow management to keep the teams together, and a late-season fade in 1989 broke Charles's heart.

He had long wanted some help from Montreal's government in getting a new ballpark to replace Olympic Stadium, which had outlived its usefulness, and it wasn't forthcoming. So Charles threw in the towel, putting the team up for sale. No one stepped up in Montreal, but Bronfman wouldn't sell to interests looking to purchase the team and relocate it to American cities. Instead he turned the team over to one of his partners, Claude Brochu, and his group of investors. They eventually sold the franchise to New York art dealer Jeffrey Loria in 1999.

A couple of years later Loria would play into a three-headed solution that I put together to help revitalize one of our most valuable franchises, the Red Sox. The team had been in the Yawkey family since 1933, when thirty-three-year-old Tom Yawkey purchased it. He owned it until he died in 1976, and then it passed to his wife, Jean. She was in charge until her death in February 1992, at which time it began to be managed by their estate, with John Harrington the point man. John and I developed a running conversation about his need to put together a sale of the club, as the estate couldn't hold it forever. This was a huge story in New England, and lots of potential ownership groups were floated by Dan Shaughnessy and others in the Boston media. The sale was complicated by the bulk of the revenue from the sale going to charity, not the estate itself, which brought the state's attorney general into the proceedings and heightened public scrutiny.

This wasn't just the franchise being sold. It was also Fenway Park and 80 percent of the New England Sports Network—not that many of the new groups were interested in Fenway. They felt it was dilapidated and looked to join baseball's building boom with a new stadium.

The only group that told me it was committed to preserving Fenway Park was headed by a longtime friend of mine, Tom Werner, who had owned the Padres from 1990 through '94. His group included Larry Lucchino, who had been the visionary behind Camden Yards and had a keen sense of baseball history, understanding the intrinsic value of a cathedral like Fenway.

Werner and Lucchino had been on different sides in Kohler, when we held our ugly battle over revenue sharing, and understood how the game was changing. They were an intriguing partnership in the early stages of a process in which a lot of people were expressing interest in the team but few of them actually had the resources to make it work. But I felt Boston needed a truly powerful ownership group, especially given the stadium work it would face, which was why I did something nobody saw coming.

I orchestrated one of the greatest triple plays in baseball history.

In November 2001, I allowed John Henry, who owned the struggling Florida Marlins, to become the lead investor in the Werner-Lucchino group. That put the process into overdrive, and on December 20 we announced the following: the Red Sox were being sold to the Henry-Werner-Lucchino group; Loria was essentially exchanging his ownership position in the Expos for one with the Marlins; and Major League Baseball was taking over the Expos, with the possibility that they'd soon become the first team to relocate since the Washington Senators moved to Texas in 1972.

It really was impossible for the Expos to stay in business without a new stadium, and there were no reasons to be hopeful we'd solve that problem. In the meantime, we'd do the best we could in Montreal, hiring Omar Minaya to be the general manager and Frank Robinson as manager.

They were both great for the three seasons we operated in Montreal before we moved the team to Washington for the 2006 season, while we were in the final stages of negotiations that would lead to the team being sold to Ted Lerner for $450 million.

Major League Baseball had suffered through ten franchise shifts from 1953 through '72, but this was the only one during my tenure. I'm asked how I could allow this to happen given my feelings when the Braves left Milwaukee. Well, there's an enormous difference. The Braves could have stayed in Milwaukee. We had put together an ownership group that could have purchased the team, and we had a workable stadium in place. The Braves' ownership was simply looking for greener pastures. This was the opposite situation.

We looked for viable solutions in Montreal and couldn't find them. There was no stadium and no ownership group. Moving was our last option, and it brought none of us joy to eventually use it.

On the other hand, I was thrilled to have Henry and Werner in charge of the Red Sox, in large part because they understood firsthand the difficulties that small-market teams face. I also knew Lucchino would work hard to put the luster back on Fenway Park, and he did. He utilized the imagination of Janet Marie Smith, who had played a huge role in executing Larry's vision for Camden Yards. I certainly wouldn't have ever pictured putting seats on top of the Green Monster in left field, but they did it, and it is a wonderful addition to the park.

Shaughnessy, who is a lifelong friend of mine, screamed in the *Boston Globe* that the Red Sox sale was "a bag job" that screwed worthy prospective buyers who were local. I favor local ownership. I always have. But in this case the creative solution, the one I engineered, was the right one.

Henry's group poured more than $280 million of its money

into improving Fenway and continues to give Boston a run of historic teams. John tried to hire Billy Beane away from the Oakland A's to be his first general manager but couldn't convince him to leave the West Coast. That probably turned out for the best, as his second choice was Theo Epstein, a Brookline native who was only twenty-eight when he took over the team he had followed passionately. Theo is one of my favorite executives in the game. He's incredibly bright, but he's also a great people person. He really treats everyone well, including players and low-level staffers. His love for the game can't be questioned, and he's one of the hardest workers anywhere.

Under Epstein, the Red Sox broke the so-called Curse of the Bambino in 2004, winning the World Series for the first time since 1918. They did it even though they hadn't won the division. That Red Sox team won ninety-eight games but finished behind the Yankees, qualifying for the postseason as a wild card team.

They were one of six wild card teams to win the World Series in an eighteen-year stretch between 1997 (Marlins) and 2014 (Giants). It's funny, looking back, how much criticism I received from Bob Costas and other purists when I expanded the postseason beyond four teams. The competition created by the fight for wild card spots has changed the late-season dynamic in baseball, exactly as I hoped it would.

Commissioners are supposed to be unbiased, I know, but I'll admit I was happy when the Red Sox pulled off their incredibly dramatic escape in the '04 AL Championship Series, somehow beating the Yankees after being on the verge of being swept.

This was great, high-wire baseball, with one of our best rivalries thrown in for no extra cost. Terry Francona was brilliant as the Red Sox manager, as were players like Pedro Martinez and David Ortiz. It was good for almost everybody not living in

St. Louis when the Red Sox swept the Cardinals in the World Series, and it's been healthy for the sport that the Sox have just continued winning, with titles in 2007, 2013, and 2018.

A similar renaissance took place with the Cubs after they were sold. Sam Zell had purchased the Tribune Company, whose holdings included the long-suffering (but tremendously popular) Cubs, and he didn't want to be in the baseball business. We went through a thorough, methodical process that led us to what would eventually be an $845 million sale to Tom Ricketts, a longtime Cub fan who had met his wife in the Wrigley Field bleachers while he was in grad school at Northwestern.

There had been talk that this would be a billion-dollar transaction, but nobody was complaining about the final price. The Tribune Company had purchased the team from the Wrigley family for $20.5 million in 1981.

Names of other potential buyers popped up along the way, of course, including Dallas Mavericks owner Mark Cuban. He told newspapers he was interested, but when I asked Zell he said he wasn't a serious factor. The only other strong group that emerged was one headed by John Canning, a former partner of mine in the Brewers, but in the end Ricketts was the choice.

Like Henry, Werner, and Lucchino in Boston, the Ricketts family was committed to improving Wrigley Field. I believe the condition of the old ballpark scared off a lot of investors, but Tom saw possibilities where others saw trouble. He poured money into the park, and both it and the neighborhood around it are looking better than ever. That makes me proud.

I'm also proud Tom Ricketts considers me a mentor to him. I certainly tried. He is one of those wise people who are smart enough to know what they don't know, and was willing to take advantage of the short commute between Chicago and Milwaukee to see me a lot after he purchased the team. We spent a long time talking about how to run a franchise as well as the right way to view the sport. He probably got tired of me telling him John Fetzer stories, but he never asked me to knock it off.

Tom moved slowly in everything he did after purchasing the team, and I really respected that. He didn't have the impulsiveness that so many new owners do, and I believe that worked for him in major ways. He had inherited Jim Hendry, a good baseball man, as his GM and left him in place for two seasons before deciding it was time to bring in a new general manager to execute his vision of a complete rebuild.

The Cubs' drought was even longer than the Red Sox drought, dating back to 1908. But there was a feeling Chicago fans wouldn't stand for a rebuild, so the Cubs were constantly patching things up by signing free agents or trading prospects for veterans. It was a cycle that had led them nowhere, and Ricketts recognized it. He was bold enough to seek a change.

His timing lined up perfectly with Epstein's timing leaving Boston, and I got involved to help him hire Theo.

It's hard to imagine the Red Sox could allow Epstein to leave, but there was tremendous tension between ownership and the front office after the run of championships began, and it boiled to the surface in 2011, when a September collapse caused the Sox to miss the postseason. Francona and the Sox had a mutual parting of the ways and Theo seemed ready to leave, too. But he had one year left on his contract, and the Sox ownership group wouldn't let him leave without compensation.

The Red Sox might have been able to keep Epstein by giving him the title of president of baseball operations and letting him report directly to Henry, but that was a nonstarter, killing any chance at a contract extension. Ricketts received permission to talk to Epstein, but the Red Sox were being difficult about letting Epstein out of his deal. They wanted to receive some of the Cubs' top prospects as compensation.

Talks were stalled, going nowhere, so I gave the teams a weekend to work out a deal. Ricketts was prepared to wait a year on Epstein if necessary, but that would have been a horrible year for everyone. It was pointless. Both teams needed to get on with their futures. I finally persuaded Henry, Werner, and Lucchino to do what was good for baseball, which was for Theo to come to Chicago. They agreed to a deal that involved some minor compensation, and Ricketts had his man.

Theo was thrilled and so thankful. He wanted to come to Milwaukee to thank me in person, but I told him it wasn't necessary. He had more important things to do, and wouldn't you know he got right to work and did a wonderful job?

The Cubs endured 101 losses in 2012, their first with a hundred losses since 1966, but by 2015 they had become a perennial postseason team. They recovered from a three-games-to-one deficit to beat Cleveland in the 2016 World Series, winning game 7 in ten dramatic innings, after the best rain delay in their history.

An estimated five million people attended the Cubs' parade and celebration in Chicago, and championship merchandise sales shattered records. I was so happy for Tom Ricketts and the baseball fans in Chicago. Wrigley Field hasn't just been preserved but has become a place for joyous gatherings, which is exactly what a ballpark should always be.

22

One of t h e lessons I learned from my father was that something is only good or bad in comparison to something else. That was one of his favorite sayings.

Major League Baseball was always being compared to the NFL, and it never really seemed fair to me. I think Bowie Kuhn had it right about baseball always being held to a higher standard. Sometimes it seems like we never get credit for doing things right even when we are doing really good work.

Our work in getting a strong policy to limit the use of performance-enhancing drugs by our players is a prime example. We have the toughest testing program in sports, and we had to go through hell to get it. You can ask all the experts, reporters who cover steroid issues, like ESPN's T. J. Quinn, or even the guys at the World Anti-Doping Association.

After the 1998 home run race exposed the steroid issue for baseball, I began meeting annually with team doctors and the professional athletic trainers working for clubs. I love those guys and really looked forward to those meetings. Every time we met, they would ask me why steroids weren't a bigger issue for the NFL. We used to sit there and get killed by the media and fans, and then Paul Tagliabue, the NFL commissioner, and Gene Upshaw, head of the football union, would say they had a great drug program and everybody believed them. End of story.

Despite all the issues with brain injuries, despite teams moving around willy-nilly, and despite a steroid policy that has far fewer teeth to it than the one in baseball, the NFL still can't do much wrong with the public. If it sounds like I'm jealous, I'm really not.

The problem with PEDs is a broad one, impacting all sports. But really the only times anyone seems to care is when a baseball player or Olympic athlete tests positive.

Look at how many chances the public was willing to give Lance Armstrong. There are probably still some people who believe he got railroaded, even though there's no question he built his career by getting around the testing rules as long as he could.

Bowie was right. Baseball is held to a higher standard. That's fine with me, too.

Our game is better. We should be held to a higher standard, even when it stings.

Our drug testing program isn't the only place where we've passed the NFL and become the industry standard. I'm also very proud of the replay system we put in place, although I will admit it took a long time to convince me we should let technology override umpires and the human element that has made baseball so intriguing.

I always worried about disturbing the game. Older fans remember the confrontations that managers like Billy Martin, Earl Weaver, and Leo Durocher had with umpires. Crowds enjoyed it, I think, except maybe when it was a big call that went against their team. The umpires didn't enjoy that. Bill Haller certainly didn't with Earl, as you may remember.

But I always wind up with a smile on my face when I watch the tape of Weaver and Haller going back and forth after Haller called a balk on Mike Flanagan. I wasn't sure I wanted to eliminate that drama—and sometimes comedic relief—from the game, especially when I watched what was happening in the NFL.

The NFL first experimented with instant replay in 1976, put it in for the '86 season, and killed it in '91. Owners didn't approve it again until the '99 season. I didn't want that to happen in baseball. We weren't going to jump into it until we knew we had a system that would work.

Shortly after the NFL first implemented replay, Peter Ueberroth was getting pressure to use television cameras to help umpires on tough calls. He never seriously considered it.

"The umpires making split-second decisions is part of the flavor of the game," Ueberroth said. "We don't want to lose that flavor. You can make a dish so bland that it's not worth sitting down at the table."

I was worried about that, too, but at some point MLB's technology became so advanced, it seemed wrong to continue to put all the responsibility for calls on umpires, who are never going to be perfect. Don Denkinger made a famous mistake in the 1985 World Series that hung over him for the rest of his career. Rich Garcia, like Denkinger an excellent umpire with a great track record, was in the right spot on the field but still made the wrong call when a twelve-year-old Yankee fan named Jeffrey Maier reached over the fence to grab a long fly from Derek Jeter, with the Orioles' Tony Tarasco waiting to catch it.

It was getting harder and harder to know if balls were home runs, in part because of the way ballparks were being built, each with its own unique lines. Brad Ausmus hit a homer in the 2005 National League Championship Series that banged off the left-field wall, just above a yellow line, but in an area of Minute Maid Park that's a real patchwork quilt. Umps got the call right, I think, but no one could blame them if they had missed it.

No longer could we go with the spirit of Hall of Fame umpire Bill Klem. He was once shown a newspaper photo of a blown call and replied, "Gentlemen, he was out because I said he was out."

We decided it was time to use replay but only in a limited way, on home run calls—whether it was fair or foul, whether the ball cleared the boundary. That was all I was willing to do initially. We experimented with it late in the 2008 season and then put it in play for the postseason and beyond, and it was a success.

It was about this time that I created a fourteen-man committee for on-field matters to study ways that we could improve the game. I included some of the best managers in the game on that committee, with active managers Tony La Russa, Jim Leyland, and Mike Scioscia joining Joe Torre and Frank Robinson, and they took the job very seriously. All of the managers were in favor of expanding replay to consider calls on the bases and catches in the outfield. Tony was especially passionate and, eventually, persuasive. I didn't lead those guys to their recommendation; they overcame my resistance to change.

I was a willing listener. Tony was really the one who kept after me. The more we would talk, the more I would like it. That's where our expanded replay came from.

I don't think this was responsible for anything we did, but I remember being really impacted by the game in 2010 when Jim Joyce, a great umpire, missed a call that cost the Tigers' Armando Galarraga a perfect game. That was both a horrible moment and a great one at the same time. Everybody involved handled the situation so beautifully, especially Joyce and Galarraga. They even got together to write a book about it a few years later.

I like Joyce. He's a nice guy. I knew he felt so bad about that call. He told me so himself the next time I saw him. I'm sure he would have liked to have replay. The umpires have been great about it. There might have been a few who resented it at the start, but I think everybody understands what we were doing when we expanded it for the 2014 season, giving managers their own challenges.

I remember that first April we put it in place. I had spent the weekend in Phoenix and was coming back to Milwaukee. I walked into my house at about seven o'clock and the phone was ringing. I debated whether to answer it, but I did. It was Tony. He said, "Did you see the games today?"

He said there were at least five or six instances where replay really worked well. He was so happy because he had been the one, more than anyone else, who helped me finally pull the trigger. With all the changes I made, I wasn't sure about this one. I guess my conservative instincts took over. I give that committee credit. They were really for it.

Now there's talk about using cameras to call balls and strikes, with an electronic eye. I know exactly how that could work because my wife Sue watches a lot of tennis. I see how quick and accurate those reviews are. But I can't imagine taking the discretion away from a home plate umpire. There's still something to be said for the human element. It just wouldn't be right if they were buzzing the umpire's left ear for a strike and right ear for a ball, or however it would work.

I can't see it. But there was a time when I couldn't see instant replay at all, and now it's not only a part of the game but it's working very well.

The business grew healthier with each passing year following the labor deal of 2002. We continued to grow the game, not simply facing one crisis after another, and everyone involved in the major leagues benefited.

Both attendance and revenue grew on an annual basis and so did player salaries, rising from an average of about $2.3 million in 2002 to a little more than $3.8 million in 2014, my last season as commissioner.

That's more than 65 percent growth, remarkable in any such stretch but truly stunning when you consider America suffered through a financial crisis that led to a major recession from December 2007 through the summer of 2009. It was the worst economic downturn since the Great Depression, and while it impacted many owners and almost all of our fans, it only slowed down our growth a little.

Derek Jeter and Albert Pujols, two of my favorite players, seemed to turn in strong work every season. We always had great story lines, like the brilliance of Ichiro Suzuki, a six-time batting champ in Japan before he arrived as both Rookie of the Year and MVP for the 2001 Mariners; Josh Hamilton gaining control over his personal demons to lead the Rangers to back-to-back World Series; and the resurgence of the Cardinals under Tony La Russa. Mike Trout hit .220 when he got to the Angels in 2011 but then turned into a modern Joe DiMaggio the next season. He hasn't slowed down yet, bless him.

Joe Torre and George Steinbrenner thrived in a partnership that lasted twelve seasons, with the Yankees winning four championships and six American League pennants. The Yankees would win the World Series again in 2009 under Joe Girardi, with the rivalry between them and the Red Sox hotter than ever, but there was more competitive balance and late-season drama in baseball than in any period in history.

Twelve different teams had won a championship in the last eighteen years through 2018, when the Red Sox won their fourth in fifteen seasons, and twenty-six of the thirty had gone to the postseason within the last eight years. All thirty teams played postseason baseball from 1992 through 2018, with twenty-two reaching the World Series.

This was the kind of competitive balance that I dreamed of when I sat through those horrific meetings over revenue sharing in Kohler, Wisconsin. It was a far cry from the sport I had grown up with, when the Yankees won fourteen of sixteen pennants and nine championships from 1949 through '64.

In fact, we had more drama on one day in 2011 than in most of those seasons when the Yankees were dominating.

If I had to pick the wildest day of my tenure, I might go to September 28, 2011, when the 162nd game of the season decided two wild card races. It would make the short list for sure.

Four of the fifteen games played that day were essentially win-or-go-home affairs, and an improbable comeback by the Rays over the Yankees—they scored six runs in the eighth, tied the game with a homer by Dan Johnson in the ninth, and finally won in the twelfth—knocked the Red Sox out of the playoffs. The Phillies, meanwhile, were busy gutting the Braves in thirteen innings, which allowed the Cardinals to slip into the postseason.

La Russa's team would have been eliminated if Chris Carpenter hadn't won in Houston that day but somehow wound up holding a World Series parade through the streets of St. Louis.

The Rangers had been set to celebrate a championship in six games, which would have brought redemption from a loss to the Giants in the 2010 Series, but Nelson Cruz allowed a ninth-inning drive by David Freese to get over his head. Hamilton gave Texas another lead with a tenth-inning home run, but the Cardinals tied the game in the tenth and won in the eleventh, setting up the decisive—and anticlimactic—game 7.

We expanded the playoffs the following November, adding a second wild card team in each league. If you didn't win your division, you'd have to beat the other wild card team to reach the division series, guaranteeing the postseason would begin with must-win games.

It can be a cruel format—just ask the Pirates, who were beaten by the Cubs' Jake Arrieta in 2015 and the Giants' Madison Bumgarner in '16—but it really rewards the teams that win divisions, giving them something to play for in September when there are two or more strong teams in the same division.

Owners noticed how smoothly things were running. I had been given a three-year contract when I was formally named commissioner in 1998, and had three more years added on to that deal in November 2001, when we were positioning ourselves for the historic labor negotiations that would conclude the next summer. That deal was due to run out in 2006, but in August 2004, the owners persuaded me to stay for three more years, through 2009.

Fred Wilpon of the Mets paid me a great compliment that day.

"I have been in baseball nearly twenty-five years, and in that time I have never known anyone more dedicated and more devoted to the game than Bud Selig," Wilpon said. "Baseball is in great shape today because of Buddy."

Revenues had grown to $4.1 billion when that first extension was announced, an increase of more than 156 percent since I stepped in for Fay Vincent in 1992, and would keep growing. I would receive two more extensions as commissioner, with the final one being announced in January 2012, after a unanimous 30–0 vote. It ran through the 2014 season, meaning I would be on the job until after my eightieth birthday.

No one believes me, but I really did mean it when I told Sue I'd have the job for only a few months, then go back to being the owner of the Milwaukee Brewers. But I arrived with a job to do and I committed myself to getting the job done. The owners appreciated the difference I was making for them, especially those like Jerry Reinsdorf who were baseball historians. They understood how I'd changed the nature of the position and how much better off baseball was with the model that I'd ultimately hand over to Rob Manfred.

At that meeting in St. Louis in 1998, I told the owners to judge me on the value of their franchises. It's fair to say they did all right while I was in charge.

Nothing speaks to that dynamic more strongly than the strange chapter we experienced with the Dodgers under Frank McCourt, who shouldn't have been allowed to buy the team in the first place.

The O'Malley family had owned the Dodgers since Walter O'Malley bought a controlling interest in the then-Brooklyn Dodgers in 1950. Like so many other valued ownership groups, the family decided to get out of the baseball business after our long run of failed labor deals, including the strike that caused us to end the 1994 season in August. When the O'Malleys sold the Dodgers in early '98, they got $311 million from Rupert Murdoch's Fox Group, at the time the most anyone had ever paid for a sports team. But Murdoch decided to sell the team himself only six years later and no one in Los Angeles stepped up to buy it.

I was shocked by the lack of interest. I didn't know why a franchise based at Dodger Stadium, with the iconic Vin Scully calling games, wasn't viewed as being more attractive. I've never figured it out. But the one person who was really banging the drum to get the team was Frank McCourt, a Boston businessman who had tried unsuccessfully to get the Red Sox from the Yawkey estate. He was into commercial real estate, especially parking lots, and we had a lot of questions about the kind of owner he'd make.

Bob Daly was running the Dodgers for Murdoch, and I really

liked Bob. He was very good with everything he did in baseball. I wasn't happy when Murdoch decided he wanted out and he didn't want the process to drag out. We had been doing business with Fox for national telecasts since 1996, and the relationship had worked well for both sides.

McCourt offered Murdoch $371 million for the team, Dodger Stadium, and the Vero Beach spring training facilities. Bob Daly implored me to take the deal because Fox wanted to sell. I can't say I knew McCourt, but I knew his name and his reputation. We approved the sale in 2004, as much as a favor to Fox ownership as anything, and we hoped for the best.

Big mistake.

A few years later, McCourt wound up in bankruptcy, which you would have thought would have hurt his leverage, especially with a franchise that hadn't had interested buyers come forward in the recent past. Rob Manfred and I wound up taking a couple of trips to Delaware to meet with the bankruptcy judge there, as we worked to unravel this mess.

Then one night, right before we were anticipating holding an auction for the team, the most surprising thing happened. I got a call from McCourt saying he was selling the club to Mark Walter and Guggenheim Partners for $2.15 billion. Magic Johnson was in the new ownership group, which would be run by my old friend Stan Kasten, who had been Ted Turner's guy in Atlanta and helped the Nationals gain footing in Washington.

I almost dropped the phone. I may have asked Frank to repeat the price he was getting for the team. I was floored, like everyone else who heard it.

In the end, we've probably never had an owner who did better for himself in baseball than McCourt, whose own performance was more like that of a ham-fisted shortstop who couldn't hit the fastball than a perennial All-Star. He didn't just become the first owner to sell a baseball team for a billion dollars. He went straight to two billion dollars, partly on the strength of their local television rights. The sale closed in 2012, and the next year the Dodgers did a deal with Time Warner Cable that is valued at $8.35 billion over twenty-five years—or $334 million per year.

That's not a great thing for disparity, as it is more revenue than many of our teams produce in a year, but it said a lot for the health of a game that I often described as a nightmare when I stepped in.

There was some gnashing of teeth in the front offices of National League teams about this windfall, which could heavily impact the Dodgers' rivals in the NL West. But in terms of our corporate bottom line, you wouldn't be wrong if you said there were twenty-nine other owners who were finally happy with something McCourt did.

23

There are times you'll never forget if you live to be a hundred. Conversations, too.

I had one of those talks with John Schuerholz on a Monday in December 2016, at the Gaylord National Harbor Hotel, outside of Washington, D.C.

I'd known John forever, maybe a little longer than forever. He had cut his teeth as a farm director and, while I was operating the Brewers and then moving into the commissioner's office, he built two baseball powerhouses, first with the Royals in the 1980s and then with the Greg Maddux–John Smoltz–Tom Glavine Braves in Atlanta in the nineties and beyond.

He served as chairman on my fourteen-person committee for on-field matters. We talked all the time on the phone and enjoyed each other's company when we got together.

But we'd never had a day or a conversation like this one. The day before we had found out that we had been elected to the Major League Baseball Hall of Fame by a sixteen-person panel of Hall of Fame players, executives, writers, and broadcasters.

It takes more than a day for something like that to sink in when it happens to you. Trust me. I'll never forget the talk we had when he and I were alone. I think we were both still in shock. I started to roll off the names of iconic ballplayers and legends who had long ago gone into the Hall of Fame in Cooperstown.

"Babe Ruth . . . Lou Gehrig . . . Joe DiMaggio . . . Ted Williams . . . Henry Aaron . . . Mickey Mantle . . . Willie Mays . . .

Jackie Robinson . . . Branch Rickey," I said, pausing for a long while before I completed my thought.

"And you and me, John?"

We both just laughed and probably cried a little bit, too. It was really hard to comprehend that I'd been elected to Cooperstown. I'm sure it was for John, too.

When you're a kid, you could not even have conceived of this honor. There will never be any doubt that being a baseball Hall of Famer is the greatest honor of my life.

We had traveled to the site of the winter meetings for a press conference with Jane Forbes Clark and Jeff Idelson of the Hall. I believe I flew, but I'm not sure I needed an airplane.

The phone calls that came in were wonderful. Hank Aaron called. Paul Molitor called. Many, many friends called, including guys like Herb Kohl and my other brothers at Pi Lambda Phi, whom I had known practically forever.

I thought back to the early years, after I'd replaced Fay Vincent and was trying to get baseball's ownership on even footing with the players union while dealing with the initially baffling, then persistent issues with steroids and other performance-enhancing drugs. I thought of that horrible day when I stepped in front of television cameras at County Stadium to announce there wasn't going to be a 1994 World Series.

Everything I did was controversial. I took daily poundings in the press and was ridiculed and mocked by Donald Fehr, Gene Orza, and Marvin Miller. It was brutal.

Who could have ever dreamed I was going to end up in the Hall of Fame?

But I persisted and wound up serving almost seventeen years as commissioner and leading baseball for twenty-three overall. These were pivotal years for the sport, and I moved it forward with clear eyes, an open mind, and a willingness to make personal sacrifices for the good of the game.

Yet me in the Hall of Fame? It stretched my imagination almost as much as it did those who had minimized me when I was getting started, who had asked what a small-town guy was doing with so much responsibility.

While players are first reviewed by ten-year members of the Baseball Writers Association of America (BBWAA), with 75 percent approval required for elections, there are a variety of paths to the Hall of Fame. The rules are adjusted from time to time to find ways to make the best judgments, but one thing never changes—it is really, really hard to get inducted.

That's the way it should be, too.

Voters are often criticized over the deserving candidates who haven't yet been elected. Everybody has their short list of guys they'd like to see in. Mine starts with Ted Simmons, the catcher who was so great for the Cardinals and the Brewers, but it is understandable why opinions are so split.

In my view, the Hall of Fame is another way in which baseball is superior to other sports. They all honor the greats in their game, but it's how you define *great* that makes the difference. It seems like there are ten or twelve NFL players elected every summer and almost as many for basketball's Hall.

I'm not knocking them, but I want to be honest. There are few automatics with baseball's Hall of Fame. I was nervous about whether I would make the cut.

The only path for executives is with what used to be called the Veterans Committee. That group has been overhauled into a trio of committees that vote by era. I was included on a ballot for the Today's Game committee, along with Schuerholz and eight others (George Steinbrenner, Lou Piniella, Harold Baines, Will

Clark, Albert Belle, Orel Hershiser, Mark McGwire, and Davey Johnson).

A sixteen-person panel met over a weekend in Washington, D.C., debating the merits of the ten candidates. It is a really thoughtful way to consider executives, umpires, and players who have been passed over by the BBWAA.

I knew it would take twelve votes for me to be elected, with word coming down on Sunday, December 4. My family gathered together in Milwaukee to await the vote.

I had been told that Jane Forbes Clark, the chairperson of the Hall, would call sometime between 4:15 in the afternoon, Milwaukee time, and 4:45 p.m. if I had been elected. I had been through the process as commissioner for almost twenty-three years, so I knew the drill.

While I was the commissioner, I'd always get the courtesy of receiving the first call from Jane. She'd call me to tell me who had gotten in before she'd notify those who had been elected. But now I was in a completely different position. It was an agonizing wait, as I'd heard from so many others.

I didn't have to wait too long, but I'll admit that when the phone didn't ring at 4:15 I began to think it might not be my time. I think it was 4:17 when it rang, and Jane was on the other end of the line.

"You've been elected to the Hall of Fame on the first ballot," Jane said. "Congratulations."

Talk about achieving something beyond your wildest dreams. This was that for me.

Adding to my excitement, the BBWAA elected a large class that year. When results of the writers' voting was announced in early January, Ivan Rodriguez was elected in his first time on the ballot and both Tim Raines and Jeff Bagwell got beyond 75 percent after slow climbs upward in voting.

Suddenly Schuerholtz and I were in a five-person class, which was great. I was more than happy to share my excitement—and my nervousness—with these men.

Abner Doubleday was a two-star general in the Union army in the Civil War, amazingly enough fighting at both Fort Sumter and Gettysburg. But that's not what he's known for, of course. He's been widely believed to have played a major role in inventing baseball in a cow pasture outside Cooperstown, New York, in 1839.

Some baseball historians consider this a myth, however, pointing to Alexander Cartwright of the New York Knickerbocker Base Ball Club or even a handful of others. It's a point of unending debate, like the designated hitter rule. But credit Stephen C. Clark for bringing the baseball world to Doubleday country in upstate New York.

The fabulous Otesaga Resort Hotel was opened by the Clark family in 1909, along the banks of Lake Otsego, which really is as pretty as a picture. Business dropped off during the Great Depression, and Clark settled on Cooperstown's ties to Doubleday and baseball as a way to bring people to the sleepy village.

Clark founded the Baseball Hall of Fame and Museum in 1936, inducting the first class of Hall of Famers in 1939, after completing construction on the building. It was an instant success, with some of baseball's legends making the long trip by train and automobile to be honored. That eleven-man group included Babe Ruth, Ty Cobb, Walter Johnson, and Cy Young.

Believe me, I was just as thrilled as any of them when induction day came on July 30, 2017. I had been to Cooperstown dozens of times before, enjoying every trip. That included one about three months before the induction.

I was invited up for an orientation visit, with the Hall of Fame staff walking me through what I could expect in July. I also met with reporters that day, and a writer from a local paper reminded me that in the past I had been booed by fans who wanted Pete Rose in the Hall. He asked if I thought I'd get booed this time by the Montreal fans there to honor Raines.

I told him that it was certainly possible. If it happened, it would be the result of having to make tough decisions. We had exhausted all options before moving the Expos to Washington, D.C., and in the time since, Montreal had yet to fix its stadium problem or identify a strong ownership group there. Having seen the Braves move from Milwaukee to Atlanta, I certainly understood the fans' pain.

But I was determined that baseball would make progress under my leadership, and the franchise's move to Washington had worked well for the sport. It would be great for Montreal to eventually get a second chance, as we got in Milwaukee, but we never really had a chance to consider one on my watch.

While I was on that orientation visit, I took part in a tradition that most visitors to the Hall never know about. I was shown where my plaque would hang and then given a Sharpie to sign the wall. My autograph is now buried forever beneath the plaque.

Every moment of that orientation visit brought me pure joy. It was the best day I'd ever had in Cooperstown, and I knew it would be nothing compared to the upcoming weekend in July.

I was nervous when induction weekend arrived. How could

I not be? I spent forever writing my speech, ultimately going through thirty-two different drafts.

The ending was always the same. I went with words that had come to me when I was honored at the New York writers' dinner in January 2015, the evening of my last night as commissioner. The New York chapter of the Baseball Writers Association of America presented me with their William J. Slocum Award for long and meritorious service.

That was almost as emotional for me as the day in Cooperstown. I had a prepared speech, but at the end I ad-libbed a finish that came to me as I stood at the podium.

"What you've seen in my career is the story of a little boy's dreams that came true," I said.

That was really the best way I could put it, and I knew I'd said it well when Sandy Koufax came over to me afterward and said I had brought tears to his eyes. He was a hero of mine, of course, but we shared the same love for baseball. That's what is so great about all the Hall of Famers.

They care about the game the same way I care about the game. It was so great to be in the company of Henry Aaron, Frank Robinson, Koufax, and all the greats that weekend.

There was a Hall of Fame party for us on Friday night, which was wonderful. All of the returning Hall of Famers were there, along with writers who had won the Spink Award and broadcasters who had won the Frick Award. That meant Bob Uecker was there, which always makes a room better.

Robin Yount came over to talk. "When we met in 1974, who could have imagined that Bob Uecker, you, and me would be in the Hall of Fame together?" he said, and he got very emotional. I never see him when I don't think about that night in 1982 at County Stadium, when he chased me out into the concourse to tell me he was playing the game no matter what the doctors and trainers said.

Remember what he said? He said he was playing because that's what ballplayers do. Well, these Hall of Famers were cut from the same cloth as Robin.

Henry, my friend of nearly sixty years, was there. He had been more nervous than I was about whether I would get in. Frank Robinson, whom I had known for more than forty years and who had been with me through much of my commissionership, was there. It was a great night and a great feeling.

On Saturday night, the Braves and Brewers got together to throw a party for John Schuerholz and me. That was great, but there were times I was almost overwhelmed. The whole experience was beginning to hit me.

I slept well Saturday night—I've never had a problem sleeping—and was excited when I got up. It was a gorgeous day in upstate New York and, as a bonus, it was my eighty-third birthday. I'd never received a gift like this.

I wasn't alone much that day, but when I was, my thoughts turned to my mother and father and all the people who had helped me along the way. I knew I would mention John Fetzer, Carl Pohlad, and George Steinbrenner in my speech, but I felt bad that I couldn't mention everyone. How could I? I had gone through three or four generations of baseball people. I trust they all know how important they are to me.

If I got booed while I was giving my speech, well, I certainly didn't hear it.

I can remember the surreal feeling I got when Jeff Idelson read the wording on my plaque to the large crowd gathered on that warm, sunny day:

"Commissioner from 1992–2015, the first seven years in acting

capacity before formally named by unanimous vote of all 30 owners in 1998. Presided over an era of vast change to the game on the field while extending its breadth and depth off it. Fostered an unprecedented stretch of labor peace, introduced three-division play and expanded the postseason. Under his leadership, umpiring was centralized and replay review was established. Celebrated the National Pastime's pioneering diversity by universally retiring Jackie Robinson's No. 42. Bridge-builder and devoted fan who returned baseball to Milwaukee before serving as second-longest tenured commissioner."

That plaque is going to hang in Cooperstown long after I'm around to visit it. That's the most humbling part of the honor.

When I made that trip to Ford School in the summer of 1958, I was a kid getting started in business with a passion for baseball. I was blessed to meet Carlos Nelson, who would introduce me to Don McMahon and Frank Torre after we had traveled together from Detroit back to Milwaukee. Who knows how my life would have turned out if not for those serendipitous events?

No one who watched me try to hit a curveball would have ever guessed I'd leave a lasting legacy on baseball. But that's where my life led me, and I couldn't be any more satisfied and proud how it turned out.

As an owner, an acting commissioner, and then commissioner, I always tried to think about the good of the game, not just my own interests. John Fetzer taught me that lesson early on, and I never forgot it.

EPILOGUE

These days, I'm more or less back to being where I was when my lifelong love affair with baseball began. I'm one of the biggest fans of the game anywhere.

I still work for Major League Baseball, having accepted the job of Commissioner Emeritus in 2015, when Rob Manfred became baseball's tenth commissioner. I moved out of my thirtieth-floor office and into one that might even be nicer, in an adjacent building. I still spend time on the phone with league officials and some owners, but now that I'm no longer the commissioner, I'm not under nearly the same stress.

I can openly root for the Brewers again, which was a lot of fun when first-time manager Craig Counsell guided them to game 7 of the National League Championship Series. Craig grew up near me, in Whitefish Bay, along the banks of Lake Michigan, and I've known him since he was a boy.

His father, John, worked in marketing for me when I owned the Brewers. He even took Craig to St. Louis for the 1982 World Series.

Until the 2018 season, I had never met Christian Yelich, who would win an MVP award after David Stearns, the Brewers' young general manager, traded for him. But I loved watching him play and discovering he's just as nice off the field as he is terrific on it. Sue wore a Yelich jersey proudly during October, as big a baseball fan as she ever was, and we entertained both Robin Yount and Bill Bartholomay in our box.

It was great to see how Bill was received. He had been a villain when he moved the Braves to Atlanta, but I told him I could re-hab his image here. He's a really good man and has been a valued friend of mine for more than forty years. It shows that it is short-sighted to hold grudges.

I loved the way it felt to let my emotions show during the postseason—not that I'd ever been very good at hiding them.

You should have seen me after the *New York Times* published this massive story about how strikeouts are ruining baseball. Some of the facts are indisputable but the conclusions the story reached were wrong.

Hitters have changed, with more of them swinging for the fences than ever, concerned with things like launch angle and exit velocity instead of choking up on the bat and making contact (although some of the smarter hitters—Anthony Rizzo and Joey Votto, to name two—do still choke up like the old-timers).

There was a record total of strikeouts in 2018—41,207, with 153 players striking out at least a hundred times. Henry Aaron never struck out a hundred times, but that was another era.

The most troubling fact about all the strikeouts is that for the first time in history big-leaguers produced more strikeouts than base hits (41,018). There was definitely something to write about, but I was disappointed the story tied the trend to a slight decline in attendance.

Here's the thing—attendance has been down across the board in pro sports. Even the NFL has experienced a decline as more and more fans choose the experience of watching at home. We'd rather have them in the stadium, for sure, but baseball continues to produce record revenue (as does the NFL).

But this story suggested baseball is somehow in trouble. I've read that nonsense since 1958, since Ollie Kuechle used to write it in Milwaukee. I have read that for sixty years—the game is dying, it's too slow, the next generation won't love it like older ones, and now this—there are too many strikeouts.

I've been hearing it's too slow since I was a young man, and the issue is usually raised by people who are looking for things they can criticize. When I watch games every night, the drama is good. Fans are into it. The people in the stands are having a great time.

I know people hold baseball to a higher standard than other sports, as Bowie Kuhn said, but I don't understand how people can keep making the same mistake. They either don't study history, don't understand history, or just want to fall for a sensational story.

People are mad about strikeouts, this and that. What about the drama during the season, with all these teams fighting for the playoffs? There were two games played on the Monday after the end of the season to break division ties, for goodness sake. Watching the Brewers overtake the Cubs and hold off the Cardinals, I can assure you things were tense.

I was reading this *New York Times* piece in my office, then thinking about it, and I remembered what my dad had told me back in the sixties.

"Buddy, what do you care about bringing a baseball team here?" he asked me. "The sport is dying."

Well, why doesn't somebody walk out on Wisconsin Avenue, in downtown Milwaukee, and count how many people are walking around in Brewers jerseys? Dying? It's the opposite, really. Baseball is thriving.

I'm thankful for so many things, including my health. I lost my brother Jerry to lymphoma in 2010 and survived a scare of my own with melanoma in 2004.

I'll never forget the day I was diagnosed. I went in for my annual physical on election day. We did the full checkup, and the doctor referred me to a see a dermatologist about a splotch on my forehead. The dermatologist did tests, and that Friday I was in the office on the phone with Rob, bitching as always about Steinbrenner and money probably, and I'm told the dermatologist is on the phone and it's urgent.

He told me I had a Grade IV melanoma, a very serious skin cancer. That night, Wendy's on the computer. So are Sari, Lisa, Sue. They're all looking this up and getting a lot of misinformation. I'm concerned, I'll tell you that. I was in shock. I figured I didn't have much time left. I thought about the things I had been worrying about, like payrolls. I started thinking, "I ought to live my life a little."

On Saturday I took all five of my granddaughters shopping, followed by lunch at McDonald's. We were really living. But after I dropped the last one off, I sat in my car and cried. I'm not ashamed to say that. I was really scared.

But I was treated by great doctors at Memorial Sloan Kettering Cancer Center in New York. It took three and a half hours in surgery and lots of follow-up treatment, but I recovered to return to my life.

The positive from this is I've become very involved with the Stand Up To Cancer program, which MLB promotes during the World Series every year. Sue and Jerry Reinsdorf set up a meeting with a number of women who were very prominent in the Hollywood film industry on a visit to Los Angeles for Dennis Gilbert's benefit for scouts. They wanted to pitch me about an organization that would pull together cancer research from institutions around the world. They called it the Manhattan Project of cancer research.

Sue knew this was something we needed to support, and so did I. That is how Major League Baseball, with a pledge of $10 million, became the inaugural donor for Stand Up To Cancer. We continue to maintain a close and active relationship. I mean it when I say baseball is a social institution with important social responsibilities. I'm very proud of the work we've done through Stand Up To Cancer.

When I was named commissioner in 1998, I put the Brewers into a trust to be run by Wendy. I could not be seen as being partial toward one team, of course, and I worked very hard to make sure there was no bias toward my city or the franchise that I had built. I so feared that criticism that I bent over backward.

The stadium issue was the primary one for Wendy, of course, and once we were in Miller Park in 2001 the franchise was flourishing.

Wendy was running the Brewers the way I did in the early days, trying to build a winner from scouting and player development, and with the help of a wise general manager, Doug Melvin, she laid the groundwork for teams that would go to the postseason.

But in 2004, shortly before I had to deal with melanoma surgery, Wendy and I decided the time was right to sell the team. It was a difficult decision that was made a lot easier after we got to know the prospective buyer, Mark Attanasio.

Mark has a brilliant mind and, just as important, a kind heart. He is quiet, humble, and understated—values that resonate in a midwestern city such as Milwaukee. He brought a family attitude with him, having his proud father sing the national anthem at Miller Park several times. He not only made the transition graceful and seamless; he has gone on to treat my family and me better than I could have imagined.

We had purchased the team for $10.8 million in 1970 and thirty-five years later sold it for $223 million. That's solid appreciation on an asset.

The team was never just a business for me, of course. It was my life. That's why it is so much fun to see the Brewers doing well under Attanasio, Stearns, and Counsell.

You should have seen me when the Brewers hosted the Rockies in the first game of the division series. I was just as much of a wreck as I was watching us play the Orioles on the last day of 1982, when Don Sutton faced Jim Palmer.

The Brewers were beating the Rockies 2–0 through eight innings, thanks to a home run by Yelich, who I'm loving the same way I loved Molitor and Yount. But the ninth inning started badly, with the Rockies getting hits off Jeremy Jeffress.

It was just like the old days. I couldn't watch, so I invoked the Seven-Minute Rule.

I got up from my seat and left the suite. I was pacing up and down the hallway behind it. I'd hear the crowd groan and know something bad was happening. I stuck my head in and asked Sue what was going on.

"You're not going to like it," she said.

Well, I knew that. Sure enough, the Rockies scored two runs in the ninth to tie it 2–2 and send me to a new level of agony. But I'm happy to report we lived to tell about it.

Yelich scored the winning run in the bottom of the tenth, and the Brewers swept the series. They beat Clayton Kershaw at Miller Park in the start of the NLCS against the Dodgers, and I was like everyone in Milwaukee.

I was dreaming of how sweet it would be to go back to the

World Series. But you don't write the script in baseball, which is why it is always so compelling. The turning point of the series was game 5, when Kershaw got his revenge, and the Dodgers finished it with a 5–1 victory in game 7.

I wasn't happy heading home that night, no question about that. But I had the sweetest thought a baseball fan can ever have.

Wait till next year.

ACKNOWLEDGMENTS

Little I've ever done made me as nervous as the visits to Ed Fitzgerald, Oscar Mayer, Bob Uihlein, and other Milwaukee leaders when I was trying to put together a group to keep Major League Baseball in my hometown. But that blend of hopefulness and anxiety put me on an incredible journey, and in some ways writing this book has been like that trip of a lifetime.

I knew a long time ago I was going to write a book to revisit the people and issues I've experienced in almost sixty years in baseball. In my final years as commissioner I was often asked about my plans after leaving the position and always said I'd write a book. It sounded easy, but I've learned it's a challenge to find the right words and a real process to commit to them.

In the end, I'm proud of the work I did to get here. It wouldn't have been possible without the support of my wife, Sue, and daughters, Wendy, Sari, and Lisa, along with Laurel Prieb, Wendy's husband.

Beyond my family, many others were essential to this project, beginning with Rich Levin, Richard Justice, and Charles Steinberg. They believed I should tell my story, and got the ball rolling in a process that would last more than four years. Tom Haudricourt, a treasure as Milwaukee's leading baseball writer, helped in many ways.

Sandy Montag, my agent, was an invaluable resource all the way. He encouraged me from start to finish and connected me to HarperCollins and its remarkable staff. I'll always be appreciative to Sandy for his support.

My old friends at Major League Baseball were generous with

their time and their recollections of many events described in the book. Rob Manfred provided guidance and clarity in many areas, especially the particulars of labor negotiations and the law behind events like the federal mediation in the painful 1994–95 strike. Dan Halem was helpful in regard to the more recent past. Pat Courtney, who succeeded Levin in the difficult PR role while I was commissioner, was with us every step of the way, and I'll be thankful to him.

My fellow owners and those I worked alongside while commissioner were there when I needed them, as always. Jerry Reinsdorf has always been a true baseball historian, and his encyclopedic knowledge and keen eye made this book better. So too did input from Jim Pohlad, Lew Wolff, Bill Bartholomay, Fred Wilpon, David Glass, Mark Attanasio, and many others.

I'll always be indebted to the great historian Doris Kearns Goodwin for writing the foreword. It put a lot of pressure on us to live up to her standard.

I owe a lot to my editor at HarperCollins, Matt Harper. He constantly pushed me to dig deeper into my memory and to go to some of the less comfortable places. He was devoted to the task from our first conversations and shaped the book in many ways. I'd also to thank others at HarperCollins, especially Lisa Sharkey, who believed in us from the start. Thanks also to copyeditor, Greg Villepique; senior production editor, David Palmer; publicist, Danielle Bartlett; marketing director, Kaitlin Harri; along with Anna Montague and Maddie Pallari.

I also need to say thanks to Phil's agent, Gary Morris of the David Black Agency, for supporting the project.

Finally, I couldn't do what I do without the staff at my Milwaukee office. Thank you, Mary Burns, Charles Hargrove, and Meredith Malone. You guys are the best. Just like the great game of baseball.